A Is for Apple

A Is for Apple

MORE THAN 200 RECIPES FOR EATING, MUNCHING,
AND COOKING WITH AMERICA'S FAVORITE FRUIT

Greg Patent and
Dorothy Hinshaw Patent

BROADWAY BOOKS   NEW YORK

Broadway Books titles may be purchased for business or promotional use or for special sales. For information, please write to: Special Markets Department, Random House, Inc., 1540 Broadway, New York, NY 10036.

BROADWAY BOOKS and its logo, a letter B bisected on the diagonal, are trademarks of Broadway Books, a division of Random House, Inc.

Visit our website at www.broadwaybooks.com.

Library of Congress Cataloging-in-Publication Data

Patent, Greg.
A is for apple : More than 200 recipes for eating, munching, and cooking with America's favorite fruit / Greg Patent and Dorothy Hinshaw Patent. —1st ed.
p.   cm.
Includes bibliographical references and index.
ISBN 0-7679-0203-3 (pb)
1. Cookery (Apples)   2. Apples.   I. Patent, Dorothy Hinshaw.   II. Title.
TX813.A6P38   1999
641.6′411—dc21
98-41926
CIP

FIRST EDITION

Designed by Barbara Balch

Illustrations by Janet Pedersen

99 00 01 02 03 10 9 8 7 6 5 4 3 2 1

For Dad

CONTENTS

ACKNOWLEDGMENTS

Those who helped make writing this book such a pleasure for us are

Harriet Bell, our editor at Broadway Books, whose uncanny instinct for what's right guided this book into its final form.

Alexis Levenson, her assistant, whose pleasant reminders made us get things in on time.

Judith Weber, our agent, who made many helpful editorial suggestions.

Art and Nancy Callan, who provided us with dozens of local apple varieties, and patiently answered our many questions.

Tom and Jill Vorbeck, who sent us boxes of apples from the Midwest and gave us lots of valuable information.

Julia Daly of the U.S. Apple Association, for information and material on apples and cider.

Jan Longone, of The Food and Wine Library, for steering us to important books on apples and apple cookery.

Elizabeth Ryan, for many stimulating conversations about apples and cider and the joys of growing and harvesting apples.

Diane Bilderback, for her cheerful assistance and advice.

The Washington Apple Commission for much useful information on the apple industry in Washington State.

And our many willing friends, who tasted and critiqued the recipes in this book.

PREFACES

Since it took two of us to write this book, we settled on a division of labor. Greg spent his time in the kitchen testing recipes and at his computer writing them up, and Dorothy researched all sorts of apple information in the library, on the phone, or on the Internet. Dorothy tasted everything Greg made, and Greg read everything Dorothy wrote. We're each writing our own preface because our history and feelings about apples are so personal. So, ladies first.

I've had a love affair with perfect apples since I was a young child. My father grew up on an apple ranch in Idaho, and every year, bushel baskets full of apples picked at their best arrived on our doorstep in Minnesota. Back then, the favorite commercial apples were Delicious, Rome Beauty, and Jonathan. My favorites were the Delicious, as they had a special unique flavor that people today,

alas, are unable to experience. Delicious apples back then were yellow with red stripes, and they were picked when just ripe. Today, we have Red Delicious, so deep red in color that even pickers can't tell whether the apples are ripe or not—they are red well before they are ripe. That redness has also come at the sacrifice of much of the unique flavor that made Delicious such a sensation when it first appeared on the scene. Also, for commercial purposes, which we'll be discussing as we go along in the book, Red Delicious apples are usually picked while their flesh is still green, before they have had a chance to mature properly.

I feel fortunate to have experienced the real thing, to have known for years what a truly wonderful apple can taste like, even if I wasn't able to find it in the store. Working on this book has given me the opportunity to rediscover true apple flavor, and this time in much more of its amazing variety, a variety I never knew existed before. By ordering apples through the mail and by buying them from our friends Art and Nancy Callan, local orchardists who grow an abundance of wonderful varieties that can thrive in Montana's often capricious climate, I've been able to rediscover my childhood enthusiasm for this most remarkable of fruits.

Dorothy Hinshaw Patent

Perfection with possibilities: perhaps more than any other food, that's what apples mean to me. One might argue that all of nature's creations are perfect. I prefer the Orwellian view that some of nature's work is more perfect than others, especially when it comes to apples. But if something is perfect, how can there be possibility? Possibility ought to lead to perfection, but perfection is an end unto itself.

Although I've been eating apples all my life, I hadn't given much thought as to why I loved the fruit so much until I began cooking the recipes for this book. Almost one thousand pounds of apples later, I think I'm beginning to understand. The raw, intact apple is perfect in its own way: an appealing compact repository of beauty, aroma, taste, and texture. But this sort of perfection, while it may be nature's goal, is only the beginning for the cook.

What can I turn this already wonderful thing into to make it new and wonderful in a different way? Cooking, as we know, transforms, and when it comes to cooking with apples, the possibilities for transformation are endless. When cooked, an apple ceases to be its own thing and becomes, instead, part of what the cook hopes will be a perfection of a different sort. This is what I have attempted to achieve with these recipes.

During testing, I asked: Do apples belong in this recipe? If so, why and how? What I learned was that apples are so versatile they can both support the flavors of more assertive foods and assume a lead role. Apples in soups, salads, and main dishes tend to be content with serving as part of the ensemble, whereas in cookies, cakes, sweet breads, and desserts, they insist on being dominant. This, I believe, is as it should be. Welcome to our world of apples. I wish you happy cooking and great eating.

Greg Patent

Our Favorite Fruit

The apple is our national fruit, and I like to see that the soil yields it;
I judge of the country so. The American sun paints himself in these
glowing balls amid the green leaves. Man would be more solitary, less
friended, less supported, if the land yielded only the useful maize and
potato, and withheld this ornamental and social fruit.

—RALPH WALDO EMERSON, *JOURNALS*

Some Apple ABCs

If someone were to ask you to name familiar fruits, chances are you'd blurt out "apple" first. Apples are the second most popular fruit in America, after bananas, but they're so much more versatile and full of meaning than that convenient tropical snack. We just love apples. We love munching them and we love them cooked in pies, turnovers, and fritters. We think of the apple as our own American fruit, although its origins and popularity extend far beyond our borders.

When you hold an apple in your hand, you possess one of nature's greatest creations. It may seem to be a simple piece of fruit, one of countless trillions, but it's a living, breathing miracle. Look closely at an apple and you'll see tiny depressions the size of a pinhole all over the surface. These are the apple's pores. The apple breathes through these as we do through our lungs, taking in oxygen and giving off carbon dioxide. Hold the apple to your nose and give it a big whiff. Its delectable perfume makes you want to bite right in. The aromatic chemicals are the apple's way of enticing you to eat it. It is nonverbal communication of the highest degree of sophistication. An apple wants to be eaten, because that is how it makes more apples. You throw the core away and the seeds germinate in the soil, sprouting new seedlings. And so the cycle begins anew. But here's where people have come in for thousands of years, selecting the most appealing fruit and improving it to suit human tastes until we have the thousands of varieties of apples growing around the world today.

The Apple's Glorious Variety

Why should we settle for anything but the finest flavor when we potentially have so much to choose from? No one knows exactly how many apple varieties exist, but the number exceeds seven thousand. That's an amazing figure, with several reasons behind it. First is the antiquity of the relationship between apples and humans. We know from the remains of lake dwellings in Switzerland that people were eating apples at least eight thousand years ago. The ancient Egyptians planted apple trees, even describing their techniques in writing. The Romans were growing at least seven apple varieties by around 200 B.C. and thirty-six by around 50 A.D., including kinds both for eating fresh and for storage. The Romans had learned how to take cuttings from favorite trees and graft them onto the roots of others, which is the only way to ensure consistent varieties of apples. At least one variety from those ancient times, called the Api, now almost certainly survives as the Lady apple here in North America. This small yellow-to-red juicy treat, with an especially flavorful skin, was a favorite of French royalty, one of only seven varieties deemed fit for that finicky king, Louis XIV.

While humans have been breeding and selecting apples for thousands of years, nature has provided plenty of material for us to work with. The genus *Malus,* to which apples belong, appears to have evolved over an area that includes Asia Minor, the Caucasus, Central Asia, and the Himalayan Mountains. Mountains tend to provide the genetic isolation vital to the development of diversity in species of plants and animals, and apples are no exception. But the species of apples and crab apples that have evolved are all closely enough related that they can hybridize with one another. While two species have done most of the work, at least seven of the twenty-five species of *Malus* have contributed significantly to the creation of the multitude of apples grown around the world today.

Much of the explosion of apple varieties occurred in America following European settlement. For one thing, settlers in new territories wanted to grow apples at their new homes. But trees weren't easy to transport over long distances by agonizingly slow wagons, so many pioneers simply carried sacks of seeds gathered from cider mills and planted the seeds at their new homes. Apple seeds, however, don't produce trees with fruit identical to the one from which they come, so no one could know what sort of apples would arise from those seeds. After they began to bear, trees that produced a disappointing harvest were cut down, or the fruit used for animal feed or cider making. But those with good fruit were treasured and tended. In addition, American apple breeders began using wild species of native crab apples in their breeding programs during the latter half of the nineteenth century, mostly to improve winter hardiness in the challenging climates of North America. By 1900, five thousand new varieties had been named in the United

a rose is a rose is an apple and so is a strawberry

the rose family, which scientists call Rosaceae, is a gift of nature we should be especially thankful for. Not only does it provide us with what might be our favorite flower, it also gives us almost all the fruits grown in home gardens, from strawberries to apricots. Of familiar garden fruits, only grapes and blueberries fall outside the rose family.

Not only are the fruits from these plants delicious, they also produce beautiful flowers. Most cultivated roses have been bred far beyond the simple design of a rose-family flower. Roses are crammed with overlapping petals, but the basic pattern is pentaradial; that is, a typical rose-family flower has five delicate petals surrounding the center, which holds the ten pollen-bearing stamens and the female part of the flower in the middle, the style. These showy flowers are designed to attract the bees that will pollinate them. In addition to their visual appeal, the flowers often carry a delicate sweet scent to lure their pollinators.

The close relationship among so many fruits allows nurseries to graft the top of one kind of tree onto the roots of a different related species, giving us trees in a variety of sizes and with enhanced disease resistance. Peaches, plums, and apricots are all grown on the same rootstocks. Dwarf plum trees have often been grafted onto seedlings of the sand cherry, and crab apples make good, hardy rootstock for full-sized apple trees. The familial bond also allows breeders to create crosses like plumcots and Pluots™.

As we all know, however, close family ties can also bring trouble. The same pests and diseases, such as fire blight and the codling moth, can infect a wide variety of fruit trees and ornamental garden plants.

States, and around two hundred of these are still known to be grown. Two especially fine and popular varieties, Newtown and Spitzenberg, come from this early period. According to some experts, Newtown is the best-tasting apple there is, while Spitzenberg comes close.

Largely because of the demanding climates of North America, most of the varieties grown here were developed here. But apple breeding today is an international affair. Of the popular and upcoming varieties, Braeburn, Gala, Freyberg, Granny Smith, Pink Lady, and Sundowner were bred in Australia and New Zealand. Arlet, Cox's Orange Pippin, and Elstar came from Europe, while Fuji and Mutsu (also called Crispin) were developed in Japan.

Does an Apple a Day Keep the Doctor Away?

The variations on this familiar saying are almost endless:

An apple a day puts the dentist to flight.
An apple a day keeps the doctor away;
an onion a day keeps everyone away.
An apple a day keeps the doctor away;
more apples than one keep him on the run.

And so forth. But just how nutritious are apples? According to the Washington Apple Commission, a medium apple has 80 calories and negligible protein, fat, and sodium; it provides 5 percent of the potassium, 20 percent of the dietary fiber, 2 percent of the vitamin A, 8 percent of the vitamin C, and 2 percent of the iron that an average person should consume in a day. Much of the vitamin A and vitamin C lie in the apple's skin.

Compared to other fruits, the apple is actually rather puny as a source of vitamins and minerals. But more than mere nutritional value has been claimed for this popular fruit. It may seem strange, but there is plenty of evidence that apples can help with both constipation and diarrhea. Recent research suggests that certain chemicals in apples, called flavonoids, may help prevent cancer. Apple cider vinegar is a popular folk medicine used to battle many foes—insect bites, dandruff, athlete's foot, and burns. We have no evidence that cider vinegar is effective for these woes, but it certainly can't hurt you.

Perhaps the most important medical effect of eating apples is the sense of pleasure that comes from biting into that crispy, sweet-tart flesh and tasting that delightful apple flavor.

Apple Basics

I tell you folks, all politics is applesauce.

—WILL ROGERS, *THE ILLITERATE DIGEST*

Today, all over the United States, apples occupy the largest fruit segment in supermarket produce sections. From Florida to California, it is not unusual to find a dozen apple varieties in any one store. This is very encouraging, because it indicates not only the desire on the part of the public to try new types of apples, but the store owners' willingness to take chances in making these different varieties available.

The varieties change during the fall and winter to reflect what's available at any given time. Moreover, even though the United States is one of the world's largest growers and shippers of apples, we import apples from New Zealand and Chile during their growing seasons, giving us the luxury of purchasing freshly picked Granny Smiths, Braeburns, and Galas during our spring months.

Supermarkets will carry apples that look good, ship well, and store well, which limits the range of what they're able to offer. The very best places to discover and taste different varieties of apples are farmers' markets. Our friends Art and Nancy Callan grow dozens of apple varieties on twelve hundred trees occupying only two and a half acres in the Bitterroot Valley of Montana. The earliest apples they bring to market are Lodis, at the beginning of August. Their season ends in late October after the last Honeycrisps are picked. In between, the selection changes weekly, depending on what's ripe.

If everything goes well, in a good year their annual crop may yield Vista Bella, Discovery, Jersey Mac, State Fair, Summer Red, William's Pride, Lyman's Large, Jonamac, McIntosh, Royal Gala, Liberty, Kidd Orange, Sweet Sixteen, Goldrush, and Wolf River, plus some others. Jonamac is their most dependable variety. It is a delicious all-purpose cooking and eating apple that can be harvested from early September to mid-October. Many of these varieties do not store well, so they must be used soon after pick-ing. Some types of apples bruise easily, for ex-ample, and have to be handled with care. For these reasons, they would not succeed in the commercial marketplace. But they do make mighty good eating and/or cooking.

When faced with an unfamiliar variety, ask to try a sample. Most growers are delighted to provide a taste. If you're not sure how good a particular kind of apple is for baking, there's a simple way to test many kinds at the same time. Follow the recipe for Spicy Apple Dumplings (page 82), using one or two pieces from each kind of apple. In half an hour, you'll have the answer.

what apples should i use?

although there are no hard-and-fast rules, here is a general guide to apple eating and cooking, based on our own experiences and information from Elizabeth Ryan, proprietor of Breezy Hill Farm and Hudson Valley Draft Cider Company in New York State.

eating—This is clearly a matter of individual preference. But crisp and juicy varieties with a good balance of sweetness and tartness are what to aim for. The following apples make excellent eating: Baldwin, Braeburn, Empire, Esopus Spitzenberg, Fuji, Gala, Golden Delicious, Golden Russet, Gravenstein, Honey-crisp, Jonagold, Jonamac, Macoun, McIntosh, Melrose, Mutsu, Northern Spy, Spigold, and Winesap.

juice—For apple juice or apple cider, choose vari-eties that have lots of flavor. Sweeter apples such as Red and Golden Delicious tend to be used in juice, and tarter varieties such as Granny Smith, Rome, Jonathan, and Winesap in cider. Sometimes so-called neutral apple varieties, those equally tart and sweet, are used in combination with sweeter apples (for juice) or tarter ones (for cider). The McIntosh family (Cortland, Empire, Macoun, Milton, and Spartan) is an example of a neutral variety.

sauce, purées, and butters—Use hearty, full-flavored apples here. Early-season apples are poor keepers and tend to have soft, mushy textures when cooked, but they make sensationally smooth, tangy apple-sauce. Lodi and Transparent are examples. Late-season apples, with heartier tastes and textures, make excellent sauce, purées, and apple butters. Any Jonathan variety, especially Jonamac, is excellent, as are Gravenstein, McIntosh, Northern Spy, and Winesap.

pies and tarts — The most important characteristic of a pie apple, besides taste, is texture. Braeburn, Cox's Orange Pippin, Empire, Jonathan, Northern Spy, and Rhode Island Greening, alone or in combination, are excellent. The old warhorses Granny Smith and Golden Delicious will also work, but why bother when you can have a far superior taste with other varieties? Avoid McIntosh and its relatives in pies and tarts unless you have access to early-season fruit; but even then, use them in combination with a sturdier apple, or the filling is apt to be too mushy. The key is to use apples in their prime.

baked apples — Here it's important that the apple hold its shape and not fall apart. Rome apples are perfect, but Gala, Gravenstein, Oren, Braeburn, and other firm-textured apples will also work. Avoid Fuji, which is too sweet and perfumey, and McIntosh.

apple crisps and cakes — In general, use the same kinds of apples recommended for pies, but you have a bit more leeway here. If softer-textured apples are more to your liking in crisps, mix some McIntosh with a firmer apple. If your cake recipe calls for applesauce, it's important to know if the applesauce is thin or thick. Thick apple-sauce should be made with late-season apples, such as Jonathan. The recipe should specify the type of sauce and the apple recommended for it. Cakes with chopped or diced apple require varieties suitable for pies.

apple stuffings — Full-flavored, dense-textured apples are called for here. Any russet variety, such as Roxbury Russet or Ashmead's Kernel, will work very well, as will any member of the Winesap family (Arkansas Black, Stayman Winesap). Less satisfactory, but still quite good, are Granny Smith, Jonathan, Northern Spy, and Spigold. Don't mix varieties. Let each one stand on its own.

chutneys and salsas — The tartest, firmest apples work best. Use any member of the Baldwin family (Baldwin, Esopus Spitzenberg), Granny Smith, or Rhode Island Greening.

The bottom line — and this is our best advice — is to use the best of what's available. During the fall and early winter, when apples are in their prime, search out local varieties. Since apples are grown in so many parts of the United States, most readers will be able to heed this advice. We cannot be more emphatic on this point. Any recommendations in our recipes are just that. Don't try finding a Cox's Orange Pippin to make an apple pie in July. Go to your market and buy Braeburns instead. Chances are they'll be from New Zealand, since July is early winter down there.

Buying and Storing

Apples are alive and breathing, and that means they need to be stored properly for maximum flavor and texture. Since we find apples displayed in produce counters all year long, we tend to assume they'll keep forever. Not so. When buying apples, check each one to be sure the skin is intact and there are no soft spots or bruises. Apples should feel firm when you squeeze them gently in your palm. When you get home, refrigerate them. Don't put them in a bowl on your counter and expect them to stay forever young and firm. Apples deteriorate rapidly at room temperature. For the best eating and cooking, buy only what you plan to use within a few days, and keep them chilled until that time.

Working with Apples

PEELING AND CORING Should you peel the apple first before coring or do it the other way around? It all depends on what you plan to cook. If it's a pie, tart, crisp, or other apple recipe calling for peeled and cut apples, the following technique works best:

1. Cut the apple into quarters with a sharp knife.
2. Place an apple quarter rounded side down on your work surface, and with a sharp paring knife, remove the core by angling the blade from one end of the apple to the center of the quarter, passing under the core. Spin the quarter around 180 degrees and repeat the procedure from the opposite end. Remove the core. Repeat with the remaining apple quarters.

3. Use the paring knife to remove the peel from each quarter. Repeat the whole process with any remaining apples; once all the apples are quartered and peeled, cut them as specified in the recipe. It will take less than ten minutes to core and peel enough apples for a pie this way.

Although there are hand-operated gadgets such as the rotary apple peeler (see Mail-Order Sources, page 261) that will peel, core, and slice apples in one operation, they have their drawbacks. Unless you're processing pounds and pounds of apples, they're probably not worth the expense. But if you like kitchen contraptions, they may prove to be useful. We use ours to cut apples for drying. However you prepare your apples, save all the trimmings to turn into apple pectin for the Apple and Blood-Orange Sauce (see page 20).

If you work slowly, the apples may start to turn brown. According to Roger Yepsen in his book *Apples,* browning is an apple's defense against dehydration and disease. When the apple is cut, the torn cells release a natural disinfectant that kills disease-causing microbes. Then other cells come into play, forming something akin to scab tissue to cover the wound. To prevent browning, drop the prepared apples as you go into a bowl of water and lemon juice. One quart of water plus the juice of one lemon should do the trick; we also throw in the squeezed lemon halves. Drain the apples and pat them dry on paper towels before proceeding with the recipe.

CORING WHOLE APPLES If an apple is to be baked whole, core it first and then peel it. But apple corers have their problems. Most are too small to do the job properly. They have diameters ranging from three-quarters to seven-eighths of an inch, which isn't wide enough to remove all of the seeds. The core of an apple isn't a symmetrical cylinder like the coring device. Cut into an apple lengthwise and you'll see that the core is fairly narrow at both ends but quite wide and bulbous in the middle. The best job a corer can do is to remove the center of the widest part of the core, leaving some of the seeds and core fibers still in the apple. Another problem with

coring a whole apple is how to aim the corer so that it actually passes through the part you want to remove. The core isn't necessarily a true vertical through the apple. Before coring, notice how the stem and blossom ends line up, then push the corer through the fruit, give it a good twist, and pull it out with the core. Look inside the cavity and remove any seeds with the tip of a paring knife. After all your apples are cored, peel them with the paring knife if the recipe indicates, and rub the surfaces with lemon juice to prevent discoloration. Or drop them into a bowl with water and lemon juice as described above. When ready to use, shake the apples to remove excess water and pat them dry on paper towels.

CUTTING UP APPLES FOR PIES, TARTS, AND CRISPS Once the apples are quartered, cored, and peeled, you have several options for how to cut them. For a pie, you should aim to preserve the texture of the fruit. If you slice the fruit too thin, the pieces may not remain intact. We've found that cutting each quarter lengthwise into three or four wedges works best, with the widest part of each slice about $1/4$ inch thick.

For tarts, the wedges should be thinner, between $1/8$ and $1/4$ inch thick. And for crisps, Bettys, cobblers, and similar desserts, we slice the quarters crosswise. Because of the shorter baking time of these desserts, the slices should not be too thick. Slices $1/4$ inch thick are about right.

DICING, JULIENNING, AND SHRED-
DING Some recipes require other than apple
slices.

Dicing—This means cutting the fruit into
small cubes. The size of the cubes will vary depending upon the recipe. If an instruction simply says "diced" without giving a dimension, this
means the cubes of apple should be about $1/4$ inch
on each side. This is not a precise measurement,
only a general guideline.

To dice apples, set a flat side of the cored and
peeled apple quarter on your cutting surface.
Slice the quarter vertically about $1/4$ inch thick.
Keeping the slices together, turn them as a unit
so that they are parallel to the cutting surface.
Cut the stack of slices lengthwise into $1/4$ inch-
thick strips, then cut these crosswise into $1/4$-inch
cubes. Some of the pieces will have rounded surfaces, which is fine. If the apples are to be diced
smaller or larger, adjust the thickness of the
slices accordingly. If a recipe calls for the apples
to be "chopped," dice them into $1/4$-inch pieces.

Julienne—This means cutting the apple into
thin strips. The procedure is exactly the same as
the first two steps for dicing, except you omit the
final step of cutting crosswise. Julienned apples
are typically $1/8$ inch thick. But they can also be
slightly thicker.

Shredding—You can use either the coarse
holes on a box grater or the regular shredding
disk of a food processor to shred apples. You must
work quickly when shredding the fruit, or it will
turn brown. The exception here is the Cortland,
which has magical brown-defying properties. As
a rule, shredded apple should be immediately
added to a batter or placed in a bowl of water and
lemon juice until ready to use. Our advice is to
opt for the former, since shredded apples may
become mushy if allowed to sit for any length of
time in water.

DRYING APPLES Perfectly ripe apples at the
peak of taste and texture are ideal candidates for
drying. Use local varieties as soon after picking as
possible. Apples can be dried outdoors in the
sun, in an oven set on the lowest heat, or in a
food dryer. Both the sun and oven methods are
chancy, so we prefer using a simple, inexpensive
food dryer. These gadgets are compact, easy to
use, and efficient.

The goal of drying is to remove the moisture
in the food that allows spoilage organisms to
grow, without cooking the food. Drying should
be a continuous process; it's not a good idea to
start drying a batch of food, stop for a number of
hours, and then start up again. The partially dried
material will begin to deteriorate. A temperature
of 130° to 140° F is best for drying apples and
other fruit.

Thin, even slices are necessary for proper
drying so that all the pieces dry quickly and
evenly. We like to use an old-fashioned apple
peeler/corer/slicer such as the rotary apple
peeler (see page 8 and Mail-Order Sources, page

261) to prepare apples for drying; it cuts the apples into evenly thick, attractive circular slices.

Since apples tend to brown when exposed to air, we dip the slices into a solution of ascorbic acid, such as Ever-Fresh, before drying. (The container gives information as to how much to use.) Then we drain the slices briefly on paper towels and load them onto dryer trays.

Drying fruit is a personal thing. We have a friend who dries everything until it's rock-hard, then on long road trips he challenges his teeth and jaws by snacking on his dried fruit. Other folks like to dry to a relatively soft stage and store the bags of fruit in the freezer. We prefer the middle ground recommended by the dryer manufacturer. Depending on your dryer, the

the family orchard

before modern farm equipment and rootstocks that could control the height of fruit trees, starting and running an apple orchard was very hard work. My (Dorothy's) grandfather, Pop Hinshaw, moved with his family to Idaho in the early 1900s when the government put in an irrigation system to turn the sagebrush desert into farmland. The sagebrush was six feet tall—good news in that big plants meant fertile soil, but bad news in that all the sage had to be removed before crops could be planted.

Pop was a bit of a visionary. He could see that this land was perfect for growing apples, even though his neighbors scoffed. Apple trees took around ten years to produce a worthwhile crop—who could survive in this land that long before bringing in vital cash? But Pop persevered, beating down the sage with a long bar pulled by horses, then wrenching out each sage plant by hand. The eventual result was a thriving apple ranch on which he and his wife raised their four children. I've seen old home movies of how work was carried out in the orchard, including footage of a man dressed in short sleeves standing in the back of a pickup truck using a long nozzle with a sprayer that went every which way to treat the trees with lead arsenate. I shudder at the thought, but my father says the powder settled on the dining table in the house, and that when the family members wanted to eat an apple, they'd pick one, wipe off the powder on their clothes, and take a juicy bite. Since Dad is now in his mid-nineties, this practice clearly wasn't fatal.

A few years ago, we visited the orchard. True to Pop's vision, much of the valley is now devoted to apple growing. And true to modern trends, the orchards are no longer owned by independent farmers but by giant corporations. However, in honor of the man who devoted so much of his life to this wonderful fruit, the old ranch still has a sign identifying it as "Hinshaw Orchards."

temperature, and the humidity, ³/₈-inch-thick apple slices can take anywhere from four to ten hours to dry. They are ready when the pieces are uniformly pliable and leathery. If you aren't sure, you can tear a piece in half to see if beads of moisture appear along the tear. If they do, test again in another half hour. Once cooled, dried fruit can be stored in clean plastic bags or in plastic or glass containers. Be sure to label as to variety and date. Dried foods keep best in the dark at a temperature of 60°F or less. If you keep them in your freezer, they should keep for well over a year. Taste your dried fruit every few months to see if its quality is declining. If so, use as soon as possible.

Choosing varieties for drying can be fun. It's amazing how differently apples can behave during the drying process. We tested eight varieties. Granny Smith slices came out unpleasantly grainy. Gala and Sweet Sixteen ended up being too sweet when dried. But Braeburn, Fuji, Liberty, McIntosh, and Wolf River all produced excellent slices.

In addition to making good, healthy snacks, dried apples are handy for making pies, cobblers, sauce, breads, and cookies.

Apple Sizes in Recipes

The recipes in this book are based on the following guidelines for apples sizes:

Small—apples weighing about 4 ounces

Medium—apples weighing between 5 and 7 ounces

Large—apples weighing about 8 ounces

Of course, there are some varieties, such as Wolf River and Spigold, whose standard size is about 1 pound per apple. But these are special cases. To have some frame of reference, we've settled on the above as a useful tool. In many recipes, we've given the total weights of apples along with the number of apples of a particular size. For example, a recipe might say "2 pounds apples (about 4 large)." Sometimes a cup measurement for cut-up apples is also given, but the weight and/or number of apples needed are also provided. In most cases, precise amounts of apple are not crucial to the success of a recipe, but where they are, several measuring guidelines are included.

like many other great Americans, the Red Delicious apple had humble beginnings. Well over a hundred years ago, sometime between 1868 and 1872, an apple seed sprouted between the rows of an orchard in Iowa owned by Jesse Hiatt. When Hiatt saw the interloper, he cut it down. He knew that seedling trees rarely produced useful fruit, and this little tree was in the way of his neat rows. But the tree grew back. Finally, the orchardist decided to let the tree have its way, and he began to tend it.

In those days, apple trees were full-sized and took a long time to come to bearing, so Hiatt had to wait years before the tree finally produced just one cluster of blossoms. Only one fruit matured from the cluster, but it had such exceptional flavor that Hiatt declared to his wife that this was the best apple ever and named it Hawkeye.

Hiatt carefully protected the tree and offered the apple to others to taste, but mostly they laughed at its unusual shape, drawn out toward the blossom end into five little bumps. Round or conical apples were the thing back then, not strange-looking fruit like Hawkeye.

Meanwhile, Clarence Stark, president of Stark Brothers Nursery in Missouri, was hunting for a new apple variety for commercial production. At the time, the most popular apple was Ben Davis, which grew and produced reliably but had poor flavor. Stark decided to sponsor a competition in 1892 in hopes of encouraging orchardists to enter their favorites. Hundreds of entries from across the country arrived and were displayed on plates of five apples arrayed on long tables, with each display labeled with the name of the grower. When Stark tasted Hiatt's Hawkeye, he knew he'd found what he was looking for. He dubbed the apple Delicious, a name he'd been saving for just such a fruit. But when he looked for the name of the grower, the entry card was missing.

Stark repeated the competition the next year, hoping the new apple would again be entered. Fortunately, Hiatt was a stubborn fellow, and even though he thought his apple had received no honors the year before, he entered it again. When Stark got the apples, he immediately contacted Hiatt and purchased the rights to propagate Delicious.

From these precarious beginnings, Delicious has become the most widely grown apple in the world. It is perfect for commercial production, producing trees with strong branches that grow at wide angles and that thrive and produce abundantly in a variety of climates. The hardy trees need little pruning, bear annually, and have significant resistance to the serious disease fire blight. The fruit is attractive to look at, keeps well, and travels well.

Consumers today, however, may wonder what the fuss over flavor was all about. Who can call one of these fruits purchased in the supermarket truly "delicious"? The original Delicious had dark red stripes on a light red and greenish yellow background. But "improvements" have led to a dark red color that develops early, making it difficult to tell when a Delicious apple is ready to pick. Following the edict that it's better to be safe than sorry, orchardists pick their apples early rather than late, knowing that at least the crispness of the fruit will be retained in storage. So, when you bite into a Delicious purchased in, say, April, you'll see that the flesh is crisp but slightly green. The fruit was picked before it was ripe, so the full flavor couldn't develop. In addition, what orchardists call "improvements," such as the darker red color and more compact trees that bear more apples, have been accompanied by a marked decline in flavor.

Scientists in Washington State are taking a look at the problem of flavor in Delicious apples. They are comparing the flavor of a number of Red Delicious strains, including the original common Delicious and the first "improved" variety, Starking. Such is the nature of commercial apple production that the latter two had almost died out. Even if the early types are found to have far superior flavor, however, it will make no difference to the business—growers will never return to growing the original common Delicious. But one bright spot in the study is that the fruit is being harvested at three different dates and held for storage for varying lengths of time. If these harvest and storage tests show differences in flavor for Red Delicious strains commonly grown today, the industry may modify some of its procedures and allow more of the flavor to develop before apples reach the store.

Through the centuries, apples have meant more to people than just something to eat. If you cut an apple in half crosswise instead of lengthwise, you'll see a perfect five-pointed star. In occult religions, this symbol, called the pentagram, is very powerful. It is used to cast evil spells, such as the one put on Snow White when she bit into an apple. Apples seem to have embodied the qualities of both good and evil. Magical golden apples that convey desirable traits like eternal youth figure heavily in European myth and legend, from the Garden of the Hesperides of Greek legend to the Celtic myths of Avalon, which translates as "Apple-land."

Now take a big bite of that apple. That snappy crunch you hear is the sound of fifteen or more pounds of pressure being liberated by your teeth as they puncture the cell walls. The delicious sweet and tangy juices that fill your mouth contain malic and citric acids and sucrose that tingle your taste buds as well as aromatic chemicals that drift into your nasal passages and communicate the message, "delicious!"

Apple scientists, or pomologists, say that apples have three basic taste characteristics—sweetness, tartness, and fruitiness. Apples that taste the best to most people have a good balance between sweetness and tartness. But it makes a difference if we're going to eat that apple raw or use it in cooking—the sweetness that we savor in a fresh Gala or Fuji dulls the flavor if we use that same variety to make a pie. Some people enjoy chomping into a bright green Granny Smith, but just about everyone gobbles down a slice of pie made with that same apple. While our tongues perceive sweetness and tartness, an apple's fruitiness is conveyed through its aroma. If the apple you sniffed earlier was a Fuji, chances are you inhaled a delightful perfume. If it was a Red Delicious, however, you may have wondered what we were talking about.

Scientists pinpoint three other features that affect an apple's appeal to us—texture, color, and shape. Bite into a Lodi apple or a McIntosh that has sat around a bit too long and you may recoil from the texture. Yet even the most tasteless firm Red Delicious will have a satisfying crisp texture. Texture is a key quality in our ability to enjoy an apple as we eat it.

Color and shape, however, are something else entirely. An overemphasis on these two traits, the ones our eyes and minds are exposed to most obviously when we decide whether or not to buy particular apples, led breeders and growers to focus less on how an apple tastes and more on how it looks. They decided that an evenly shaped apple was more important than a flavorful one and that a bright red or green fruit was more likely to be put into the grocery cart than a pale yellow one with a few feeble red streaks.

The truth is that shape and color have nothing to do with flavor, and for a long time we were given little choice in the supermarket. During most of the year, we could choose between Red Delicious and Golden Delicious and precious little else. While other familiar varieties such as Jonathan, Rome Beauty, and Winesap occasionally graced the produce section, they were the exception rather than the rule. Then Granny Smith came along and began a revolution. People discovered that they liked apples with character, and soon, other newcomers from down under joined the battle for the hearts and pocketbooks of consumers.

Today, the forces of flavor and quality seem to be winning. In Washington State, Red Delicious still rules the orchard, but Fuji is replacing Golden Delicious as the second most abundant variety of tree. In the market, we have many apples to choose from now—Gala, Braeburn, Criterion, and others with a variety of uses. But we still need to guard against being seduced by the narrow views of some breeders and growers—they have developed a Red Fuji, for example, that looks pretty but lacks the wonderful flavor of the original variety. We're supposed to respond to that bright red fruit by mindlessly choosing it over and over again, even if we're disappointed by its flavor.

Applesauces

Applesauce is one of the simplest things to make, but the choice of apple may be important, depending on the intended use. If you're making it just to eat on its own, consistency may not be a factor. For taste, however, use what pleases you. For texture, there are some kinds of apple with more body than others.

McIntosh Applesauce

This sauce is a quick and simple version for those who don't like the bother of coring and peeling apples. In addition, it yields a thick, delicate pink sauce perfect for eating fresh or for using in other recipes. We don't add any additional sugar, since ripe McIntosh apples have a perfect balance of sweet and tart flavor. For best results, use early-season apples and fresh cider.

MAKES ABOUT 6 CUPS

4 pounds McIntosh apples, quartered
Three 3-inch cinnamon sticks
1 cup fresh apple cider

1. Put the apples into a heavy medium saucepan along with the cinnamon and cider. Cover the pan and bring the mixture to a boil over medium-high heat, stirring frequently. Be careful not to scorch the apples.

2. Lower the heat to medium and cook, covered, stirring occasionally, until the apples are mushy and the consistency of a sauce, about 20 minutes. Cool to room temperature.

3. Remove the cinnamon and pass the sauce through the fine disk of a food mill. Cover and refrigerate for 3 or 4 days, or freeze for up to 6 months.

Summer Applesauce

First-of-the-season apples such as Lodi and Transparent make silky-smooth, tart, thin applesauce. Look for them at the end of July or early to mid-August. They are best used in soups and desserts where you want an especially smooth quality. Both varieties are available for only a short time, two to three weeks, in apple-growing regions all over the country. The apples do not store well and must be used right after picking. Vista Bella, another late-summer apple, may be substituted. Or if you live where apples are grown, ask the growers what varieties are comparable. Note that no sugar is included in this applesauce, so it can be used in sweet or savory recipes. If you're a fan of this sauce, make batches of it and freeze for later use. It will keep for months.

MAKES ABOUT 5 CUPS

4 pounds Lodi or Transparent apples
Zest and juice of 1 lemon—zest removed in
    strips with a vegetable peeler
One 3-inch cinnamon stick

1. Quarter, core, and peel the apples. Drop them as you go into a bowl with 2 cups water and the lemon juice. When all the apples are prepared, drain them and put them into a large saucepan with 1 cup water, the lemon zest, and cinnamon stick.

2. Cover the pan and set it over medium-low heat. Cook at a simmer, stirring occasionally, until the apples fall apart, 20 to 30 minutes. Cool, then remove the cinnamon and zest.

3. Use an immersion blender or hand-held electric mixer to whip the mixture into a smooth purée. Transfer to airtight containers and store in the refrigerator for 3 or 4 days, or freeze for up to 6 months.

---

the most famous apple of all

how many paintings must there be of Eve reaching for that irresistible bright red apple in the Garden of Eden? It turns out that Eve couldn't have been tempted by an apple—apples were unknown in the region at that time. The Hebrew word used for the instrument of her downfall is *tappauch,* a generic word for fruit. *Tappauch* could include apricots, oranges, peaches, and quinces, all of which were known at the time and place Genesis was written. But the early translators of the Bible into English came from northern areas where the apple was the most familiar fruit, so "apple" it became, and the apple has borne that responsibility in our culture ever since.

Thick Apple Purée

Five pounds of apples are cooked down to a thick, concentrated purée that proclaims "apple." Once you've made it, you'll have it on hand for several recipes in this book: Apple Soufflés, Crème Brûlée, and Apple Ice Cream, among others. You must use an apple that will not turn watery when cooked. Jonamac is our first choice because of its tart taste and firm texture, but other Jonathan varieties will also work.

MAKES ABOUT 4 CUPS

5 pounds crisp cooking apples, such as Jonamac, quartered, cored, peeled, and cut into 1-inch pieces
1 cup sugar
1 tablespoon pure vanilla extract
2 tablespoons Calvados or Applejack
1 teaspoon ground cinnamon
4 tablespoons (½ stick) unsalted butter

1. Place the apples in a large, heavy nonreactive pot. Cover the pot and cook slowly over low heat for about 45 minutes, stirring occasionally with a wooden spatula, until the apples are tender. Uncover the pot and stir the apples to break them up.

2. Add the remaining ingredients, increase the heat to high, and boil, stirring constantly, until the mixture cooks down to a thick purée that holds its shape on the tip of the spatula, about 20 minutes. Just when to stop cooking can be a bit tricky, but as you stir, keep your eye on the bottom of the pot. If you swipe the spatula quickly across the bottom and the apple mixture immediately runs together, it is not ready. When the apple mixture stays put and the bottom of the pot remains visible after swiping, the purée is ready. (Here are a couple of other tests: 1. If the apple mixture wants to stick to the bottom as a thin film and you no longer see obvious bubbles even though the mixture is boiling hot, it is ready; and 2. If you spoon some of the purée in a mound on the tip of the wooden spatula and quickly turn the spatula upside down, the apple mixture should not immediately fall off; it may stay put.)

3. Remove the pot from the heat and stir occasionally until cool. If necessary, use a potato masher to make a smooth purée. When completely cool, transfer to an airtight container. Cover and refrigerate up to 2 weeks, or freeze for up to 6 months. Bring the purée to room temperature before use.

Applesauce Slices

This is an updated version of what Dorothy's mother called "apple sauce." Some might refer to this as stewed apples. Her version consisted of lovely intact apple slices in a heavy, sweet syrup. I can still feel the grains of powdered cinnamon on my tongue when I think of sitting in the breakfast nook eating a bowl of Mother's sauce. The pinch of salt is my grandfather's touch. I've modified the recipe by using cinnamon sticks instead of powdered cinnamon and fresh cider for the liquid. I've also used a minimum amount of extra sugar so the flavor of the apples isn't drowned out by sweetness. If you use a sweeter variety of apple, such as Roxbury Russet, you won't need to add any sugar at all. This dish is very versatile—it makes a good breakfast fruit, after-school snack, or children's dessert. It is best served warm. The recipe can be doubled easily.

MAKES ABOUT 3 CUPS

1 pound (2 large) Granny Smith apples, quartered, cored, peeled, and sliced into ⅛-inch-thick wedges
2 cups fresh apple cider
One 3-inch cinnamon stick
Pinch of salt

Place the apples in a medium saucepan along with the other ingredients. Cover the pan and bring the mixture to a boil over medium-high heat. Uncover the pan, stir the apples gently, and lower the heat to medium. Simmer, partially covered, until the apples are translucent and tender, about 20 minutes. Stir frequently to make sure the slices cook evenly. Cool slightly and serve warm.

Variations: Add some dried cranberries to the apples as they cook for tanginess and color. · A little freshly grated ginger adds liveliness · Fuji apples cooked in orange juice instead of cider are also a good combination. · For a chunky applesauce, break up the slices into small to medium pieces with a wooden spoon or potato masher.

APPLE BASICS

Apple and Blood-Orange Sauce

Apples are high in pectin, which means sauces and gels made with them thicken naturally. Instead of throwing away the trimmings from an apple recipe, turn them into apple pectin. Here the pectin is cooked into a bright red syrup to serve with pancakes or waffles or to use as a topping for ice cream or sorbets. Blood oranges are available in the winter months. If you can't find them, other oranges may be substituted. You'll need a candy thermometer.

MAKES ABOUT 1½ CUPS

Peels, cores, and seeds from 2 pounds apples
¼ cup blood-orange juice
3 tablespoons fresh lemon juice
1½ cups sugar
1 tablespoon Grand Marnier
1 tablespoon Calvados or Applejack

1. Combine the apple trimmings with 4 cups water in a medium saucepan, bring to a boil, and boil for 15 minutes, stirring occasionally. Strain, pressing on the solids to extract as much liquid as possible. You'll have about 2½ cups apple pectin.

2. Return the pectin to the saucepan and stir in the blood orange juice, lemon juice, and sugar. Bring the mixture to a boil over high heat, stirring occasionally, and cook until the liquid reaches a temperature of 220°F on a candy thermometer.

3. Immediately remove the pan from the heat and add the Grand Marnier and Calvados. Cool and serve warm, at room temperature, or cold, or store, covered, in the refrigerator for up to 1 week.

Dried Apple Chips

These make a delicious snack or a beautiful garnish for apple sorbets and ice creams. Firm, crisp apples, such as Granny Smith, Fuji, or Honeycrisp, are sliced paper-thin and dried in the oven. You will need a mandoline or other manual slicer to slice the apples and reusable silicon baking pan liners (see Mail-Order Sources, page 261) or a food dehydrator to dry them. They keep crisp in zip-top plastic bags for weeks.

MAKES 2 TO 3 DOZEN CHIPS

2 large firm, crisp apples

1. Adjust two oven racks to divide the oven into thirds and preheat the oven to 225°F. Line two large baking sheets with silicon pan liners.

2. Cut the apples crosswise into paper-thin slices (less than $1/16$ inch thick). Arrange the largest, most attractive ones close together on the prepared pans, (nibble on the trimmings). Bake for 2 to $2^1/4$ hours, rotating the sheets top to bottom and front to back every 30 minutes. The apple slices should turn just a pale golden color; they may still be flexible.

3. Immediately peel the slices off the baking-pan liners and set them on cooling racks. When completely cool, store them airtight.

pectin

pectin is a high-fiber carbohydrate found in the flesh, skins, and seeds of most fruits and some vegetables. The long, stringlike molecules are natural thickeners in jams and jellies. Apples, blueberries, cranberries, sweet cherries, lemons, papayas, and oranges are high in pectin.

The pectin content of a fruit varies with ripeness. Fruits have their highest levels of pectin just before they are fully ripe. For pectin to work effectively as a jelling agent, there must be enough of it present relative to the acidity and sugar in the mixture. That's why pectin manufacturers recommend sticking to the quantities of fruit and sugar in recipes packed with commercially sold packets of pectin. Even so, sometimes a jam won't set properly because the fruit was not at its peak ripeness.

Juice or Cider?

Chop up a bunch of apples, press them to expel their amber-colored liquid, and what do you have, juice or cider? In Colonial America or in Europe today, the answer would be juice, with the word *cider* used to describe what happens to the juice after fermentation, when it has become a fizzy, mildly alcoholic beverage.

In today's supermarkets, you find bottles of sparklingly clear golden apple juice and apple cider. They look exactly the same. They've been filtered to give them their pristine clarity. Why is one called juice and the other cider? One cider maker told me that if the pressed juice is left alone and not filtered, it's cider. To him, cider meant something that you couldn't see through. But a Tree Top representative explained that cider is higher in acidity than juice, and that different varieties of apples are used for each, depending on the time of year and their availability. Sweet apples, such as Red and Golden Delicious, normally go into apple juice, whereas tarter varieties like Rome Beauty, Granny Smith, Jonathan, and Winesap are used for cider.

Although nationally marketed brands of apple juice and cider have been filtered and pasteurized and may look the same, they don't taste the same. Cider is definitely tarter. Bottled brands of unfiltered but pasteurized juices and ciders—opaque brown-colored liquids—should also taste differ-

ent, the juices being sweeter than the ciders. We say "should" because we have to rely on the manufacturer. According to Julia Daly of the U.S. Apple Association, there are no national standards to distinguish between apple cider and apple juice. One brand's cider may be another's juice.

So, what's the difference between apple cider and apple juice? Frankly, we think the terms have become interchangeable today. *Cider* has a nicer ring to it than *juice,* for it conjures up a bucolic scene where groups of people gather together for a social activity, sharing the fall harvest, commemorating summer's passing into fall, and producing a delicious beverage all can share.

SWEET AND HARD CIDER In Europe, cider is centuries old, and hundreds of varieties of apples are grown specifically for making it. These apples have a very dense texture and high sugar content, and they are highly tannic. *Cider* in Europe means hard, or sparkling, cider, whereas in America, *cider* means sweet cider—there has been no fermentation of the juice pressed from apples—unless otherwise specified.

In America, we usually make cider from a mixture of apples all ground together and pressed at the same time. In Europe, on the other hand, single-variety pressings are blended to produce ciders with highly specific characteristics.

Americans have been drinking cider ever since the Mayflower landed at Plymouth Rock in 1620. Everyone drank cider. It was considered to be a healthful drink, and it was served at every meal. Because there was no refrigeration, cider underwent a natural fermentation, producing a beverage with a slight kick. For children, the cider was cut with water. By the early 1890s, cider was the most popular drink in America.

The first time we made cider, we were amazed at how simple the process is. My friend Larry had invited us over for a cider party one September afternoon, and we all pitched in. We sorted through the apples, a mixture of local varieties, to make sure they were good. A few bruised or wormy ones are okay, but rotten apples should be relegated to the compost pile. Cider shouldn't be made from windfalls, because they may contain

golden delicious

like its namesake, the Red Delicious, the Golden Delicious came from a chance seedling and might have remained unknown if the grower hadn't recognized its quality. In 1914, Lloyd and Paul Stark, Clarence Stark's sons (page 13), tasted a pretty yellow apple sent to the company by mail. One bite and they recognized a golden opportunity. Never before had they tasted such a delightful, spicy apple. And not only was the apple juicy and tasty, it had arrived in April, long after any other yellow variety would have become inedible.

That fall, Paul Stark set out to find the tree that had produced this exciting new apple. It had come from A. H. Mullins of Odessa, West Virginia, a town too tiny to appear on the map. Stark reached the town by narrow-gauge railway, then traveled on horseback until he found Mullins's mailbox. No one answered his knock on the cabin door, so he looked around the orchard. Up on a hillside he spotted a tree with lovely yellow fruit, the original tree from which the apple had come. Mullins appeared, and the men struck a deal. Stark

paid five thousand dollars for the tree and surrounding ground, a good sum in those days, and had a cage built around it so no one could cut wood from it to propagate it. The apples were similar in shape to the Red Delicious, so it was named Golden Delicious.

Today, this apple is almost as popular as its namesake. But like it, Golden Delicious has suffered from its own success. The fruit is usually picked too early, while still green—and once picked, these apples don't develop further flavor. So most consumers don't know just how tasty a Golden Delicious apple really can be.

Golden Delicious is a good variety for home orchards in most of the country. It blooms over a long period, so it is a good pollinator for most other varieties. It grows best where summers are warm and dry, and it ripens from mid-September to late October. For best eating, the fruit should be pale yellow. Green fruit is underripe, and dark yellow is a sign of overripeness.

APPLE BASICS

Acetobacter, a bacterium used in making vinegar; and they may also have a toxin, patulin, if they've been on the wet ground for a few days.

For the best cider, the apples must be ripe. We cut into a few to make sure, looking for the brown seeds that signal ripeness. Next, we washed the apples with a garden hose. Then came putting the apples through a chopper. We cranked the handle as Larry dumped the fruit into the hopper. What came out was a coarse-looking mush, or pomace, with a marvelous aroma. As the apples were chopped, they fell into a fine-meshed nylon basket, and when the basket was almost full, we stopped cranking.

Larry removed the hopper and placed a wooden press over the fruit, nestling it snugly in place. As he turned the press handle to extract the juice, amber-colored cider flowed into a plastic bucket below. The cider was warm from the sun and tasted both sweet and tangy. We seemed to be in summer and fall at the same time. Maybe that was part of cider's magic.

Other Apple Brews

APPLE CIDER VINEGAR Cider vinegar is prepared from alcoholic, or hard, cider by fermentation in the presence of oxygen. We use it in recipes where we want tang with apple overtones. Cider vinegar varies greatly in strength and quality. We have tried several widely available brands with an acidity of 5 percent and found them all to be good. If you use a vinegar with higher acidity, you may need to adjust for tartness.

APPLE WINE Apples can be made into wine in the same way as grapes and other fruits. Fermentation produces a crisp, dry, or sweet wine depending on the apple varieties used and the length of the fermentation process. It's important to eliminate any active bacteria during wine production, or vinegar will be produced. Apple wine is not used in any recipes in this book, but if it is available, it can be substituted for hard cider.

CALVADOS OR APPLEJACK When hard cider is distilled, it becomes a brandy. In France it's called Calvados, named for the *département* in Normandy famed for its cider and brandy; in the United States, it's sold as applejack. Both are typically 80 proof, and they can be used interchangeably in recipes.

Ingredients

River City's gonna have her Boys Band! As sure as the Lord made little green apples, and that band's gonna be in uniform!

—PROFESSOR HAROLD HILL,
IN MEREDITH WILLSON'S, *THE MUSIC MAN*

Always purchase the best-quality ingredients. You can't go wrong that way. Today, organically grown produce and other products are becoming increasingly available all over the country, and we use them in our cooking whenever possible. Not only do they taste better, they're better for our planet. Where we live in Montana, we're fortunate to be able to buy organic dairy products such as butter, milk, cream, and cheese. They cost more, but their taste is remarkable. We also buy eggs from local ranchers who raise their chickens on organic feed. These eggs not only taste terrific, they also have orange-yellow yolks that impart an appealing color to cakes and ice creams. Local farmers' markets and health-food stores are great places to shop for all these foods. For baking, we use organic flours whenever possible. One national brand, Gold Medal, is marketing an organic unbleached all-purpose flour in local supermarkets. We recommend it.

A dear friend said to us a long time ago, "You have to put in good to take out good." We always remember that when cooking.

BUTTER When butter is called for, we mean unsalted butter. If you use salted butter instead, bear in mind that each stick (4 ounces) contains the equivalent of about ½ teaspoon salt.

CIDER Both sweet and hard ciders are used in these recipes. Sweet cider is simply called cider. We prefer unfiltered pasteurized sweet cider, found in refrigerated cases. They have complex flavors and are more aromatic than filtered pasteurized ciders.

Hard ciders can be as wonderful as a fine Champagne, golden with a natural sparkle. The choice of hard ciders is quite broad, as there are many national brands available. For a juicy apple taste, try HardCore Crisp Hard Cider. If you want something zingier, give Ace Fermented Apple Cider a try. Purpom is a typical French cider, with delicate flavors. Any of these or other hard ciders are suitable for our recipes. Hard ciders are in the process of achieving microbrew status, so seek out local suppliers and sample, sample, sample to discover what suits your taste. Hard cider should always be drunk chilled.

CREAM When heavy cream is called for, you can use either it or whipping cream. Although the former contains a bit more fat, the results will be the same with either cream.

EGGS Unless stated otherwise, these recipes all use eggs graded large.

FLOUR For general cooking, we use unbleached all-purpose flour, which is what most of these recipes call for. It is a mixture of hard (high-gluten protein) and soft (low gluten) wheats, and its gluten content is suitable for just about any type of cooking. Cake flour is made from soft wheat and is much less likely to toughen during cake and pastry making. It is bleached, which means it is pure white, and typically is sold in two-pound boxes. Be sure to use it whenever it is specified. Bread flour has a higher gluten content than all-purpose flour, which gives breads a pleasant elasticity and chewiness. Two national brands, General Mills's Better for Bread and Pillsbury's Bread Flour, are available all over the country. If you can't get bread flour, unbleached all-purpose flour will work quite well.

The success of a recipe often depends on how the flour is measured. The best way to measure flour is to weigh it. In the absence of a scale, however, just follow these simple guidelines.

To sift flour before measuring, place more than you need in a sifter set on a sheet of wax paper. Once the flour is sifted, spoon it into a dry metal measuring cup to overflowing. Do not pack or shake the cup. Simply sweep off the excess flour with a metal spatula or any straight-edged object. (A chopstick works perfectly fine.) A cup of sifted flour measured this way weighs about 4 ounces.

Most of the time you will measure flour by stirring it in its container to aerate slightly, spooning it to overflowing into a cup, and sweeping off the excess with a metal spatula. A cup of flour measured this way weighs about $4^1/_2$ ounces.

A third way to measure flour is to stir the flour in its container to aerate it slightly, scoop a dry metal measuring cup into the container to overflowing, and sweep off the excess as described above. This cup of flour will weigh about 5 ounces.

To be sure we are speaking the same language, baking recipes specify both the weight of

johnny appleseed

Remember Johnny Appleseed,
All ye who love the apple;
He served his kind by word and deed,
In God's grand greenwood chapel.

—WILLIAM HENRY VENABLE, "JOHNNY APPLESEED"

the image of Johnny Appleseed, head topped by a tin-pan hat, striding barefoot across the countryside strewing apple seeds from a sack slung over his shoulder is imbedded in the American imagination. But who, in reality, was Johnny Appleseed? Born John Chapman in Leominster, Massachusetts, on September 26, 1774, he was an individualist in the American tradition.

Chapman loved nature and knew how important apples could be to the new Americans as they settled the continent. He wanted to provide them with trees and tried to keep one step ahead of the settlers. In his travels, he befriended all he met, from the animals of the forest to Native Americans and settlers alike. He never carried a gun.

He was too intelligent to think that just scattering seeds along his path would lead to the growth of productive apple trees, as legend would have you believe he did. Instead, he planted seeds collected at cider mills in nurseries along the path of settlement, offering the trees to grateful settlers for their gardens.

Johnny began his mission early in life. He left home when he was twenty. By the age of twenty-five, he was already at work in western Pennsylvania. He established nurseries stretching from the Allegheny River to Central Ohio. Eventually, Johnny Appleseed made his way to Indiana, Illinois, and Iowa, continuing his work for forty years, sometimes traveling hundreds of miles to tend his seedlings. The establishment of apple nurseries in Iowa was particularly important, because it was from there that the first apples were taken to Oregon and the rest of the Pacific Northwest.

Johnny Appleseed was a man with a mission who aided pioneers in establishing their homes, but the eastern farmers who were actively settling the areas in which he worked often brought their own seeds or seedlings along, so he wasn't alone in his endeavor. He died in Fort Wayne, Indiana, in March 1845, at the age of seventy-one, while staying at a friend's home on his way to tend one of his orchards.

the flour and how to get it into your measuring cups. *The above weights apply to all-purpose and bread flours only.* Cake flour is much lighter and airier in texture and weighs less when measured by these methods. Whole wheat flour tends to weigh a bit more. Generally speaking, measuring flour accurately for bread making is not as critical as when you are making a delicate pastry.

Why not just pick one method to measure flour? The answer is, to keep things simple. For example, when we want 5 ounces of flour, we specify a cup of flour measured by stir, scoop, and level method. If we want 4½ ounces of flour, we specify a cup measured by the stir, spoon, and level method. Using the scooping and leveling method in this case would result in an inaccurate measure.

NUTS Because nuts are high in fat, they can turn rancid quickly. Therefore, they must be very fresh. Buy only what you need and keep any leftovers airtight in the freezer. Frozen nuts will keep well for up to six months.

When using walnuts and pecans, always check for pieces of shell just in case. (Pine nuts and macadamia nuts are rarely packaged with any shells.)

A nut requiring special handling is the hazelnut. You can usually purchase hazelnuts shelled but with their skins on. The skins should be removed before using the nuts by blanching or skinning them: Spread the nuts in a single layer in a shallow baking pan and toast them in a 350°F oven for 10 to 15 minutes, stirring the nuts occasionally, until they are a toasty brown and have a delicious aroma. Transfer the nuts to a kitchen towel and wrap the nuts in the towel. When the nuts are cool, rub them vigorously with the towel to remove the skins. Some skins stubbornly refuse to come off, so just leave them. There is no harm including a few nuts with some skin in recipes.

YEAST All the yeast recipes in this book use active dry yeast. During recent years, we've become fans of SAF-Instant yeast, and that's what we use in our yeast recipes. It can be ordered by mail (see page 261).

Pies and Tarts

Apple pie without cheese is like a kiss without a squeeze.

—OLD ENGLISH RHYME

Why not begin with pies and tarts? You'd probably be heading for the sweet stuff anyway, so here's a head start.

Apples and pastry are like love and marriage. Although you can have one without the other, the partnership is far superior and satisfying. All the recipes in this chapter are proof of this belief.

The bottom line with these desserts, whether you call them kuchen, pie, or tart, is the union of apples and pastry. The pastry can be thick or thin, flaky or cookie-like. It can be a platform for a glorious display of glossy slices or enrobe the filling completely, hiding the contents from view. A lattice top adds elegance, while a streusel topping provides a delightful texture contrast.

In each recipe, the crust is specific to the particular filling because that's what gave the best results. Although we recommend specific apple varieties, they are only suggestions. Do try local apples as they become available. The flavor of tarter apples can withstand the rigors of a hot oven better than sweeter ones, but where texture is important you may have to make a compromise. Don't be afraid to combine apple varieties in a pie, for example, where you can intermingle tart with sweet and firm and softer textures.

Apple Pie

This is the classic two-crust apple pie perfected during twenty years of baking. The pastry is tender and flaky, and the fruit remains in separate pieces that aren't mushy. What's the best kind of pie apple? Perhaps Cox's Orange Pippin or Northern Spy or Empire or Liberty, or maybe half a dozen other types. What's important is to use apples that will not turn mushy. Avoid McIntosh and its cousins, although first-of-the-season fruits hold up better in pies than ones held in storage. Actually, I like using more than one variety of apple in a pie for taste, texture, and interest. Sweet Fujis, and Tart Newtown Pippins, for example, are a good combination. Similarly, Braeburns and Granny Smiths make a good mix too.

The apples in the pie should hold together when cut and served. To achieve this, the ideal consistency of the surrounding juices should be a thick, silky syrup. Cornstarch or tapioca flour are the best thickeners in an apple pie. Tapioca flour produces a slightly smoother result. It can be ordered by mail (see page 261). There's always a bit of guesswork in knowing how much thickener to use since the pectin content (and hence the juice-thickening ability) of apples can vary from batch to batch in the market. I prefer using less rather than more, since a slightly runny pie is infinitely preferable to one whose filling is adamant. For a great floral flavor and aroma, I like adding a small amount of Fiori di Sicilia, a combination of citrus oils and vanilla, to the filling (see Mail-Order Sources, page 261).

Ideally, the crust for an apple pie is crisp, tender, flaky, and buttery, and it clings to the fruit. The formula here will give you this result. I've made many pies where the crust bakes up into a lovely dome but the fruit has sagged, leaving an airspace. Too much butter makes for a firmer crust, so it can't settle along with the fruit.

Let the pie cool completely and leave it at room temperature for several hours before serving. Otherwise, the filling may run.

MAKES 8 SERVINGS

2¼ cups (11¼ ounces) unbleached
all-purpose flour (scooped into the cups
and leveled)

¾ teaspoon salt

10 tablespoons (1¼ sticks) chilled unsalted
butter, cut into tablespoon-sized pieces

½ cup chilled vegetable shortening

2 teaspoons cider vinegar

FILLING

¾ cup sugar

½ teaspoon ground cinnamon

½ teaspoon freshly grated nutmeg

2 to 3 tablespoons tapioca flour or cornstarch

¼ teaspoon salt

3 pounds apples (about 7 large), quartered,
cored, peeled, and sliced into ¼-inch-thick
wedges

1 tablespoon fresh lemon juice

¼ teaspoon Fiori di Sicilia, optional

2 tablespoons chilled unsalted butter, cut into
small pieces

1 tablespoon sugar

1. *To make the pastry in a food processor,* with the metal blade in place, process the flour with the salt for 3 seconds. Scatter the butter pieces over the flour; pulse 4 times. Divide the shortening into 4 lumps and add them to the work bowl; pulse 3 times. Scrape the work bowl. Combine the cider vinegar with 6 table-spoons ice water in a 1-cup glass measure. While pulsing very rapidly, add the liquid in a steady stream through the feed tube. Keep pulsing until the dough *almost* gathers into a ball. There should be several largish clumps of dough in the bowl. Remove the dough from the work bowl and press it gently so that it holds together. Divide in two, with one piece slightly larger than the other. Shape each piece into a 6-inch disk, dust lightly with flour, and wrap tightly in plastic wrap. Refrigerate for 1 hour or longer.

To make the pastry by hand, combine the flour and salt in a mixing bowl. Use a pastry blender to cut the butter into the flour until the pieces are pea-sized. Add the shortening and cut it in until the particles of fat resemble coarse meal. Combine the cider vinegar with 6 tablespoons ice water in a 1-cup glass measure and drizzle the mixture over the dry ingredients while tossing and stirring with a fork. Keep mixing until the dough gathers into a ball. Divide, wrap, and chill as described above.

2. When ready to bake, adjust two oven racks with one in the lowest position and the other in the center position. Place a heavy baking sheet on the lower rack and preheat the oven to 450°F.

3. Roll out the larger disk of pastry on a lightly floured surface into a 13-inch circle. Fold the dough into quarters. Center the point of the dough in the center of a 9-inch pie plate, then unfold the dough. Lift the overhanging edge of pastry all

around the pie plate so that the pastry lines the pan loosely but snugly; do not stretch the dough. Leave the excess pastry hanging over the edge. Roll out the second piece of dough into a 12-inch circle. If your kitchen is warm, refrigerate both crusts, placing the top crust on a baking sheet.

4. To prepare the filling, combine the sugar, cinnamon, nutmeg, tapioca flour, and salt in a large bowl. Add the apples and toss to combine well. Mix the lemon juice with the Fiori di Sicilia, if using, and drizzle it over the fruit; toss again to combine well.

5. Turn the filling into the pie shell, mounding the apples in the center. Distribute the butter bits evenly over the filling. Brush the overhanging edge of the pastry lightly with water and cover the filling with the top crust. Press the edges firmly to seal. Using scissors, trim away the excess pastry to within 1/2 inch of the pan's rim. Fold the edge of pastry back on itself to make a standing rim, and flute it. Brush the top crust lightly with water and sprinkle with the sugar. With a small sharp knife, make four slits at right angles to each other between the center and edge of the top crust.

6. Place the pie on the baking sheet and bake for 15 minutes. Transfer the pie on the baking sheet to the center shelf, reduce the temperature to 350°F, and continue baking for about 1 hour longer, until the crust is well browned and you can see thickened juices bubbling up through the slits. Cool the pie on a wire rack for at least 6 hours before serving. Refrigerate any leftovers.

Note: A good sharp Cheddar cheese is always welcome with apple pie. Simply place a thin slice or two atop or alongside each serving. Or bake some cheese into the pie by placing a thin layer of Cheddar cheese over the apple filling before putting on the top crust. Cheese and apple pie are best when the pie is eaten warm; if the filling oozes, that's all right.

apple pie and motherhood —and don't

forget our flag!—are among our favorite symbols, the things we identify most closely as American, the things you'd better not criticize. But just how American *is* apple pie? We might have to argue with the British about that, because they claim apple pie for their own. As early as 1615, British cookbooks featured recipes for apple pie. As late as 1937, Edward Bunyard, in *The Epicure's Companion,* insists that apple pie is uniquely English:

> Apple pie may not be English in its origins, but centuries of use have made it so.
>
> "Pie," says the *Oxford Dictionary,* "not known outside England." Of course not! "A dish composed of meat, fowl, fish, fruit, or vegetables, enclosed in or covered with a layer of paste and baked. . . ." A pie is enclosed, a tart exposed. A tart is a foreign idea; all good things in England are enclosed: commons, gardens, remittances, and pies.
>
> But *the* pie, the pie of all pies, the quintessence of pie-ity is the apple pie. . . . The apple pie is part of our English heritage which we should be careful to preserve in its integrity.

Early English recipes contained familiar ingredients still used today, except that the cinnamon and cloves weren't powdered—presumably, the diner would remove the pieces while eating. A very common ingredient, used only rarely in American cooking today, was rose water. Apple pie recipes in early American cookbooks were clearly derived from their English ancestors, since they included the typical spices and the rose water. Often the apples were cooked at least partially before putting them into the crust.

While apple pie might have originated in England, Americans from the early colonists on have embraced apple pie, sometimes in colonial days making it the main dish at suppertime. American inventiveness has also transformed the simple apple pie into countless variations, combining it with ingredients such as pumpkin, sour cream, pecans, and green tomatoes to create completely new, quite un-British, pies.

Deep-Dish Apple Pie

This is an unusual two-inch-high square apple pie with a very short and buttery pastry crust. A layer of pastry is also used in the filling, not only for structural support, but also for added richness. The pastry can be difficult to work with because it has a tendency to tear, but it's well worth it. My friend Alice Schroeder gave me the original version of this recipe, which she got from her grandmother. Select a firm tart apple for this recipe, such as Braeburn, Granny Smith, Kidd's Orange, or Northern Spy. A combination of one of these varieties with a McIntosh-type apple will also give you excellent results.

This pie keeps well for several days in the refrigerator, but the pastry is at its most tender and best when freshly baked.

MAKES 12 SERVINGS

PASTRY

1/2 pound (2 sticks) unsalted butter, at room temperature
2 tablespoons sugar
1/2 teaspoon salt
3 large egg yolks
2 1/2 cups (10 ounces) sifted unbleached all-purpose flour

FILLING

1 cup sugar
1 teaspoon ground cinnamon
1/2 teaspoon ground ginger
1 tablespoon cornstarch
3 pounds crisp cooking apples, quartered, cored, peeled, and thinly sliced crosswise
1/3 cup golden raisins or dried sour cherries
1/3 cup diced dried pears
1/3 cup diced dried apricots
1 cup chopped toasted pecans
2 tablespoons fresh lemon juice
1 tablespoon pure vanilla extract

GLAZE

1 large egg white
1 tablespoon sugar

1. To make the pastry, in a large bowl, beat the butter with an electric mixer until softened and smooth. Add the sugar, salt, and egg yolks and beat well. Add the flour, stirring until the dough gathers into a ball. (If you have a mixer with a flat beater, use it to incorporate the flour on low speed.)

2. Transfer the dough to your work surface, shape it into a log about 2 inches in diameter, and turn it so that one end faces you. Using the heel of your hand, rapidly break off and smear bits of dough away from the far end of the log until the entire log of pastry has been "broken" away. Gather the pieces of pastry together and shape it into a ball. Divide the dough into two pieces, one slightly larger than the other.

(If you have a scale, one piece should weigh about 13 ounces and the other about 9 ounces.) You can work with the pastry right away, but if your kitchen is very warm, it's best to wrap each piece of pastry in plastic wrap and refrigerate for 30 minutes to an hour. (The pastry can be made a day or two ahead and refrigerated.)

3. To prepare the filling, combine the sugar, cinnamon, ginger, and cornstarch in a small bowl. In a large bowl, toss together the apples, dried fruits, nuts, lemon juice, and vanilla. Add the sugar mixture and combine well. You will have about 10 cups of filling.

4. Roll the smaller piece of pastry on a lightly floured pastry cloth or work surface to a 14-inch square. Lightly butter a 9 × 2-inch square baking pan. Carefully fold the pastry in quarters and place it in the pan with the point of the pastry in the center of the pan. Gently unfold the pastry. Nudge, don't stretch, the pastry from the top edges of the pan until the sides and bottom of the pan are covered and press gently on the pastry so that it adheres to the pan. If the pastry tears at any point, simply press the pieces together. Leave the excess pastry overhanging the rim for now. Set aside.

5. Divide the larger piece of pastry in half. Roll one piece into a 9-inch square and the other into a 9½-inch square. Refrigerate on a baking sheet.

6. Adjust an oven rack to the center position and preheat the oven to 350°F.

7. Place half the apple mixture in the pastry-lined pan. Spread the filling evenly and press gently to remove any air pockets. Lay the 9-inch square of pastry over the filling. Place the remaining filling in the pan and spread it evenly. (The pan will be very full.) Beat the egg white with 1 teaspoon water to combine well. Brush the edges of the overhanging pastry with the egg wash and carefully place the remaining square of pastry on top of the filling. Seal the edges of the pastry with the tines of a fork and cut away the excess pastry with a sharp knife. Brush the top of the pie with the egg wash and sprinkle with the sugar. Prick the top all over at 2-inch intervals with a fork.

8. Bake for 65 to 80 minutes, until the pastry is a rich golden brown and the apples are tender when tested with a sharp knife. Set the pan on a wire rack to cool completely.

9. To serve, cut into squares with a sharp knife. (The first piece is always hard to remove intact; keep it for a snack.) Refrigerate leftovers.

PIES AND TARTS

Individual Deep-Dish Apple-Rhubarb Pies

We've always loved individual fruit pies, and this is one of our favorites. The filling is tart and tastes distinctly of apple and rhubarb. The sauce is slightly runny, so we use only a top crust to eliminate the problem of a soggy bottom crust. You will need to start this a day ahead, as the rhubarb needs time to "sweat" and release its juices. Use any crisp, tart apple, such as York Imperial, Northern Spy, Cox's Orange Pippin, Newtown Pippin, or Granny Smith. The pies are baked in clear glass, 10-ounce Pyrex bowls, which make an especially pretty presentation.

MAKES 6 SERVINGS

RHUBARB

1 pound rhubarb, trimmed and cut into 1/2-inch pieces (about 4 cups)

1 cup sugar

1/4 teaspoon ground cloves

PASTRY

2 cups (10 ounces) unbleached all-purpose flour (scooped into the cup and leveled)

3/4 teaspoon salt

8 tablespoons (1 stick) chilled unsalted butter, cut into tablespoon-sized pieces

1/2 cup chilled vegetable shortening

FILLING

3 tablespoons cornstarch or tapioca flour (see Mail-Order Sources, page 261)

Finely grated zest of 1 lemon

3 tablespoons fresh lemon juice

1 tablespoon pure vanilla extract or Calvados

1/2 cup sugar

1/2 teaspoon ground cinnamon

1/4 teaspoon salt

2 pounds crisp, tart apples, quartered, cored, peeled, and thinly sliced crosswise

Sugar for sprinkling

3/4 cup heavy cream

1. Combine the rhubarb, 1 cup of the sugar, and the cloves in a medium bowl. Cover and let stand in a cool place overnight. (Refrigerate if your kitchen is very warm.) The sugar should be completely dissolved and the rhubarb will be swimming in a pool of juices.

2. *To make the pastry with a food processor,* with the metal blade in place, add the flour and salt to the work bowl. Scatter the butter pieces over the flour. Pulse 4 times. Scrape the work bowl and add the shortening in 4 or 5 lumps. Pulse 3 times. While pulsing rapidly, gradually add 6 tablespoons ice water in a slow steady stream. Continue pulsing with rapid on/off bursts until the dough *almost* gathers into a ball. It should be in several large lumps. Stop pulsing and remove the dough from the work bowl. Di-

vide it in half and shape each half into a 6-inch disk. Wrap the dough in plastic and refrigerate for at least 1 hour. (The dough can be made 1 to 2 days ahead.)

To make the pastry by hand, combine the flour and salt in a large bowl. Scatter the butter pieces over the flour and cut in the butter with a pastry blender until the pieces are about pea-sized. Add the shortening to the bowl in 4 lumps and toss with your hands to coat the shortening with flour. Use the pastry blender to cut the shortening into the flour mixture until the fat particles resemble coarse crumbs. While tossing and stirring the pastry mixture with a fork, gradually drizzle in 6 tablespoons ice water. Keep stirring and tossing until the dough gathers into a ball. Divide the dough, wrap it, and chill as above.

3. Turn the rhubarb and juices into a large strainer set over a bowl. Drain well, reserving the juices, and set the rhubarb aside.

4. Measure 1¼ cups of the rhubarb juice. (Add water if necessary to reach 1¼ cups.) Put the cornstarch in a heavy saucepan. Gradually add the rhubarb juice, stirring with a heatproof rubber spatula until smooth. Set the pan over medium heat and cook, stirring gently with the spatula, until the juices come to a boil and thicken. Reduce the heat slightly and continue cooking and stirring gently for 1 to 2 minutes. If you have used tapioca flour, the mixture will seem very thick and pasty; do not be concerned. Remove the pan from the heat and stir in the lemon zest, lemon juice, and vanilla. Set the sauce aside to cool.

5. In a large bowl, combine the remaining ½ cup sugar with the cinnamon and salt. Add the apples and toss to coat well. Add the rhubarb and cooled sauce and fold together to combine well. Set aside.

6. Adjust an oven rack to the center position and preheat the oven to 400°F. Lightly butter six 10-ounce deep-dish bowls.

7. Roll out half the pastry on a lightly floured pastry cloth or work surface until it is about ⅛ inch thick. Measure the diameter of the tops of the molds you are using, and use a circular template (a dish, large cookie cutter, or vol-au-vent cutter) 1 inch larger in diameter to mark three circles on the rolled-out dough. With a sharp knife, cut the circles of dough from the pastry. (If your kitchen is warm, carefully transfer the rounds of dough to a cookie sheet and refrigerate while you roll out the second piece of dough.) Repeat with the remaining dough.

8. Divide the fruit mixture evenly among the molds. Wet the rim of one of the molds with a dampened pastry brush. Lift a circle of dough and center it over the top of the dish. Lower it gently onto the dish so that the edges of pastry overhang the rim, then fold the overhanging edge of pastry under itself to make a double thickness with about ¼ inch of overhang. Gently press down on the thickened edge of pastry so that it sticks to the rim of the mold. Use the back of a fork to press firmly on the edge of the pastry to seal it to the rim of the mold and make a decorative border. Repeat with the remaining pastry and molds.

9. Brush the tops of the pies lightly with water and sprinkle each lightly with sugar. With a small sharp knife, make a 2-inch slit in the top of each pie and wriggle the tip of the knife to widen the slit slightly. Place the molds on a large baking sheet with an edge, leaving an inch or so of space between the dishes, and place the pan in the oven.

10. Bake for 35 to 45 minutes, until the pastry tops are well browned and the filling is bubbly; the apples should feel tender when tested with the tip of a sharp knife. Reverse the position of the baking sheet, back to front, halfway during baking. Remove the pan from the oven and let the pies cool on the pan on a cooling rack.

11. Just before serving, slowly pour 2 tablespoons heavy cream through the slit in each pie. (If you are not serving all the pies, don't pour the cream into those not being served. Refrigerate the leftover pies and serve them cold, pouring in the cream just before bringing them to the table.)

Rustic Apple Cider Pie

Boiled and reduced apple cider combined with thinly sliced, firm cooking apples and spices bakes into a luscious pie. Use Braeburn apples if possible, mixed with a couple of Fujis, or a locally grown not-too-tart, firm pie apple. The crunchy/flaky pastry for this pie is made in an old-fashioned way, and the results are foolproof.

MAKES 8 SERVINGS

PASTRY

2 cups (9 ounces) unbleached all-purpose
    flour (spooned into the cup and leveled)
1/2 teaspoon salt
6 tablespoons (3/4 stick) chilled unsalted butter
1/4 cup plus 2 tablespoons chilled vegetable
    shortening

FILLING

2 1/2 cups apple cider
1/3 cup sugar
3 tablespoons tapioca flour (see Mail-Order
    Sources, page 261) or cornstarch
1 teaspoon pumpkin-pie spice
1/2 teaspoon ground ginger
2 tablespoons fresh lemon juice
2 teaspoons pure vanilla extract
3 pounds crisp, firm cooking apples,
    quartered, cored, and peeled

1 tablespoon sugar

1. To make the pastry, whisk together ⅓ cup of the flour and ⅓ cup ice water in a small bowl to make a smooth mixture; set aside. Combine the remaining 1⅔ cups flour and the salt in a medium bowl. Cut in the butter and vegetable shortening with a pastry blender until the particles resemble coarse meal. Add the flour paste and stir with a fork until the pastry gathers together. Divide the dough into two portions, one slightly larger than the other. Wrap tightly in plastic wrap and refrigerate for at least 1 hour.

2. To make the filling, place the apple cider in a heavy, medium saucepan and boil over medium-high heat, swirling the pan occasionally, until reduced to ⅔ cup, 10 to 15 minutes. Watch carefully toward the end of cooking to prevent burning. Set aside to cool to room temperature.

3. Adjust two oven racks so that one is at the lowest position and the other in the center. Place a heavy baking sheet on the lower shelf and preheat the oven to 450°F.

4. In a large mixing bowl, combine the sugar, tapioca flour, pumpkin-pie spice, ginger, lemon juice, vanilla, and cooled cider until smooth. Cut each apple quarter crosswise into thin slices, adding them as you go to the cider mixture and tossing to combine well.

5. Roll out the larger piece of pastry on a lightly floured surface to a 12- to 13-inch circle. Without stretching the dough, fit it into a 9-inch pie pan, making sure the pastry sits snugly on the bottom and sides. Let the excess pastry hang over the rim of the pie plate. Roll out the second piece of dough to a 12-inch circle.

6. Place the apples in the pie shell, leaving most of the juices in the bowl. Mound the apples slightly in the center and pat them down gently to eliminate air spaces. Carefully pour the juices in the bowl over the apples. Brush the edges of the pastry lightly with water and carefully place the second piece of dough on top. Press the edges firmly together to seal. Trim the pastry to leave a ½-inch overhang, then form a standing rim and flute it to give the pie a rustic look. Use a small sharp knife to make four slits in the top of the pie at right angles to each other between the center and edge of the top crust to allow steam to escape. Brush the top of the pie and the fluted edge lightly with water and sprinkle with the sugar.

7. Place the pie on the baking sheet. Bake for 15 minutes. Transfer the pie on its baking sheet to the center shelf, reduce the temperature to 350°F, and continue baking until the crust is browned and apples are tender when tested with a sharp knife, another 45 to 60 minutes. (If the apples were very firm, the pie may need to bake for more than 1 hour at 350°F.) If the crust is getting too brown, cover it loosely with aluminum foil.

8. Cool the pie on a wire rack and serve it warm or at room temperature.

Cranberry-Apple Streusel Pie

Streusel, a buttery crumb topping, brings the classic combination of apples and cranberries to the fore in this appealing pie. Make this when McIntosh apples and cranberries just come to the market. If McIntosh apples aren't available, substitute Braeburns.

MAKES 8 SERVINGS

PASTRY

1¼ cups (6¼ ounces) unbleached all-purpose flour (scooped into the cups and leveled)

¼ teaspoon salt

8 tablespoons (1 stick) chilled unsalted butter

FILLING

Grated zest of 1 lemon

1½ cups fresh cranberries, chopped

⅓ cup sugar

1 pound McIntosh apples (about 3 medium), quartered, cored, peeled, and thinly sliced crosswise

1 tablespoon fresh lemon juice

TOPPING

⅓ cup unbleached all-purpose flour (scooped into the cup and leveled)

½ cup firmly packed light brown sugar

½ teaspoon ground cinnamon

¼ teaspoon freshly grated nutmeg

4 tablespoons (½ stick) chilled unsalted butter

½ cup chopped pecans

1. To make the pastry, combine the flour and salt in a mixing bowl. Cut in the butter with a pastry blender until the particles resemble coarse crumbs. Gradually add 5 tablespoons ice water while tossing the mixture with a fork. Keep tossing and stirring until the dough gathers into a ball. Shape the dough into a 6-inch disk and wrap it in plastic wrap. Refrigerate for at least 1 hour.

2. Adjust an oven rack to the center position and set a heavy baking sheet on the rack; preheat the oven to 350°F.

3. Roll out the pastry on a lightly floured surface to a 13-inch circle. Fit it without stretching into a 9-inch pie pan. Trim the excess pastry, leaving ½ inch of overhang. Fold the pastry back on itself to form a high standing rim and flute it.

4. Combine the lemon zest, cranberries, and sugar in a bowl and spread the mixture evenly in the pastry shell. Arrange the apple slices over the cranberry layer and sprinkle with the lemon juice.

5. To prepare the topping, combine the flour, brown sugar, cinnamon, and nutmeg in a medium bowl. Add the butter and cut it in with a pastry blender until the mixture resembles coarse meal. Stir in the

pecans. Sprinkle the topping evenly over the apples, covering them completely. Pat gently into place.

6. Set the pie pan on the baking sheet and bake for 55 to 60 minutes, or until the topping is browned and bubbling slightly. The edges of the crust should be a rich golden brown color. Remove the pie from the oven and cool it on a wire rack. Serve warm or completely cool.

the earliest apple pie

fortunately, some very early English cooking manuals survive to give us a glimpse at how apples were used in early days. *The Forme of Cury,* a collection of recipes put together around 1390 by chefs to King Richard II, contains the earliest-known apple pie recipe:

Leshes Fryed in Lenton
Drawe a thick almande mylke with water. Take dates and pyke hem clene, with apples and peers and mynce hem with prunes damsyns. Take out the stones out of the prunes, and kerve the prunes a two. Do thereto raisons, sugar, floer of canel, hool macys and clowes, gode powdors and salt. Color hem up with sandres. Meng thise with oile. Make a coffyn as thou didest before, and do this fars thereinne, and bake it wel and serve it forth.

Jan Longone, owner of the Wine and Food Library in Ann Arbor, Michigan, mercifully provides a translation:

Fruit Slices Fried for Lent
Make a thick almond milk with water. Take dates and pick them over. Take apples and pears and mince them with damson prunes. Take the stones out of the prunes and carve the prunes in two. Add raisins, sugar, cinnamon powder, whole mace and cloves, good spices, and salt. Color them with sandalwood. Mix these with oil. Make a coffin (two-crust pie) as you have done before, and put the stuffing inside, and bake it well and serve it forth.

In 1615, John Murrell, in *A New Booke of Cookerie,* published in London, described an apple pie much like what we would serve today, once you remove the whole spices:

To Make a Pippin Pye
Take their weight in Sugar, and sticke a whole clove in eavery piece of them, and put in pieces of whole Cinamon, then put in all your Sugar; with a slice or two of whole Ginger; sprinkle Rosewater on them before you close you Pye: bake them, and serve them in.

Apple Chiffon Pie

The filling for this pie, made with an Italian meringue, is light, airy, and a contrast to the crunchy walnut crust. The pie makes a great finale for a dinner party.

MAKES 8 SERVINGS

PASTRY

$^1\!/_4$ **cup walnuts**

$^1\!/_4$ **cup sugar**

$^1\!/_2$ **teaspoon ground cinnamon**

$1^1\!/_4$ **cups ($5^3\!/_4$ ounces) unbleached all-purpose flour (spooned into the cups and leveled)**

$^1\!/_4$ **teaspoon salt**

6 **tablespoons ($^3\!/_4$ stick) chilled unsalted butter, cut into tablespoon-sized pieces**

1 **large egg**

FILLING

$1^1\!/_2$ **teaspoons unflavored gelatin**

$^1\!/_2$ **cup sugar**

1 **tablespoon cornstarch**

Scant $^1\!/_2$ **teaspoon salt**

$^3\!/_4$ **cup milk**

2 **large eggs, separated**

1 **cup smooth unsweetened applesauce**

1 **teaspoon pure vanilla extract**

2 **tablespoons Calvados**

2 **large egg whites**

$^1\!/_4$ **teaspoon cream of tartar**

TOPPING

1 **cup heavy cream**

1 **teaspoon pure vanilla extract**

2 **tablespoons confectioners' sugar**

Ground cinnamon

1. To make the pastry, combine the walnuts, sugar, and cinnamon in a food processor and pulse 6 to 8 times. Add the flour, salt, and butter and pulse 5 times. Lightly beat the egg in a 1-cup glass measure and add ice water to come to the $^1\!/_4$-cup line. While pulsing rapidly, add the egg mixture to the work bowl through the feed tube. Continue pulsing rapidly 20 to 30 times until the mixture forms a dough that *almost* gathers into a ball. (At first you may think this will never happen, but it will.) Remove the dough from the work bowl, press it together into a ball, and flatten it into a 5-inch disk. Wrap it in plastic wrap and refrigerate it for 1 hour.

2. Roll out the dough on a lightly floured surface to a 12-inch circle. Fit the dough loosely into a 9-inch pie plate and trim the edge of the dough flush with the rim of the pan. If the dough tears, simply press it together. Refrigerate the pie shell for 1 hour. (The dough trimmings make good cookies.)

3. Adjust an oven rack to the lower third position and preheat the oven to 350°F.

4. Line the chilled pie shell with aluminum foil and fill with dried beans. Bake for 20 minutes. Carefully remove the foil and beans and continue baking until

the shell is completely cooked and golden brown, about 15 minutes more. Cool completely.

5. To prepare the filling, sprinkle the gelatin over 2 tablespoons water in a custard cup; set aside. Whisk together $\frac{1}{4}$ cup of the sugar, the cornstarch, salt, and $\frac{1}{4}$ cup of the milk in a medium saucepan. In a blender, blend the remaining $\frac{1}{2}$ cup milk with the egg yolks and applesauce until smooth, about 30 seconds. Combine with the mixture in the saucepan, set the pan over medium-high heat, and cook, stirring constantly with a heatproof rubber spatula, until the mixture boils and thickens. (Don't be concerned about the egg yolks scrambling; the cornstarch protects them.) Continue cooking and stirring for 1 minute longer. Add the gelatin, remove the pan from the heat, and stir until the gelatin is completely dissolved, about 1 minute.

6. Place the saucepan in a bowl with ice and water and stir *just* until the mixture reaches room temperature; do not let the mixture get cold. Remove the pan from the ice water bath and stir in the vanilla and Calvados. Set aside. Save the ice-water bath.

7. In a large bowl, beat the 4 egg whites with an electric mixer at medium speed until foamy. Add the cream of tartar and continue beating at medium speed until soft peaks form. Set aside while you make the sugar syrup.

8. Place the remaining $\frac{1}{4}$ cup sugar in a small heavy saucepan and add 3 tablespoons water; do not stir.

Set the pan over high heat and swirl the pan by its handle occasionally as the mixture comes to a boil. When the sugar is dissolved and the mixture is boiling and looks clear, cover the pan and boil for 1 minute. Uncover the pan and continue cooking for 1 to 2 minutes longer, until the syrup is thick and has large bubbles. The temperature should be 240°F, but since there is such a small amount of syrup, it is difficult to measure and it's easier to judge it by eye.

9. Meanwhile, once the sugar syrup boils, resume beating the egg whites until they form stiff peaks. When the syrup is ready, quickly pour a little of it into the egg whites with the mixer off, then *immediately* beat at high speed for about 10 seconds. Continue this process until all the syrup is used. Don't scrape the saucepan; just use the syrup you can pour out of the pan. Beat at high speed for several more minutes, until the meringue is cool and forms stiff shiny peaks. Set aside.

10. Return the gelatin mixture to the ice bath and stir with the rubber spatula until the mixture feels cold and begins to set. Remove the pan from the water, add about 1 cup of the Italian meringue, and beat until smooth. In three or four additions, gently fold the gelatin mixture into the remaining meringue.

11. Pour most of the filling into the prepared crust. You won't have room for all of it at this point. Reserve the excess filling at room temperature. After

43

20 minutes, when the top of the pie has set, carefully spoon the remaining filling over the center of the pie. It will stay put and not run over. Refrigerate the pie for at least 4 hours before serving.

12. When ready to serve, beat the cream with the vanilla and confectioners' sugar until stiff peaks form. Spread it over the filling and dust lightly with cinnamon.

ugly ducklings

one of the most important reasons for growing your own apple trees is to obtain the tastiest fruit. Even the best commercial apples, such as Fuji and Braeburn, can't compare in taste to some varieties available only to home growers. There are several reasons for this, perhaps the most important being that commercial growers want to grow varieties they know will sell, and people won't give ugly fruit a chance. But an apple's appearance has little to do with its taste.

Take Knobbed Russet, offered by Southmeadow Fruit Gardens, for example. The catalog refers tactfully to this as "probably the most unusual looking apple" in their collection, but the description sounds distinctly unattractive: "the uneven surface is overlaid with rough grey and black russet and welts and knobs worthy of its name." Yet the flavor is outstanding: "crisp, rich, sugary, highly flavored flesh of the highest quality, superb with cheese at a winter evening's dessert."

Another Southmeadow offering is Lord's Seedling, described by apple expert George H. Howe as "nothing to look at, yellow and more or less russeted . . . and one of the most aromatic, deliciously flavored apples I know."

In general, commercial apple producers assume that russeted apples, which have rough, often brownish patches on the skin, won't sell. Perhaps they believe consumers will think the uneven roughness of the russeted surface indicates a fungus infection or other unpleasantness, not a normal condition. In any case, this prejudice precludes the commercial availability of many wonderful varieties, such as Roxbury Russet, the oldest American variety, with dense, crisp, sweet flesh and a unique flavor, and Pitmaston Pineapple, neglected both for its russeted skin and its small size, but one of the best, described by apple expert E. A. Bunyard as having "a most deliciously scented and honeyed flavor."

Other delicious apples are rejected commercially for any number of reasons—poor yield, short storage period, poor shipping qualities, or uneven shape. None of these qualities is related to the most important thing about an apple, its flavor.

Charlotka

"Our number one fruit is apples. Our number two fruit is apples. And our number three fruit is also apples." So proclaimed our tour guide on a bus excursion through the Polish countryside one October. A few days later, I devoured a huge serving of an incredible charlotka, a Polish apple tart, at a café in Warsaw. Although I have eaten many versions of charlotka, none have compared to that one. It was a thick layer of butter-smooth apple purée baked between two layers of thin, crisp, tender pastry. This charlotka, re-created from memory, comes mighty close to the one I remember. Bells and whistles went off in my mouth at first bite. The amount of apples needed seems staggering, but they will cook down more than you might think. The key to the success of this recipe is using a firm, sweet-tart cooking apple that will hold its shape when turned into applesauce, such as Jonamac, Northern Spy, Winesap, or Pippin. The filling and pastry can be made ahead and refrigerated for a day or two; assemble and bake the charlotka when you want to serve it.

MAKES 8 SERVINGS

FILLING

5 pounds crisp cooking apples quartered, cored, peeled, and coarsely chopped
1 cup sugar
1 tablespoon pure vanilla extract
2 tablespoons dark rum
1 teaspoon ground cinnamon
1/2 cup apricot preserves, strained
4 tablespoons (1/2 stick) unsalted butter

PASTRY

2 cups (9 ounces) unbleached all-purpose flour (spooned into the cup and leveled)
1/4 teaspoon salt
8 tablespoons (1 stick) chilled unsalted butter, cut into tablespoon-sized pieces
1 cup confectioners' sugar
2 large egg yolks
1/4 cup milk
1 teaspoon pure vanilla extract

1 large egg yolk
Confectioners' sugar for dusting

1. To make the filling, place the apples in a large, heavy nonreactive pot. Cover and cook slowly over low heat, stirring occasionally with a wooden spatula, for about 45 minutes, until the apples are tender.

2. Uncover the pot and stir the apples to break them up. Add the remaining filling ingredients, increase the heat to high, and boil, stirring constantly, until the mixture cooks down to a thick purée that holds

its shape on the tip of the spatula, about 20 minutes. Just when to stop cooking can be a bit tricky, but as you stir, keep your eye on the bottom of the pot: If you swipe the spatula quickly across the bottom and the apple mixture immediately runs together, it is not ready. When the apple mixture stays put and the bottom of the pot remains visible after swiping, the purée is ready. (Here are a couple of other tests: 1. If the apple mixture wants to stick to the bottom as a thin film, and you no longer see obvious bubbles even though the mixture is boiling hot, it is ready; and 2. If you spoon some of the purée in a mound on the tip of the wooden spatula and quickly turn the spatula upside down, the apple mixture should not immediately fall off; it may stay put.)

3. Remove the pot from the heat and stir occasionally until cool. If necessary, use a potato masher to break up any large apple pieces, but don't overdo it. It's nice to have an uneven texture. You will have about 4 cups of filling. (The filling can be made ahead and stored in an airtight container in the refrigerator for up to 2 weeks. Bring it to room temperature before using.)

4. To make the pastry, stir the flour and salt together in a medium bowl. Cut in the butter with a pastry blender until the mixture resembles coarse meal. In a small bowl, combine the remaining pastry ingredients with a fork. Add to the flour mixture and stir and toss until the dough gathers into a ball.

5. Divide the dough into two portions, one about one and a half times the size of the other (if you have a scale, one piece should weigh about 12 ounces and the other about 8 ounces). Flatten each to form a disk about 1 inch thick; wrap tightly in plastic and refrigerate for at least 30 minutes.

6. When ready to bake the charlotka, adjust two oven racks so that one is at the bottom and the other is in the center of the oven. Place a heavy baking sheet on the lower shelf and preheat the oven to 450°F.

7. Roll the larger piece of pastry out on a lightly floured pastry cloth or work surface to a 14-inch circle. Fit it into a 10-inch fluted tart pan with a removable bottom. Be sure not to stretch the pastry. Gently nudge it down from the top edge of the pan so that it fits snugly into the corners. Leave the excess hanging over the edge. Roll out the smaller piece of pastry to a 12-inch circle.

8. Spread the filling in the tart pan; the pan will be completely full. Combine the egg yolk and 1 teaspoon water with a fork in a small bowl. Brush the rim of the pastry in the pan with the egg glaze and lay the circle of pastry on top of the filling. Press the edges firmly together to seal, cutting off the excess pastry in the process. (Shape the scraps into a disk, wrap it securely in plastic, and refrigerate. Use to make sugar cookies.) Brush the top of the charlotka with the glaze, taking care not to let any run down between the pastry and the edge of the pan. Prick the top all over with a fork.

9. Set the pan on the baking sheet in the oven and bake for 15 minutes. Transfer the charlotka on its baking sheet to the center shelf, reduce the temperature to 375°F, and continue baking for another 30 to 35 minutes, or until the charlotka is puffed and the pastry is very well browned. Cool the charlotka completely on a wire rack. It will settle during cooling.

10. Carefully remove the charlotka from its pan and transfer it to a serving platter. Dust the top with a thin layer of confectioners' sugar, cut into wedges with a sharp knife, and serve.

Tarte Tatin

If there's one recipe that proclaims "apple" in all its glory, this is it. Slices of apple are baked in a caramel syrup of butter and sugar, topped with pastry. Then the tarte is turned upside down, cooled, and served. What makes this so special is the texture of the apples. As they imbibe the delicious caramel, they become smooth and velvety, with an irresistible flavor. The pastry, also rich and buttery, combines with the apple in the mouth and makes the taste buds do cartwheels. Over the years, tarte Tatin has become legendary, partly because of its seeming simplicity but mostly, I think, because of its uniqueness.

The key to a great tarte Tatin lies in the choice of apple. The best apple I've found for the tarte is something called Ashmead's Kernel, an old russet variety. It's a small, ugly-looking, homely thing that is firm, tart, crisp, and, well, ideal, but it's not widely available. The apples that are available and that make wonderful tartes Tatin are the kinds that hold their shape and don't fall apart during cooking. I've had excellent results with Northern Spy, Jonamac, Jonagold, Golden Delicious, Granny Smith, Liberty, Sweet Sixteen, Braeburn, and Kidd's Orange. Select just about any firm apple variety that is more tart than sweet. Although tarte Tatin is delicious plain, a small portion of lightly sweetened whipped cream (perhaps flavored with a touch of Calvados), crème fraîche, or top-quality vanilla ice cream is always welcome.

PASTRY

1 cup (5 ounces) unbleached all-purpose flour (scooped into the cup and leveled)

1 tablespoon sugar

¼ teaspoon salt

8 tablespoons (1 stick) chilled unsalted butter, cut into tablespoon-sized pieces

FILLING

7 tablespoons unsalted butter

1 cup sugar

2½ pounds apples (about 5 large or 7 medium), quartered, cored, and peeled

1. To make the pastry, combine the flour, sugar, and salt in a large bowl. Add the butter and use a pastry blender to cut the butter into the flour until the particles are in largish lumps. Then work the mixture rapidly between your fingertips to flatten the pieces of butter into flakes. Don't be too thorough, or the butter will soften. Add ¼ cup ice water and toss and stir with a fork (a large blending fork works really well) just until the dough gathers together into a mass.

2. Shape the dough into a 6-inch log and put it on your work surface with one end facing you. Working quickly, with the heel of your hand, starting at the far end of the dough, break away and smear pieces of the dough until all the dough has been used. Gather up the dough, reshape it into a log, and repeat the process. This entire procedure should take you about 30 seconds. Shape the dough into a 6-inch disk, wrap it tightly with plastic wrap, and refrigerate for at least 2 hours. (The dough can be prepared up to 3 days ahead.)

3. When ready to bake the tart, adjust an oven rack to the center position and preheat the oven to 375°F.

4. To prepare the filling, melt the butter in a 10-inch cast-iron frying pan or a tarte Tatin pan over medium-low heat. Stir in the sugar, raise the heat to medium, and cook, stirring occasionally with a wooden spoon, until the mixture becomes a smooth, dark caramel syrup, about 15 minutes. At first the mixture will look granular, then it may lump up. Don't despair. The sugar will gradually melt and become smooth and a rich, dark brown color; however, the butter and sugar will not be completely combined. What's important is that the sugar is properly caramelized; don't go too far, or the caramel will burn. Remove the pan from the heat and set it aside to cool slightly.

5. Cut each apple quarter lengthwise into two or three slices: two if the apples are of medium size, three if the apples are large. Arrange a single layer of apples in the pan in an attractive pattern of concen-

tric circles. Add the remaining apples to the pan in no particular order, mounding them slightly in the center.

6. Roll the pastry out on a lightly floured surface to a 10-inch circle. Don't be concerned about rough-looking edges. Carefully lay the pastry over the filling, and tuck the excess dough down inside the pan. With the tip of a small sharp knife, make 4 small steam vents in a square pattern about 2 inches from the center of the dough.

7. Bake for about 1 hour, until pastry is browned and you can see the caramel syrup bubbling around the edges.

8. Now comes the tricky part. Is the apple filling too juicy? Has the caramel been diluted to the point where it needs more cooking? Chances are the answers are yes. Even with Ashmead's Kernel apples, I find a final top-of-the-stove cooking of the tart is needed. Carefully tilt the pan and observe how liquid the filling is. If the juices are so thick that they've been almost entirely absorbed by the apples, the tart is done. If the juices are runny, set the pan over medium heat and cook, shaking the pan occasionally (use a potholder, as the handle will be hot), until the liquid is very thick and syrupy and almost completely absorbed by the apples. This can sometimes take 10 to 15 minutes, depending on the type of apple you've used.

9. When the tart is done, place a serving platter over the pastry, hold it in place with a potholder, and grasp the handle of the pan with another potholder. Quickly invert the two and set the platter and pan down on your countertop. Wait a few seconds and slowly lift off the pan. If everything has worked out properly, the top layer of apples should be in a neat pattern. If the slices have moved apart a bit, use a small metal spatula to realign them. Cool the tart and serve it warm or at room temperature.

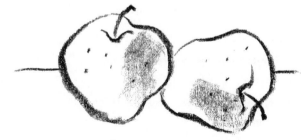

French Apple Tart

This is a classic. Apples are sautéed in butter and sugar until tender. The mixture is roughly mashed and spread into a partially baked, flaky pastry shell. Thin apple slices are arranged attractively over the top, brushed with butter, sprinkled with sugar, and baked until deliciously browned. Be sure to use a firm, tart apple for this. Granny Smith, Kidd's Orange, Northern Spy, and Empire are all good choices. This tart is best when very fresh, so bake it within a few hours of serving.

MAKES 8 SERVINGS

PASTRY

1¼ cups (5¾ ounces) unbleached
    all-purpose flour (spooned into the cups
    and leveled)
1 tablespoon sugar
½ teaspoon salt
4 tablespoons (½ stick) chilled unsalted
    butter, cut into tablespoon-sized pieces
⅓ cup chilled vegetable shortening

FILLING

2½ pounds firm, tart apples (about 5 large),
    quartered, cored, and peeled
4 tablespoons (½ stick) unsalted butter
½ cup sugar

TOPPING

2 large firm, tart apples, quartered, cored,
    peeled, and cut lengthwise into
    ⅛-inch-thick slices
2 tablespoons unsalted butter
1 tablespoon granulated sugar
Confectioners' sugar for dusting

1. To make the pastry, combine the flour, sugar, and salt in a large bowl. Add the butter and shortening, and use a pastry blender to cut the butter and shortening into the flour until the particles are in largish lumps. Then work the mixture rapidly between your fingertips to flatten the pieces of fat into flakes. Add 4 to 5 tablespoons ice water by the tablespoon and toss and stir with a fork just until the dough gathers together into a mass.

2. Shape the dough into a 6-inch log and put it on your work surface with an end facing you. Working quickly, with the heel of your hand, starting at the far end of the dough, break away and smear pieces of the dough until all the dough has been used. Gather up the dough, reshape it into a log, and repeat the process. This entire procedure should take you about 30 seconds. Shape the dough into a 6-inch disk, wrap it tightly with plastic wrap, and refrigerate for at least 1 hour. (The dough can be prepared up to 3 days ahead.)

3. Roll the pastry out on a lightly floured pastry cloth or work surface to a 12-inch circle. Fit it into a

9-inch fluted tart pan with a removable bottom. Be sure not to stretch the pastry: Gently nudge it down into the pan from the top edge so that the dough fits snugly into the corners and the sides are a bit thicker than the rest of the pastry. Roll the rolling pin over the top of the pan to cut away the extra dough, then press on the sides gently to form a rim of pastry that rises slightly above the edge of the pan. If you wish to decorate the edge of the tart shell, use the blunt side of a paring knife to score it slightly at 1/4-inch intervals. Refrigerate the shell for at least 30 minutes.

4. Adjust an oven rack to the center position, place a heavy baking sheet on the shelf, and preheat the oven to 400°F.

5. Line the chilled pastry shell with a square of aluminum foil or parchment and fill it with dried beans or rice. Place the tart pan on the baking sheet and bake for 20 to 25 minutes, or until the edges of the pastry are golden brown. Remove the tart pan with the baking sheet from the oven and set it on a cooling rack. Remove the foil and beans. Let the shell cool completely. Reduce the oven temperature to 375°F.

6. To make the filling, cut each apple quarter lengthwise in half and then crosswise into thirds. Melt the butter in a large skillet. Add the apples and sugar. Cook, stirring occasionally with a large heatproof rubber spatula, over medium-high heat until the apples are tender and the juices are very thick and syrupy and have been almost entirely absorbed, 8 to 10 minutes. The apples should maintain their shape. Remove from the heat and cool the apples in the skillet.

7. To assemble the tart, mash the apples in the skillet with a potato masher to a coarse texture. Turn the apples into the cooled tart shell and pack them in gently; smooth the top. Beginning at the edge of the crust, arrange the apple slices, overlapping them a good 1/4 inch, to form a circle of tightly packed apple slices. The center of the filling will still be exposed. Arrange enough apple slices over it to cover the exposed filling, cutting them to fit as necessary; it doesn't matter how the center of the tart looks at this point. Arrange a second circle of overlapping apple slices in the center of the tart.

8. Melt the butter in a small saucepan and add the granulated sugar. Stir well and, using a small brush, brush gently all over the apple slices, being careful not to disturb the pattern you've created. Sift 1 to 2 tablespoons of confectioners' sugar over the apples in a thin, even layer.

9. Place the tart, on its baking sheet, in the oven and bake until the top is a golden brown and the apples are tender, 50 to 60 minutes. The edges of some of the apple slices may take on a darker hue, but that is fine. If the top of the tart is browned before the apples are tender, simply tent the tart loosely with foil (shiny side out) and bake for another few minutes. Remove the baking sheet and tart from the oven and transfer the tart to a cooling rack.

10. When it is completely cool, carefully remove the tart from its pan and place it on a serving platter. Before serving, dust the top of the tart with confectioners' sugar. Serve warm or at room temperature.

Apple Lattice Tart

This is easy to make yet looks fancy. Serve it as a dessert after a large meal or for afternoon tea or coffee. Use a mixture of sweet and tart apples, such as a combination of Granny Smith or Newtown Pippin with Fuji and Spigold.

MAKES 8 SERVINGS

PASTRY

1½ cups (6¾ ounces) unbleached all-purpose flour (spooned into the cups and leveled)

½ cup (2 ounces) cake flour (spooned into the cup and leveled)

I tablespoon sugar

¼ teaspoon salt

8 tablespoons (I stick) chilled unsalted butter, cut into 6 pieces

3 tablespoons chilled vegetable shortening

¾ teaspoon cider vinegar

FILLING

⅓ cup dried sour cherries

½ cup sugar

½ teaspoon apple pie spice

⅓ cup skinned and chopped hazelnuts (see page 28)

3 large apples (I¼ to I½ pounds), quartered, cored, peeled, and thinly sliced (about 4 cups)

Finely grated zest of I lemon

2 tablespoons fresh lemon juice

I teaspoon pure vanilla extract

I tablespoon sugar

1. To make the pastry, place the flours in the work bowl of a food processor with the metal blade in place and add the sugar and salt. Add the butter along with the vegetable shortening. Pulse 4 times

(about 1 second each). Combine the cider vinegar with ⅓ cup ice water in a 1-cup glass measure. While pulsing very rapidly, pour the liquid through the feed tube in a slow steady stream. After about 30 pulses, the dough will almost gather into a ball; stop before it actually forms a ball.

2. Carefully remove the dough from the work bowl and press it together gently to form one mass, then divide the dough into two pieces, one slightly larger than the other. (If you have a scale, one piece should weigh about 10 ounces and the other about 8 ounces.) Shape each into a 1-inch-thick disk, wrap tightly in plastic wrap, and refrigerate for at least 1 hour. (The pastry can be made 2 to 3 days ahead.)

3. When ready to bake the tart, adjust an oven rack to the lower third position and set a heavy baking sheet on the rack. Preheat the oven to 450°F.

4. Soak the cherries in hot water to cover for 15 minutes, or until plumped. Drain well and pat dry with paper towels.

5. In a large bowl, combine the sugar, apple-pie spice, and hazelnuts. Add the apples, lemon zest, lemon juice, vanilla, and cherries and fold together to combine well.

6. Roll the larger piece of pastry out on a lightly floured surface to a 13-inch circle. Fit it into a 10-inch fluted tart pan with a removable bottom, without stretching the dough. Leave the overhanging

pastry alone for now. Roll out the second piece of dough to an 11-inch circle and cut it into ½-inch-wide strips.

7. Distribute the filling evenly in the tart shell, gently pressing it down. Brush the edge of the pastry lightly with cold water and arrange the strips of pastry on top in a lattice pattern. Press the ends of the pastry strips firmly onto the edge of the pastry shell. Trim away any overhanging pastry with a sharp knife. Brush the lattice strips with water and sprinkle with the sugar.

8. Set the tart pan on the baking sheet and bake for 10 minutes. Reduce the temperature to 400°F and continue baking for 40 minutes longer, or until the tart is golden brown and the apples are tender when tested with the tip of a sharp knife. Cool the tart in its pan on a rack, then carefully remove the tart from its pan and transfer it to a serving platter. Cut with a sharp knife.

Apple and Plum Galette

A galette is a rustic French fruit tart. Its hallmark is a thin pastry that is crisp yet flaky. The pastry is rolled and shaped more or less free-form and the rough-looking edges folded over the fruit. It is one of the easiest of all baked tarts to make.

Use any firm, crisp apple. If you can find Sweet Sixteen, an apple with a background taste of anise, it is particularly good in this galette. It's important not to underbake the galette. It might look done in less than one hour, but the pastry must be very brown in order for it to have its special texture. The best way to achieve this is to line your oven rack with a large baking stone and set the galette pan on it. Serve this plain or with some heavy cream drizzled over the top.

MAKES 8 SERVINGS

$^1/_2$ **cup walnuts**

2 tablespoons sugar

$^1/_2$ **teaspoon ground cinnamon**

PASTRY

$1^1/_2$ **cups ($6^3/_4$ ounces) unbleached all-purpose flour (spooned into the cups and leveled)**

$^1/_4$ **teaspoon salt**

8 tablespoons (1 stick) chilled unsalted butter, cut into 6 pieces

FILLING

3 large apples ($1^1/_2$ pounds), quartered, cored, and peeled

12 to 14 Italian prune plums, halved and pitted

3 tablespoons chilled unsalted butter, cut into small pieces

$^1/_4$ **cup plus 1 tablespoon sugar**

1. Process the walnuts, sugar, and cinnamon in the work bowl of a food processor until powdery. Remove and set aside.

2. To make the pastry, add the flour to the work bowl along with the salt and butter. Pulse 4 times. While pulsing rapidly, pour $^1/_3$ cup ice water through the feed tube in a steady stream. Keep pulsing just until the dough *almost* gathers into a ball. Remove the dough from the work bowl and gently press it into a 6-inch disk. The pastry may be used right away. (The dough can be wrapped in plastic wrap and refrigerated for up to 2 days.)

3. Roll the dough on a lightly floured surface to a 16-inch circle. Don't be concerned about rough edges. Fold the dough in quarters and center the point of the dough in a 14-inch pizza pan. Unfold the dough and allow the excess to drape over the sides. Refrigerate while you prepare the apples.

4. Adjust an oven rack to the center position and preheat the oven to 400°F; if using a baking stone, place it on the center rack and preheat for at least 40 minutes.

5. Cut each apple quarter lengthwise into 6 or 7 slices. Remove the dough from the refrigerator and sprinkle it with the nut mixture to within 1 inch of the edge of the pan. Arrange the apple slices, slightly overlapping, in concentric circles to cover the nut mixture. Place the plums about 2 inches apart in concentric circles, cut sides down, over the apples. Dot the top of the galette with the butter. Sprinkle with ¼ cup of the sugar. Bring up the overhanging pastry and press it firmly onto the outer circle of apples. Sprinkle the edge of the pastry with the remaining 1 tablespoon sugar and place the pan in the oven.

6. Bake until the dough is well browned and the filling is bubbly, about 1 hour. Cool the galette in its pan on a wire rack and serve warm or at room temperature.

granny smith

most of us think of Granny Smith as a relatively new apple, but it has been around for more than 125 years. Like so many other fine varieties, Granny Smith appeared as a chance seedling. Marie Ann Smith, who lived in a suburb of Sydney, Australia, threw some rotting Tasmanian apples into her yard. Some years later, an apple tree that grew from one of the seeds produced attractive green fruit, and in 1868, Mrs. Smith invited a successful fruit grower, Mr. E. H. Small, to give his opinion. Mr. Small thought the apple might be good for cooking, but he wasn't especially excited—several good cooking varieties were already available. (His young son, Tom, tasted the apple as well and thought it was a good eating apple.) The Smith family continued to grow the new variety, however, and a relative eventually became its first commercial grower.

In the early 1900s, interest in this bright green beauty grew. It met both the needs of the grower and the home cook. The trees produced an abundant crop, and it shipped and stored well. Consumers liked it. Granny Smith is now popular not only down under and in the United States, but also in South Africa, Chile, and France. While most people agree that Granny Smith is a fine cooking apple, some don't like it for eating. The Granny Smiths sold in the supermarket have been picked underripe—that's why they are so green and so tart. But if you sort carefully through a bin, you may be lucky enough to find some Granny Smiths that are riper, with a yellowish cast to the skin. If so, by all means, try one—it will be sweeter than what you're used to, yet still crunchy and juicy. Granny Smith ripens late, so it won't mature in the north. Even in the apple-growing regions of eastern Washington, the fruit may freeze slightly on the trees before it is ripe enough to harvest. It does, however, grow well farther south than most apples, bearing well even in Southern California.

Apple Mascarpone Tart

This is a tart of poached apples baked in a creamy mascarpone cheese mixture. The contrast among the apples, filling, and buttery pastry is heavenly. Make this for a special occasion. Use any firm, sweet/tart apple, such as Jonamac, Braeburn, Northern Spy, York Imperial, or Granny Smith.

MAKES 10 SERVINGS

PASTRY

1 cup plus 2 tablespoons (5¾ ounces) unbleached all-purpose flour (scooped into the cup and leveled)

⅓ cup (1¼ ounces) cake flour (scooped into the cup and leveled)

¼ teaspoon salt

2 tablespoons sugar

10 tablespoons (1¼ sticks) chilled unsalted butter, cut into tablespoon-sized pieces

1 large egg, separated

SYRUP

1½ cups sugar

One 3-inch cinnamon stick

½ teaspoon allspice berries

3 whole cloves

2 pounds crisp, tart cooking apples (about 5 medium), quartered, cored, and peeled

FILLING

⅔ cup mascarpone

½ cup sugar

4 large eggs

¼ cup amaretto

1. *To make the pastry in a food processor,* add the flours, salt, and sugar to the work bowl with the metal blade in place. Add the butter to the work bowl. In a 1-cup glass measure, combine the egg yolk with enough ice water to make ⅓ cup. Pulse the butter into the dry ingredients, about 4 times. While pulsing very rapidly, gradually add the egg yolk mixture through the feed tube. Pulse only until the dough *almost* gathers into a ball. Carefully remove the dough from the work bowl and shape into a 6-inch disk. Wrap tightly in plastic wrap and refrigerate for at least 1 hour.

To make the pastry by hand, combine the dry ingredients in a large bowl and cut in the butter with a pastry blender until the particles resemble coarse meal. In a 1-cup glass measure, combine the egg yolk with enough ice water to make ⅓ cup. While tossing with a fork, gradually add the egg yolk mixture to the flour mixture. Keep mixing until the dough gathers in a ball. Shape, wrap, and chill as directed above.

2. Roll the pastry out on a lightly floured surface to a 15-inch circle. Carefully fit the pastry into an 11-inch tart pan with a removable bottom: Nudge the pastry into the pan from the top edge without

stretching, making sure the dough fits snugly on the bottom and in the corners. Trim the excess pastry away so that only a $^1/_2$-inch edge hangs over the rim. Fold this edge into the shell, giving the sides a double thickness of pastry. Press firmly on the dough so that the sides extend about $^1/_4$ inch above the rim. Refrigerate for 30 minutes.

3. Adjust an oven rack to the center position, place a heavy baking sheet on the rack, and preheat the oven to 400°F.

4. Line the chilled pastry with a square of aluminum foil and fill with dried beans. Set the tart pan on the baking sheet and bake for 20 minutes. Remove the pan from the oven and carefully lift away the foil and beans. Beat the egg white with a fork just to break it up and brush the shell with the egg white. Bake the pastry for another 5 minutes, or until it is set and looks dry, and the edges are golden brown. Cool the shell in its pan on a rack.

5. To prepare the syrup, combine the sugar, $1^1/_2$ cups water, the cinnamon stick, allspice berries, and cloves in a medium saucepan. Bring to a boil over medium heat, stirring occasionally. Reduce the heat to medium-low and simmer for 5 minutes. Add the apples to the syrup and cook, covered, until tender, about 20 minutes; do not overcook them. Push the apple pieces down into the syrup from time to time with a rubber spatula. Cool the apples in the syrup with the lid on. Drain the apples, place on paper towels, and set aside.

6. When ready to bake the tart, adjust an oven rack to the center position, place a heavy baking sheet on the rack, and preheat the oven to 325°F.

7. To prepare the filling, beat the mascarpone cheese, sugar, and 1 of the eggs together until smooth. Add the remaining eggs one at a time, beating only until each is incorporated. Stir in the amaretto. Pour a thin layer of the mascarpone mixture into the pastry shell. Arrange the apples in two concentric circles on the filling. Carefully pour the rest of the mascarpone mixture over the apples. The pan will be very full.

8. Set the tart pan on the baking sheet and bake for about 45 minutes, or until the filling is puffed and a rich brown color; the center may be a bit paler. Set the tart pan on a cooling rack and let stand until completely cool, then carefully unmold the tart, transfer to a dessert platter, and refrigerate. This tart is best served cold. Cut it with a sharp knife.

PIES AND TARTS

Apple Tart Flambé

Flambéed tarts are a specialty of Alsace in eastern France. Wafer-thin pastries with all manner of toppings are baked in wood-fired ovens. The tarts get their name from the flames that lick at them during their brief stint in the inferno. One October, while in the picture-postcard town of Colmar, we ate lunch at a restaurant that specialized in *tartes flambées*. Each course was a different tart—a first-course bacon tart, then a cheese main-course tart, followed by an apple tart for dessert. Before the last was served, our waitress placed a small carafe of Calvados and a box of matches on the table; then she vanished. We were expectant. In less than a minute she scurried back, carrying a wooden board with the apple tart. She set the board on the table and immediately poured the Calvados all over the top. Without missing a beat, she struck a match and ignited the brandy before our eyes. An unpretentious dessert had suddenly been transformed into something spectacular. She uttered a happy, *"Bon appétit,"* and disappeared. As soon as the flames died down, we cut into the tart, and before we knew it, it too had disappeared.

This is very easy to make, but as with so many seemingly easy endeavors, attention must be paid. The three most important things to keep in mind are: That the pastry must be rolled very thin, the apples have to be sliced very thin, and the apple of choice is a crisp one on the tart side. Macoun, McIntosh, Arlet, and Northern Spy are some suggestions. For variety, you can mix a sweet apple, such as Fuji or Honeycrisp, with a tart one.

For best results, bake the tart on a baking stone or on quarry tiles. I roll the dough out on a pastry cloth and transfer it to a reusable silicon baking pan liner (see page 261 for Mail-Order Sources) set on a baking sheet or baker's peel. Then I simply slide the whole thing off onto the stone. Do not dally once the tart is out of the oven. Pour on the Calvados, immediately ignite it, and turn out the lights so you can see the beautiful blue flames wafting upward. If you're making this for guests, invite them into the kitchen to witness this step. Do not even think of serving this with ice cream or whipped cream or anything else. Although the recipe says it makes four servings, two hungry souls can easily polish it off.

MAKES 4 SERVINGS

½ recipe Tarte Tatin pastry (page 48) (about 5½ ounces), shaped into a disk and well chilled

2 to 3 medium crisp, tart apples, quartered, cored, peeled, and sliced ¹⁄₁₆ inch thick

1 tablespoon sugar

¼ cup heavy cream

3 tablespoons Calvados or Applejack

1. Adjust an oven rack to the center position. If possible, line the shelf with a large rectangular baking stone or quarry tiles. Preheat the oven to 450°F.

2. Roll out the pastry on a lightly floured pastry cloth or work surface to a 14-inch circle about ¹/₁₆ inch thick. You must be patient with this step and you must work the rolling pin gently. Roll with a forward motion, not a downward one. Rotate the dough frequently, turn it over from time to time, and dust it very lightly with flour as necessary. If you're going to bake the tart on a baking stone or tiles, line a large cookie sheet (having a rim on one side only) with a silicon baking-pan liner, fold the dough in quarters, and transfer it to the sheet. Unfold the dough. If you're not baking the tart on a baking stone, transfer the folded dough to a 14-inch pizza pan with the point in the center of the pan and unfold the dough. (You can do this hours ahead if you want; cover with plastic wrap and refrigerate.)

3. Arrange the apple slices on the dough in concentric circles, starting at the rim and with their sides touching. Sprinkle with the sugar and drizzle the cream evenly over the top.

4. If baking on a stone, slide the pan liner with the tart onto the stone. If using the pizza pan, simply place the pan in the oven. Bake for 5 to 8 minutes, until the pastry is cooked through and crisp and the apples are tender. Ideally, the top of the tart will be flecked with brown spots. If not, place it under the broiler for a few seconds, watching it constantly.

5. Remove the tart from the oven by sliding a baker's peel under the pan liner, or take the pizza pan out of the oven. Immediately pour the Calvados evenly over the tart and carefully ignite it with a match. When the flames die down, cut the tart into quarters and serve.

pie or tart?

what is the difference between a pie and a tart? Pamella Z. Asquith, in her *Fruit Tart Cookbook*, claims "the difference between a pie and a tart is that a pie is usually baked with a fruit filling (prepared with plenty of sugar); a tart is made with uncooked or poached fruit, and is not as sweet." Others make a more simple distinction: If it has a top crust, it's a pie. If it's open-faced, call it a tart. But where does that leave pecan, chiffon, or meringue-topped pies?

A tart is a continental European dessert, generally made in a straight-sided shallow pan. Some tarts have cooked fillings; others are made by artfully arranging raw fruit and holding the pieces in place with a clear glaze. A tart always has a bottom crust and sometimes is topped with a lattice crust. Even with the lattice, you can tell it's a tart by its shallowness and its straight sides. The pie originated in England and is baked in a pan with slanted sides. Even when served with a lattice or crumb topping, the pie has a fluted rim and a cooked filling.

Bavarian Apple Kuchen

While driving across southern Germany on our way to Munich, we stopped in Stuttgart for a museum fix. It was late afternoon when we emerged back into the October sunlight, and we were hungry. Tables at a nearby outdoor café were occupied by patrons eating all manner of pastries and desserts, but what caught our eye was a deep-dish apple kuchen. One bite and we knew we were onto something special. The pastry was cookie-like and the filling tender chunks of lemon-scented apple. A mixture of firm apples like sweet Fujis and tart Granny Smiths works very well. Northern Spy or Cox's Orange Pippin are wonderful. You will need a 9 × 2-inch-deep tart pan with a scalloped edge and removable bottom.

MAKES 8 SERVINGS

PASTRY

3 large egg yolks

½ cup sugar

½ teaspoon salt

1 tablespoon milk

2 teaspoons pure vanilla extract

12 tablespoons (1½ sticks) chilled unsalted butter, cut into tablespoon-sized pieces

2 cups (9 ounces) unbleached all-purpose flour (spooned into the cup and leveled)

FILLING

4 tablespoons (½ stick) unsalted butter

⅔ cup sugar

Grated zest and juice of 1 lemon

3½ pounds apples, quartered, cored, peeled, and cut into 1-inch chunks (about 10 cups)

1 tablespoon cornstarch

Confectioners' sugar for dusting

1. *To make the pastry in a mixer with the paddle attachment,* combine the egg yolks, sugar, salt, milk, and vanilla in the mixer bowl and beat on the lowest speed only until combined, about 30 seconds. Add the butter and beat until the butter is in smallish pieces, about 1 minute. Add the flour and beat on lowest speed until it is incorporated and the dough cleans the side of the bowl, about 1 minute. The dough should be malleable and not at all sticky. You will notice visible pieces of butter in the dough.

If not using a mixer, combine the egg yolks, sugar, salt, milk, and vanilla in a large mixing bowl and mix with a fork. Add the pieces of butter and mash them into the yolk mixture with the fork until the pieces are on the small side (about ¼ inch). Gradually add the flour, mixing and tossing with the fork. Continue stirring until the dough gathers into a ball and cleans the side of the bowl.

2. Transfer the dough to an unfloured work surface, shape it into a log about 12 inches long, and position

it with a short end of the log facing you. Working rapidly, use the heel of your hand to smear golf ball–sized pieces of dough from the far end of the log away from you. Continue until all the dough has been used. Gather the dough together, reshape into a log, and repeat this process once more. This entire procedure should take no more than 30 seconds. The butter should be thoroughly blended into the dough, but if you still see a few bits of butter here and there, it's all right. Divide the dough into two pieces, one twice as large as the other. (If you have a scale, the pieces should weigh 14 ounces and 7 ounces.) Shape each piece into a disk, wrap securely with plastic wrap, and refrigerate for at least 1 hour.

3. Meanwhile, prepare the filling: Melt the butter in a large heavy skillet over medium-low heat. Stir in the sugar and lemon juice and cook for about 30 seconds. Add the apples and mix well. Cover the pan and cook until the apples begin to release their juices, about 5 minutes.

4. Uncover the pan, increase the heat to medium, and continue cooking, stirring frequently with a heat-proof rubber spatula, until the apples are just tender when pierced with a toothpick, about 10 minutes more. Turn the apples into a wire strainer set over a bowl and let stand until cool. Reserve the apple juices.

5. Adjust an oven rack to the center position and place a heavy baking sheet on the rack. Preheat the oven to 350°F.

6. Roll the larger piece of dough on a lightly floured surface to a 13-inch circle. Coat a 9 × 2-inch tart pan with vegetable cooking spray. Fit the pastry into the tart pan, being careful to avoid stretching the dough. Leave the overhanging pastry alone for now. Roll out the smaller piece of dough to a 10-inch circle.

7. Whisk the cornstarch into the cooled apple juices. Add the apples and lemon zest and fold together gently to avoid breaking the apple pieces. Turn the apple mixture into the tart pan and pat it gently to level it; the pan will be full. Brush the edge of the pastry lightly with water and set the circle of dough on top. Press firmly on the edges to seal, then roll the rolling pin over the top to cut away the excess pastry. (Use the pastry scraps to make sugar cookies.)

8. Prick the top of the pastry in several places with a fork and place the tart pan on the baking sheet in the oven. Bake for about 1 hour, until the pastry is golden brown. Cool the kuchen in its pan on a rack.

9. When the kuchen is completely cool, carefully remove it from the tart pan. Dust with confectioners' sugar before serving.

Desserts

Coleridge holds that a man cannot have a pure mind who refuses apple dumplings. I am not certain but he is right.

—CHARLES LAMB, *ESSAYS OF ELIA*

Although I've often wondered what kind of dumplings so captivated Coleridge and Charles Lamb—was it a tender biscuit-like dough cooking atop a stew of apples? or cored apples filled with spices and butter and wrapped in a pastry? or something akin to Spicy Apple Dumplings (see page 82)—it ultimately doesn't matter because it's all good. Apple dessert terminology seems to have its own subculture. Besides dumplings, apples can become cobblers, grunts, slumps (similar to cobblers but cooked on top of the stove in a covered vessel), crumbles, crisps, pandowdys, and brown Bettys. Definitive answers to what these terms mean depend on who you read.

Despite this confusion, what is clear is that apples make great desserts alone and in partnership with other fruits. The tart natures of cranberries, rhubarb, and apricots are all mollified by apple's sweet presence. When they are baked with sweeter fruits like pears and dates, the tarter aspect of apple's personality becomes evident. In just about any combination, the fruits maintain their individuality, yet the whole is greater than the sum of its parts.

Apples can be dominant or subtle in a dessert. They can stand alone and be the star as they are in Whole Baked Apples in Pastry (call these dumplings if you want to), or assume the role of a supporting player, as in Apple Rice Pudding. In some desserts they may not even be present as apples. Pink Apple Sorbet is made with apple pectin, and Apple Cider Ice Cream relies on the concentrated flavors of boiled cider. Never mind. The desserts still taste of apple.

Cran-Apple Crisp

This crisp is a bit unusual because you actually slice the cranberries. Silly, you say? Not at all. It makes all the difference in the world in terms of appearance, taste, and texture. And it is very easy to do with the slicing disk of a food processor. In fact, you can prepare the dessert entirely in the food processor. Use McIntosh, Macoun, or any other apple from the McIntosh family.

MAKES 8 SERVINGS

1 cup (5 ounces) unbleached
    all-purpose flour (scooped into the
    cup and leveled)
1¼ cups firmly packed light brown sugar
¼ teaspoon salt
6 tablespoons (¾ stick) chilled unsalted
    butter, cut into tablespoon-sized pieces
1 cup old-fashioned rolled oats (not instant)
4 medium McIntosh apples (1¼ pounds),
    quartered, cored, and peeled
3 cups (10 ounces) fresh cranberries

1. Adjust an oven rack to the center position and preheat the oven to 350°F.

2. Add the flour, brown sugar, and salt to the work bowl of a food processor with the metal blade. Pulse 10 to 12 times to combine well. Add the butter and oats. Pulse about 10 times, until the butter is cut into small pieces. Remove the mixture from the work bowl and set it aside.

3. Insert the standard slicing disk into the work bowl and slice the apples. Remove and set them aside. If you have a thin slicing disk, use it to slice the cranberries. If not, slice the cranberries with the same disk used for the apples. Set aside.

4. To assemble the crisp, spread 2 cups of the brown sugar mixture over the bottom of a 9-inch square baking pan. Press the mixture firmly in place. Layer half the apple slices, then half the cranberry slices on top, then repeat with the remaining apples and cranberries. Top with the remaining brown sugar mixture, spreading it evenly. Gently pat it down. The pan will be completely full.

5. Bake for about 1 hour, until the top of the crisp is evenly browned. Serve warm.

Note: If you want to make the crisp by hand, combine the flour, brown sugar, and salt in a large bowl. Add the butter and cut it in with a pastry blender until the particles resemble coarse meal. Stir in the oats. Thinly slice the apples with a sharp knife, and chop the cranberries. Assemble the crisp as directed.

Apple Crisp with Apricots and Ginger

Apples, ginger, and apricots are a marvelous trio. Chopped hazelnuts add taste and crunch. Any good baking apple, such as Rome Beauty, McIntosh, or whatever else happens to be in season, will do for this crisp.

MAKES 6 TO 8 SERVINGS

TOPPING

1 cup (5 ounces) unbleached all-purpose flour
    (scooped into the cup and leveled)
1/2 cup firmly packed light brown sugar
1 teaspoon pumpkin-pie spice
1/4 teaspoon salt
8 tablespoons (1 stick) chilled unsalted butter
1/2 cup toasted and skinned hazelnuts
    (see page 28), chopped

FILLING

3 1/2 pounds apples (about 7 large),
    quartered, cored, peeled, and thinly
    sliced crosswise
Grated zest of 1 lemon
3 tablespoons fresh lemon juice
1/2 cup diced dried apricots
1/4 cup finely chopped crystallized ginger
1/2 cup sugar
1 tablespoon pure vanilla extract

1. Adjust an oven rack to the lower third position and preheat the oven to 400°F.

2. To make the topping, combine the flour, brown sugar, pumpkin-pie spice, and salt in a medium mixing bowl. Cut in the butter until the texture resembles coarse meal. Stir in the hazelnuts; set aside.

3. To make the filling, place the apples in a large mixing bowl. Add the lemon zest, lemon juice, apricots, ginger, sugar, and vanilla. Combine well. Turn the mixture into an ungreased 2-quart baking dish (such as a glass 10 × 2-inch round dish; a 9-inch square baking pan will also do just fine). Sprinkle the topping evenly over the apples.

4. Bake for about 45 minutes, until the top is browned, the juices are bubbly, and the apples are tender when tested with the tip of a sharp knife. Cool and serve warm or at room temperature.

Apple-Rhubarb Cobbler

Use a crisp, sweet apple such as Fuji, Gala, Spartan, or Golden Delicious in this scrumptious cobbler. The melt-in-your-mouth pastry will win anybody's heart. Feel free to vary this according to which fresh fruits are available. Two cups of raspberries or blueberries or one cup of each may be substituted for the rhubarb. Leftovers make a great breakfast. You will need a 2-quart baking dish about 2 inches deep; mine is a round 10 × 2-inch glass dish and makes a beautiful presentation, but a 9-inch square baking pan will work just fine.

MAKES 8 SERVINGS

PASTRY

1¼ cups (6¼ ounces) unbleached all-purpose
    flour (scooped into the cups and leveled)
½ teaspoon baking powder
¼ teaspoon salt
6 tablespoons (¾ stick) chilled unsalted
    butter, cut into tablespoon-sized pieces
½ cup buttermilk

FILLING

2 tablespoons unsalted butter
2 pounds sweet cooking apples, quartered,
    cored, peeled, and cut into ¾- to 1-inch
    chunks (about 6 cups)

½ pound rhubarb, sliced ½-inch-thick
    (about 2 cups)
⅔ cup sugar
1½ teaspoons cornstarch
1 teaspoon pumpkin-pie spice
Finely grated zest of 1 orange
¼ cup fresh orange juice
2 teaspoons pure vanilla extract or
    1 tablespoon Grand Marnier or Calvados

1 tablespoon sugar

1. To make the pastry, combine the flour, baking powder, and salt in a medium bowl. Add the butter and cut it in with a pastry blender until the mixture resembles coarse crumbs. Add the buttermilk and stir with a fork until the dough gathers into a ball.

2. Dust a pastry canvas or work surface lightly with flour. If you are using a 10-inch round baking dish, roll the dough gently and smoothly into a 10-inch circle; if you are using a square dish, roll the pastry to fit the top of your pan. Now you will need to transfer this delicate pastry to a baking sheet to refrigerate it: Line a large cookie sheet with wax paper or cooking parchment. Using another cookie sheet without sides as a large spatula, slowly and carefully slide it under the pastry. Transfer the pastry to the lined cookie sheet. Refrigerate until needed.

3. Adjust an oven rack to the center position and preheat the oven to 400°F.

4. To make the filling, melt the butter in a large nonstick skillet over medium-high heat. Add the apples and rhubarb. Cook, stirring frequently, until the apples begin to soften and are lightly browned, 6 to 8 minutes. The rhubarb will be falling apart. Remove the pan from the heat and set it aside.

5. In a large bowl, combine the sugar, cornstarch, pumpkin-pie spice, orange zest, orange juice, $1/4$ cup water, and the extract with a rubber spatula. Add the apple and rhubarb mixture and fold everything together gently. Transfer the mixture to your baking dish. Remove the pastry from the refrigerator and carefully slide it over the filling. Use the tip of a sharp knife to score the pastry fairly deeply into 8 portions. Brush the pastry lightly with water and sprinkle the top with the sugar.

6. Bake for about 40 minutes, until the pastry is golden brown and the filling is very bubbly. Cool on a wire rack and serve warm or at room temperature. Refrigerate leftovers.

Apple-Cranberry Cobbler

Cranberries tint the apples a seductive pink color in this homey, tart old-fashioned cobbler. McIntosh is our first-choice apple, but use any apple that will become soft and tender during the brief baking period. Wolf River, an enormous old variety of apple, is also delicious. Serve this plain or with vanilla ice cream.

MAKES 8 SERVINGS

FILLING

$1/2$ cup sugar
$3/4$ teaspoon pumpkin-pie spice
$3/4$ cup fresh orange juice (grate the zest of 1 orange before juicing to use in the topping)
$1 1/2$ cups (5 ounces) fresh or frozen cranberries
2 tablespoons dark rum
$1 1/2$ pounds McIntosh apples, quartered, cored, peeled, and cut into $1/2$-inch cubes (about 6 cups)

TOPPING

1 cup ($4 1/2$ ounces) unbleached all-purpose flour (spooned into the cup and leveled)
$1/4$ cup sugar
1 teaspoon baking powder
$1/4$ teaspoon baking soda
$1/4$ teaspoon salt
4 tablespoons ($1/2$ stick) chilled unsalted butter, cut into tablespoon-sized pieces
Grated zest of 1 orange
$2/3$ cup buttermilk

1. Adjust an oven rack to the center position and preheat the oven to 400°F.

2. To make the filling, combine the sugar, pumpkin-pie spice, orange juice, and cranberries in a heavy medium saucepan. Cook over medium-high heat, stirring gently but constantly with a wooden spatula, until the mixture comes to a boil. Cover the pan, reduce the heat to low, and simmer for about 5 minutes, until the cranberries are tender and the sauce is slightly thickened. As the sauce cooks, mash the cranberries with the flat side of the spatula. Cool uncovered, then stir in the rum and apples.

3. To make the topping, sift the flour with the sugar, baking powder, baking soda, and salt into a medium bowl. Add the butter and cut it in with a pastry blender until the particles resemble coarse meal. Add the grated orange zest and buttermilk and stir with a fork just until the batter is thoroughly moistened.

4. Transfer the apple mixture to a shallow 2-quart baking dish (such as a glass 10 × 2-inch round dish; a 9-inch square baking dish will also do just fine). Place the cobbler batter on top in eight even mounds, seven around the side and one in the middle, leaving some space between them.

5. Bake for about 35 minutes, until the filling is bubbly and the top is well browned. (During baking, the batter will run together, giving the top a "cobbled" look.) Cool on a rack and serve warm or at room temperature.

waxing apples

if you pick an apple from a tree, its finish is dull. But if you rub it against your sleeve, it shines right up. That's because apples have a natural waxy coating that protects them from drying out.

However, when commercially raised apples are washed in the packing shed to remove dust and chemical residues, about half the natural wax is removed. In order to protect the apples from drying out and shrivelling, they are waxed before packing. One of two substances is used—carnauba or shellac. You may wonder—isn't carnauba used to wax floors? Am I really eating shellac when I bite into an apple? But actually, both these products are completely natural and are approved by the FDA for human consumption. Carnauba wax comes from the leaves of a Brazilian palm tree. Shellac has what may sound like a more alarming origin—it's refined from a secretion produced by certain Asian tree-dwelling insects. The coating is very thin. A pound of coating will cover about 160,000 apples, as it takes only one or two drops to cover and protect each apple.

Sourdough Apple Brown Betty

Just what or who the "Betty" is in this old American dessert is a mystery. But never mind. It probably came about as a way of using up stale bread and whatever fruit happened to be around. Buttered bread crumbs are layered with sugared and spiced apples and baked until the apples are tender and the crumb topping is browned and crisp. The crumbs thicken and flavor the dessert. Here we've specified sourdough as the bread of choice because of its texture and sour tang. For extra toastiness, we brown the butter before combining it with the crumbs. Use any tart semifirm apple, or a combination of varieties. Macoun, Jonathan, Winesap, and Newtown Pippin are all good choices. Serve this warm with the Calvados Crème Anglaise (recipe follows).

MAKES 6 TO 8 SERVINGS

12 ounces day-old sourdough bread
6 tablespoons (¾ stick) unsalted butter
⅔ cup sugar
1 teaspoon ground cinnamon
¼ teaspoon ground allspice
¼ teaspoon ground cardamom
Pinch of salt

2 pounds apples (about 5 medium or
    4 large), quartered, cored, peeled, and
    sliced crosswise about ½ inch thick
½ cup apple cider
2 tablespoons fresh lemon juice
Calvados Crème Anglaise (recipe follows)

1. To make the sourdough crumbs, preheat the oven to 225°F.

2. Slice the bread about ¾ inch thick and trim away the crusts. Place the slices on a cookie sheet and bake them until they feel firm and are dry, about 1 hour. Do not let the bread brown. Cool the bread, then crush the slices coarsely with a rolling pin. You want crumbs of varying size ranging from a fine texture to pieces about ½ inch. Measure 2 cups of crumbs (about 4 ounces) and set them aside. Reserve the remainder for another use.

3. Adjust an oven rack to the center position and preheat the oven to 375°F.

4. Melt the butter in a medium skillet over medium-low heat. Cook until the butter solids and liquid are golden brown, 8 to 10 minutes. Swirl the pan occasionally to check the process. The butter will have a wonderful, nutty aroma when it is ready. Add the 2 cups of crumbs and stir to coat with the butter. Cook, stirring gently, for 2 to 3 minutes, until the crumbs begin to toast and turn golden brown. Remove the pan from the heat and set it aside.

5. In a large bowl, stir together the sugar, cinnamon, allspice, cardamom, and salt. Add the apples, apple cider, and lemon juice and fold together to combine well. Sprinkle ½ cup of the toasted crumbs evenly over the bottom of an unbuttered 8-inch square baking pan. Add half the apple mixture, spreading it evenly, and sprinkle with another ½ cup of crumbs. Spoon the remaining apple mixture into the pan, distributing it evenly, and sprinkle the remaining crumbs on top.

6. Bake for about 1 hour, until the fruit is tender, the juices bubbly, and the crumb topping is a rich brown color. Cool on a rack until warm and serve in dishes with the crème anglaise poured on top.

Calvados Crème Anglaise

MAKES ABOUT 3 CUPS

2 cups half-and-half
½ cup milk
5 large egg yolks
Pinch of salt
½ cup plus 2 tablespoons sugar
2 tablespoons Calvados
1 teaspoon pure vanilla extract

1. Scald the half-and-half and milk in a heavy saucepan over medium heat. (The mixture is ready when you see small bubbles around the edge of the pan and steam rising from the surface.) If a wrinkled "skin" is present, just leave it alone. Remove the pan from the heat and set it aside.

2. In a medium bowl, whisk the yolks and salt just to combine, then gradually whisk in the sugar. Very gradually whisk the hot half-and-half mixture into the yolk mixture. Scrape it into the saucepan and set the pan over medium-low heat. Cook, stirring constantly but gently with a heatproof rubber spatula, going all around the side and bottom of the pan, until the sauce thickens enough to coat a metal spoon, about 10 minutes. An instant-read thermometer will register 180°F. Do not allow the mixture to boil, or the sauce will curdle.

3. Immediately remove the pan from the heat and pour the sauce through a fine strainer into a bowl. Stir in the Calvados and vanilla. Cool the sauce, uncovered, stirring occasionally, to room temperature; then cover and refrigerate. It must be very cold when served. If you want to speed this process, cool the sauce in a bath of ice and water, stirring it from time to time, until it is cold. (The sauce will keep in the refrigerator for up to 4 days.)

DESSERTS

Apple Bavarian

This will knock your socks off. It is creamy, smooth, and loaded with apple taste. The essential component is a gossamer applesauce, which is best made from early-season apples such as Lodis or Transparents. Lacking those, use a flavorful cooking apple that will fall apart when cooked, such as McIntosh.

MAKES 6 SERVINGS

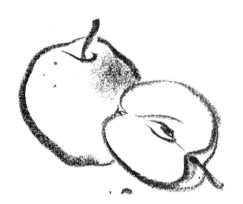

I envelope unflavored gelatin

$1/3$ cup apple juice

5 large egg yolks

Pinch of salt

I cup sugar

I teaspoon cornstarch

$1^{1}/_{2}$ cups milk

2 tablespoons Calvados

I cup Summer Applesauce (page 17)

I cup heavy cream

6 candied violets, for garnish

1. Sprinkle the gelatin over the apple juice in a 1-cup heatproof glass measuring cup. Set aside to allow the gelatin to soften.

2. Beat the egg yolks and salt with an electric mixer until the yolks are very thick, about 5 minutes. Gradually add the sugar, beating a few seconds after each addition. Continue beating for several minutes more, until the mixture is very thick and pale and forms a ribbon when the beaters are raised. Beat in the cornstarch.

3. Bring the milk to a boil in a heavy medium saucepan. Very gradually, add the milk in a thin stream to the yolk mixture, beating on low speed. Pour the mixture into the saucepan and set the pan over medium-low to medium heat. Cook, stirring gently but constantly with a heatproof rubber spatula, until the mixture thickens into a custard-like sauce and coats a metal spoon. The temperature

will be between 175° and 180°F. Add the gelatin mixture and stir briefly until dissolved. Test by placing some of the mixture in a metal spoon and rubbing it between your fingers. There should be no graininess.

4. Remove the pan from the heat and place it in a large bowl of ice and cold water. Stir gently but constantly with a rubber spatula only until the mixture feels cool to the touch. Do not allow it to get cold enough to set. Stir in the Calvados and applesauce. Remove the pan from the ice bath and set it aside.

5. Beat the cream in a medium bowl until it is firm but is not stiff. Fold some of the applesauce mixture into the cream, then fold this into the remaining applesauce mixture. To ensure thorough mixing, pour gently from the bowl to the saucepan, going back and forth as many times as necessary. Divide the Bavarian among six 8-ounce dessert glasses. Cover tightly with plastic wrap and refrigerate for at least several hours, or overnight.

6. Just before serving, top each portion with a candied violet.

Note: Another nice way to serve this dessert is with some raspberries mixed with a bit of sugar and Calvados and spooned on top.

a bushel and a peck

just how much do I love you when "I love you a bushel and a peck"? That song was written back in the days when folks bought apples in large quantities for feeding large families and for keeping in long-term storage. A bushel basket of apples weighed about forty to forty-two pounds and, in the old days, consisted of the number of apples that fit into a bushel basket. I (Dorothy) remember those baskets well: round flimsy-looking constructs of vertical veneer-thin strips of wood held together by circular bands stapled around the bottom, middle, and top. They did the job, however, holding the delightful cargo of perfect fruit, picked at just the right time, from my grandfather's apple ranch. Nowadays, apples in bulk are sold in lidded cardboard boxes. But in deference to history, these boxes contain the traditional quantity of about forty pounds of fruit.

Apple Pandowdy

My, how the name of this dessert brings back old memories! I can still hear Dinah Shore singing those words along with "shoofly pie" and how they'll make one's eyes light up when the heavens are cloudy. Cloudy or not, apple pandowdy will more than light up your eyes. It'll tickle your toes, tweak your taste buds, and give you a squeal of pleasure.

A decidedly old-fashioned American dessert, apple pandowdy is a dish of spiced apples topped with a flaky crust. Sounds like a cobbler, you say. It starts out that way, but halfway through baking, you remove the dish from the oven, cut the pastry into small pieces (dowdying it), and press it down into the apples and their juices. The crust becomes saturated with the apple juices during the final stint in the oven and when cooled just until warm, the pandowdy is ready to eat. In fact, it's irresistible. We like it best soon after it's baked, but leftovers make a great breakfast.

Use any tart, crisp apple that will hold its shape when cut up and baked. Granny Smith, Northern Spy, and Braeburn are good choices. You might want to use more than one variety. Although classic recipes for pandowdy don't call for any thickener, we like to add a small amount of tapioca flour or cornstarch to give

the juices a little body. Serve this plain or with whipped cream or ice cream.

MAKES 8 SERVINGS

PASTRY

1 cup (5 ounces) unbleached all-purpose flour (scooped into the cup and leveled)
¹/₂ teaspoon salt
1 tablespoon sugar
8 tablespoons (1 stick) chilled unsalted butter, cut into 4 pieces
1 teaspoon cider vinegar

FILLING

2 cups apple cider
¹/₃ cup sugar
¹/₂ teaspoon ground cinnamon
¹/₄ teaspoon ground cloves
¹/₄ teaspoon ground allspice
¹/₄ teaspoon salt
1 tablespoon tapioca flour or cornstarch
3 pounds tart, crisp apples (about 6 large), quartered, cored, peeled, and sliced cross-wise ¹/₄ inch thick
¹/₄ cup fresh orange juice or blood-orange juice
2 tablespoons chilled unsalted butter, cut into small pieces

TOPPING

Milk or cream for brushing
1 tablespoon sugar

1. To make the pastry, combine the flour, salt, and sugar in the work bowl of a food processor. Add the butter and pulse 4 or 5 times to begin cutting the butter into the dry ingredients. Combine ¼ cup ice water with the cider vinegar in a 1-cup glass measure. While pulsing very rapidly, add the water-vinegar mixture through the feed tube in a steady stream. Continue pulsing until the dough *almost* gathers into a ball. Remove the dough from the work bowl, press it into a 5-inch disk, and wrap it in plastic wrap. Refrigerate for at least 1 hour.

2. To make the filling, boil the cider in a heavy saucepan over medium-high to high heat, swirling the pan occasionally, until it is reduced to ⅔ cup. Set aside to cool.

3. Adjust an oven rack to the center position and preheat the oven to 400°F. Lightly butter a 2-quart baking dish (such as a round 10 × 2-inch glass dish; a 9-inch square baking pan will also do just fine).

4. In a large bowl, combine the sugar, cinnamon, cloves, allspice, salt, and tapioca flour. Add the apples, cooled cider, and orange juice and fold everything together well. Turn the mixture into the prepared baking dish and dot the top with the butter. Set aside while you roll out the crust.

5. Roll out the pastry on a floured surface so that it just fits the top of the baking dish. Place the pastry over the apples and press it down gently so that it sits directly on the apples. Brush the pastry with a little milk or cream and sprinkle with the sugar. Cut a few slits in the crust to allow steam to escape.

6. Bake for 30 to 35 minutes, or until golden brown. Remove the dish from the oven and reduce the temperature to 350°F. With a small sharp knife, cut the crust into 2-inch pieces in a cross-hatch pattern. Press the crust down into the apples with a wide metal spatula. Your aim here is not to sub-merge the pastry, but to bring it into closer contact with the juices. Some of the juices may bathe the top of the crust, but that's okay. Return the pan to the oven and bake until the pastry is a deep golden brown, about 30 minutes longer. Cool on a rack until warm, and serve.

Apple Profiteroles

Profiteroles are small cream puffs filled with whipped cream or ice cream and topped with sauce, usually chocolate. They are fun to make and to eat. Here the puff shells are filled with Apple Cider Ice Cream and drizzled with a caramel Calvados sauce. You will need a large pastry bag fitted with a plain 1/2-inch tip and a small ice cream scoop for filling the puff shells. This makes a marvelous dessert for a party since the ice cream must be made ahead, the sauce can be made a few days ahead and refrigerated, and the profiteroles can be assembled in advance and stored in the freezer for up to one day.

MAKES ABOUT 32 PROFITEROLES; 8 SERVINGS

PUFFS

3 large eggs

2 large egg whites

1/4 teaspoon salt

6 tablespoons (3/4 stick) unsalted butter, cut into tablespoon-sized pieces

1 cup (5 ounces) unbleached all-purpose flour (scooped into the cup and leveled)

SAUCE

2 cups sugar

2 tablespoons unsalted butter

1 1/3 cups evaporated milk (not sweetened condensed milk)

2 tablespoons Calvados

1 teaspoon pure vanilla extract

1/8 teaspoon salt

Apple Cider Ice Cream (page 91)

1. Adjust an oven rack to the center position and preheat the oven to 425°F. Line a 14 × 17-inch baking sheet with a silicone baking pan liner or heavy-duty aluminum foil. Fit a large pastry bag (16 to 18 inches) with a plain 1/2-inch tip.

2. To make the puff shell dough, beat together the eggs, egg whites, and salt in a small bowl with a fork just to combine thoroughly. Remove 1 teaspoon of the mixture and set it aside.

3. Place 1 cup water and the butter in a heavy medium saucepan and set the pan over medium heat. When the butter is melted, raise the heat to medium-high and bring the mixture to a rolling boil. Immediately remove the pan from heat and add the flour. Stir vigorously with a wooden spoon or spatula until the dough gathers into a ball. Return the pan to medium heat and cook, stirring constantly, for about 1 minute to evaporate excess moisture. The dough will begin to film the bottom of the pan. Transfer the dough to a medium bowl.

4. Add about 1/4 cup of the egg mixture to the dough and beat it in with a wooden spoon or a hand-held

electric mixer. Beat only until the egg mixture is incorporated. Continue adding the remaining egg mixture in $^1/_4$-cup installments, beating until incorporated after each. After the last addition, beat vigorously for about 1 minute, until the mixture is smooth and shiny.

5. Transfer the dough to the pastry bag. Holding the bag vertically with the tip close to the surface of the lined baking sheet, pipe out 1-inch mounds of dough about $1^1/_2$ inches apart. Dip the tip of an index finger into the reserved egg mixture and smooth the tops of each mound.

6. Bake for 20 minutes, until the dough is puffed and a deep golden brown. Remove the pan from the oven and quickly stab the side of each puff with the tip of a sharp knife to release steam. Return the pan to the oven, turn the oven off, and leave the puffs in the oven for 5 minutes, then transfer the puffs to cooling racks.

7. When the puffs are completely cool, slice them crosswise in half and remove any soft dough. Replace the tops and set the puffs aside. (The puffs can be made hours ahead.)

8. To make the caramel sauce, put the sugar and $^1/_2$ cup water in a heavy medium saucepan, but do not stir. Set the pan over medium-low heat and cook, swirling the pan gently by its handle occasionally, for about 12 minutes, until the sugar dissolves. Cover the pan, increase the heat to medium-high,

and boil the mixture for 1 minute. (This will dissolve any sugar crystals clinging to the side of the pan.) Uncover the pan and boil for 10 minutes longer, swirling the pan occasionally, or until the syrup is a deep amber.

9. Immediately remove the pan from the heat and let it stand for 1 minute. Carefully add the butter, stirring with a wooden spoon until the butter melts. Gradually add the evaporated milk, stirring constantly. (The caramel will harden and stick to the spoon.) Place the pan over medium heat, and cook, stirring constantly, for 3 minutes, or until the caramel melts and the mixture is smooth. Remove the pan from heat and stir in the Calvados, vanilla, and salt. Cool the sauce to room temperature, stirring occasionally. (You will have 2 cups sauce. The sauce can be made ahead and refrigerated for up to 1 week; bring to room temperature before serving.)

10. Fill the puff shells with the ice cream, using a small ice cream scoop. Replace the tops, set the filled shells on a baking sheet, and place it in the freezer until ready to serve. (The profiteroles can be filled hours ahead; when completely frozen, wrap the profiteroles and the sheet securely in plastic wrap.)

11. When ready to serve, place 4 profiteroles on each dessert plate, drizzle $^1/_4$ cup of the sauce over each portion, and serve immediately.

Apple Rice Pudding

This is creamy and subtle. It'll be creamier if you use whole milk rather than low-fat milk, but it's up to you; don't use skim milk. If you like, serve the puddings with fresh raspberries and/or a raspberry sauce. The rice in rice pudding tends to become hard if the pudding is refrigerated for more than one day. This is most likely to happen with long-grain rice, because of its high content of amylose starch. The starch becomes tender during cooking, but during cooling it forms hard crystals. Arborio rice, a medium-grain rice, is lower in amylose than long-grain rice, and it will remain tender in rice pudding for two days or so; longer than that, though, and it also begins to harden. So, eat your rice pudding within one to two days.

MAKES 6 TO 8 SERVINGS

5 cups milk
3/4 cup sugar
Pinch of salt
1/2 cup arborio rice
Pinch of freshly grated nutmeg
2 large eggs
1 cup smooth unsweetened applesauce
1 teaspoon finely grated lemon zest
1 teaspoon pure vanilla extract

2 tablespoons Calvados or Applejack
Ground cinnamon for dusting

1. Place the milk, sugar, and salt in a heavy medium saucepan and bring to a simmer over medium heat. Sprinkle in the rice while stirring with a wooden spoon. Add the nutmeg. Cook, uncovered, at a simmer, stirring occasionally, until the rice is very tender, about 40 minutes.

2. While the rice cooks, place the eggs, applesauce, lemon zest, vanilla, and Calvados in a blender jar and blend until very smooth, about 30 seconds.

3. Add the egg mixture to the hot rice mixture all at once, stirring thoroughly. Cook, stirring constantly with a heatproof rubber spatula, until the mixture is very hot and has the consistency of a medium-thick custard sauce, about 5 minutes. Do not allow the pudding to boil.

4. Spoon the pudding into six 8-ounce stemmed water goblets or eight 6-ounce wineglasses, leaving a bit of headroom. Refrigerate for at least several hours, or overnight. Once the pudding has set, cover each glass with plastic wrap. Before serving, dust the top of each pudding with a little cinnamon.

Apple Crème Brûlée

Individual crème brûlées are much more elegant than one made in a large dish. In this version, a creamy classic custard is baked atop a thin layer of Thick Apple Purée. Round ceramic molds measuring about 5 inches in diameter and 1 inch deep are ideal for these (see page 261 for Mail-Order Sources). You can use either a blowtorch (see page 261 for Mail-Order Sources) or the broiler to caramelize the sugar topping. Either way, refrigerate the dessert after caramelization for at least one hour; however, keep in mind that the sugar crust will lose its crispness if refrigerated for longer than four hours. Crème brûlée is best eaten very cold.

MAKES 6 SERVINGS

¾ cup Thick Apple Purée (page 18)
3 cups heavy cream
Pinch of salt
10 tablespoons plus 1 teaspoon sugar
6 large egg yolks
2 tablespoons Calvados or Applejack
1 teaspoon pure vanilla extract

1. Adjust an oven rack to the center position and preheat the oven to 300°F.

2. Spread 2 tablespoons of the apple purée over the bottom of each of six 5 × 1-inch-deep crème brûlée molds. It will make a very thin layer. Place the molds on a large jelly-roll pan and set aside.

3. Combine the cream, salt, and ¼ cup of the sugar in a heavy medium saucepan. Cook over medium heat, stirring occasionally, until the mixture just comes to a boil. Remove the pan from the heat.

4. In a medium bowl, stir the yolks and 1 teaspoon of the sugar together with a wire whisk just to mix well. (The sugar helps to liquefy the yolks and ease their mixing with the hot cream mixture.) Do not whisk the yolks vigorously, or you will produce unwanted bubbles. Very gradually, about a tablespoon or so at a time at first, gently whisk the cream into the yolks. When about half the hot cream has been used, add the rest about ¼ cup at a time, whisking gently. Strain the mixture into a pitcher and stir in the Calvados and vanilla.

5. Carefully pour the cream mixture into the crème brûlée dishes. The dishes will be almost full. Set the pan in the oven and slowly add hot water to come halfway up the sides of the dishes.

6. Bake for 30 to 35 minutes, or until the custard is set. The tip of a paring knife inserted into the center should come out clean. Do not overbake. Remove the pan from the oven and carefully lift the crème brûlée dishes from the water bath. Cool the dishes to tepid, then wrap each airtight in plastic wrap and refrigerate for 6 to 8 hours, or overnight.

7. When ready to prepare the sugar topping, if using a broiler, adjust an oven rack about 6 inches below the broiler and preheat the broiler. Sprinkle 1 tablespoon of the remaining sugar evenly over each dish and wipe the rims clean. Place two of the dishes under the broiler. Watch carefully and do not leave the oven for an instant as the sugar caramelizes and turns a golden brown color. Rotate the dishes as necessary to promote even caramelization. Remove the dishes from the oven and repeat the procedure with the remaining desserts. Or use a blowtorch to caramelize the sugar topping, holding it at a slight angle as you work. Refrigerate the crème brûlées, uncovered, for at least 1 hour or until ready to serve.

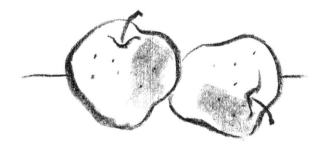

Date-Stuffed Baked Apples with Cider Cranberry Sauce

These are not-so-humble baked apples. And because the apples are large, they make a stunning presentation. Dates, orange, and cranberries all complement apples, and they're all here. You must use an apple that will hold its shape when baked. When it comes to truly large apples, the choice can be limiting. Rome Beauties are our first pick, but Spigold, Golden Delicious, and members of the Spy and Winesap families will also work. If you cannot find really large apples, substitute six smaller ones.

MAKES 4 OR 6 SERVINGS

4 large Rome Beauty or other baking apples
   (about 12 ounces each) or 6 smaller apples
   (about 8 ounces each)
$^1/_2$ lemon
4 ounces (1 cup) pitted dates
2 tablespoons unsalted butter
Grated zest of 1 orange
$^1/_2$ teaspoon ground cinnamon
1 teaspoon pure vanilla extract
$^1/_4$ cup Grand Marnier
$^1/_2$ cup fresh orange juice
$^1/_4$ cup honey

CIDER CRANBERRY SAUCE

2 cups apple cider

1 cup sugar

1 cup fresh or frozen cranberries

2 tablespoons fresh lemon juice

2 tablespoons Calvados or Applejack

1 cup heavy cream, optional

1. Adjust an oven rack to the center position and preheat the oven to 375°F.

2. Core the apples and peel them (see page 9). Rub the apples with the cut lemon as you work.

3. In a food processor fitted with the metal blade, process the dates, butter, orange zest, cinnamon, and vanilla to make a smooth paste. Divide the mixture into 4 or 6 parts, depending on how many apples you have, and shape them into cylinders. Stuff them into the apple cavities and place the apples in an 8 × 12 × 2-inch baking dish.

4. Stir together the Grand Marnier, orange juice, and honey until the honey is dissolved and pour the mixture over the apples. Bake for about 1 hour, basting every 15 minutes with the pan juices, until the apples are tinged with brown and are tender when pierced with a skewer or toothpick. Remove the pan from the oven, baste the apples again, and let them stand until warm or cool.

5. Meanwhile, prepare the sauce: Boil the cider in a heavy medium saucepan until it is reduced to 1 cup, about 10 minutes. Swirl the pan by its handle occasionally as the cider reduces. Remove the pan from the heat and stir in the sugar. Return the pan to high heat and cook, stirring constantly, for several minutes, or until the syrup measures 3/4 cup. Add the cranberries and lemon juice and boil, stirring, until you hear the cranberries "pop" and the mixture becomes bubbly and foamy, 1 to 2 minutes. Stir in the Calvados and cook 1 minute more. Remove the pan from heat and set it aside to cool slightly.

6. Before serving, add any syrup from the baked apples to the cranberry syrup. Reheat, if necessary, to warm the syrup. Place the apples on dessert plates or in bowls and spoon some of the sauce over the apples. Pass the remaining sauce at the table. Accompany with the cream if desired.

Whole Apples
Baked in Pastry

One of the most elegant and delicious ways to serve apples is to wrap them in a buttery flaky pastry and bake them. The apple centers are stuffed with raisins that have been soaked in Grand Marnier overnight. The apples can be readied for the oven several hours ahead and refrigerated. Bake them a couple of hours before serving so that they'll be nice and warm. Accompany them with Calvados Crème Anglaise. Leftovers make a great breakfast.

Use any medium-size crisp apple that will hold its shape during baking. Galas, even though they're sweet, are excellent prepared this way. Other good choices are Granny Smith, Braeburn, Northern Spy, Mutsu, Rome Beauty, Spartan, and any of the russet varieties. Avoid McIntosh and their relatives. Whichever apple you use, it must be medium in size. Use leftover pastry for pie or tart shells.

MAKES 6 SERVINGS

FILLING

1 cup (5 ounces) golden raisins
2 tablespoons Grand Marnier
Finely grated zest of 1 orange

PASTRY

3 cups (15 ounces) unbleached all-purpose flour (scooped into the cup and leveled)
1 teaspoon salt
12 tablespoons (1½ sticks) chilled unsalted butter, cut into tablespoon-sized pieces
¾ cup chilled vegetable shortening

1 lemon, cut in half
6 medium apples (6 to 7 ounces each; no larger)

GLAZE

1 large egg
¼ teaspoon salt

Calvados Crème Anglaise (page 69)

1. Combine the raisins, Grand Marnier, and orange zest in a small container with a tightly fitting lid. Let stand overnight.

2. *To make the pastry in a food processor,* you must have a larger-than-standard-size processor. With the metal blade in place, add the flour and salt to the work bowl. Scatter the butter pieces over the flour. Pulse 4 times. Scrape the work bowl and add the shortening in 4 or 5 lumps. Pulse 3 times. While pulsing very rapidly, gradually add ½ cup ice water through the feed tube in a steady stream. Continue pulsing with rapid on/off bursts until the dough *almost* gathers into a ball. It should be in several large lumps. Remove the dough from the work bowl.

Divide it in half and shape each half into a 6-inch disk. Wrap the dough in plastic and refrigerate for at least 1 hour. (The dough can be made 1 to 2 days ahead.)

To make the pastry by hand, combine the flour and salt in a large bowl. Scatter the butter pieces over the flour. Cut the butter into the dry ingredients with a pastry blender until the particles are about pea-sized. Add the shortening to the bowl in 4 lumps and toss with your hands to coat the shortening with flour. Use the pastry blender to cut the shortening into the flour mixture until the fat particles resemble coarse crumbs. While tossing and stirring the pastry mixture with a fork, gradually drizzle in $1/2$ cup ice water. Keep stirring and tossing until the dough gathers into a ball. Shape, wrap, and chill the dough as described above.

3. Squeeze the juice from the lemon into 1 quart water. Core the apples (see page 9) and peel them; add to the lemon water as you prepare them. Leave the apples in the acidulated water until you're ready to assemble the pastries.

4. Adjust an oven rack to the lower third position and preheat the oven to 400°F. Line an $18 \times 11 \times 2$-inch rimmed baking sheet with parchment.

5. Drain the apples and pat them dry on paper towels. Spoon the raisin mixture (all of the Grand Marnier should have been absorbed) into the apple centers, packing it in.

6. Roll one piece of dough on a lightly floured surface to a thickness of $1/8$ inch. The pastry must be thin, or it will taste doughy when baked. Flour the dough and your work surface lightly as necessary. Using an 8-inch-diameter saucer or cake pan as a guide, cut 3 circles of pastry from the sheet of dough with the tip of a sharp knife. For the decoration, cut three 2-inch circles of dough with a scalloped cutter and set aside. (Gather the scraps of dough, wrap them in plastic, and refrigerate for another use.) Roll out the second piece of dough and repeat the cutting of the large and small circles.

7. Place one apple in the center of a large pastry circle. Starting from the base of the apple, gather the dough around it in pleats, gently drawing them together and enclosing the apple completely in pastry. You'll have a topknot of dough. Trim away the excess with a small sharp knife and press the ends of pastry together to seal over the apple. Set the apple on the baking sheet. Repeat this process with the remaining large pastry circles and apples, spacing them well apart on the baking sheet.

8. Beat the egg and salt together with a fork. Lightly brush each pastry-wrapped apple with the egg glaze. Set a small pastry circle atop each and brush with the glaze. Pierce the top of each apple with a skewer to allow steam to escape. Bake for 40 minutes, or until the pastry is a rich golden brown color and the apples are cooked through. Cool slightly and serve the apples warm with a pitcher of the cold Calvados Crème Anglaise.

Spicy Apple Dumplings

This is my version of the recipe that won the grand prize at the Tenth Pillsbury Bake-Off. Pastry-wrapped wedges of apples are brushed with butter, Calvados and vanilla are poured around them, and they're baked. That's it. As the pastries cook, a delicious sauce forms in the pan. Be sure to use an apple that will hold its shape when baked, such as Braeburn, Jonamac, Northern Spy, or Granny Smith. These dumplings are delicious warm. Serve them plain or with whipped cream, vanilla ice cream, or vanilla yogurt. If you're unsure of how a particular variety of apple will hold up when baked, this recipe is a great way to try several varieties at once to see how they perform.

MAKES 16 PIECES

PASTRY

1¹/₂ cups (6³/₄ ounces) unbleached
    all-purpose flour (spooned into the cups
    and leveled)
¹/₂ teaspoon salt
¹/₄ cup chilled vegetable shortening
4 tablespoons (¹/₂ stick) chilled unsalted butter
¹/₄ cup untoasted wheat germ

2 tablespoons unsalted butter, softened

APPLES AND SAUCE

2 large tart, crisp apples, quartered,
    cored, and peeled
5 tablespoons unsalted butter, melted
¹/₂ cup sugar
1 teaspoon apple pie spice
3 tablespoons Calvados or Applejack
2 tablespoons pure vanilla extract
    (yes, tablespoons)

1. To make the pastry, stir the flour and salt together in a large bowl. Add the vegetable shortening and butter and cut them in with a pastry blender until the particles resemble coarse meal. Stir in the wheat germ. Sprinkle 5 tablespoons ice water over the flour mixture as you toss with a fork. Keep tossing and stirring until the dough gathers into a ball. Shape the dough into a square about ¹/₂ inch thick. Wrap in plastic wrap and refrigerate for at least 30 minutes.

2. Adjust an oven rack to the center position and preheat the oven to 450°F.

3. Roll the pastry out on a lightly floured surface to an 8 × 12-inch rectangle. Spread the softened butter over two-thirds of the dough. Fold the dough in thirds, like a business letter beginning with the un-buttered portion. Roll out again to a 10 × 16-inch rectangle. Cut the dough crosswise into sixteen 1-inch-wide strips.

4. Cut each apple quarter into two wedges. Wrap a pastry strip around each apple wedge and arrange the apples, seam side down without touching, in a 9 × 13 × 2-inch baking pan. Brush the apples with the melted butter. Combine the sugar and apple pie spice and sprinkle evenly over the apples. Combine $2/3$ cup water, the Calvados, and vanilla and carefully pour the mixture around, not over, the apples.

5. Bake for about 25 minutes, until the pastries are nicely browned and the sauce bubbly. Cool on a rack. Serve warm or at room temperature, with the sauce spooned over the pastries.

apples in washington state

washington state is the most productive apple-growing region in the United States. The Yakima and Wenatchee Valleys, just east of the Cascade Mountains, have a volcanic soil, which apples love, and a perfect climate for growing apples—warm, sunny days supply plenty of energy-providing sunshine, while cool nights help color up the apples. Before 1890, however, the western part of the state, famous for its abundant rainfall, was where apples were mostly grown. Not only did nature water the trees, but the people who would eat the apples lived there, in cities such as Seattle and nearby Portland, Oregon.

Even so, before the century was out, apples bloomed in both the Yakima Valley and the Wenatchee Valley. The arrival of the first irrigation project in 1889 was a boon to orchardists in that part of the state. But growers were concerned about getting their fruit to market. While the area was wonderful for growing apples, it didn't attract many settlers. Getting the apples to the people who would buy them was a problem. In 1894, the first railroad shipment of apples from the Yakima Valley went out, proving that indeed the fruit could be transported and sold at a distance. Ten years later, the first commercial cold-storage warehouse was built in Yakima, allowing shipments to be staggered in time.

Today, Washington state provides more than half of all the apples eaten raw in the United States. New York is a distant second at 10 percent, followed by California (9 percent), Michigan (8 percent), Virginia (3 percent), and Oregon (2 percent).

Individual Apple Strudels

Fresh apples and a variety of dried fruits are rolled in phyllo to celebrate the fall harvest. The crisp buttery phyllo encases the port wine-orange-and-cinnamon-scented fruit mixture. The dried fruits we like to use are pears, apricots, and prunes, but feel free to use what you like. Dried cranberries, blueberries, sour cherries, and figs are all possibilities. Any tart, crisp apple that will remain in distinct pieces after baking is okay, including the supermarket standbys Granny Smith and Braeburn. These are best when very fresh, but they can be assembled ahead and refrigerated for a few hours or overnight, or they can be frozen. Bring them to room temperature before baking.

MAKES 16 STRUDELS

1 cup (6 ounces) dried pears, cut into ½-inch pieces

1 cup (6 ounces) dried apricots, quartered

½ cup (3 ounces) pitted prunes, quartered

½ cup port wine

1 tablespoon finely grated blood-orange or regular orange zest

⅓ cup fresh blood-orange or regular orange juice

½ cup sugar

One 3-inch cinnamon stick

2 pounds tart, crisp apples, quartered, cored, peeled, and diced

6 tablespoons (¾ stick) unsalted butter

2 tablespoons vegetable oil

½ cup fine dry bread crumbs

½ teaspoon freshly grated nutmeg

16 sheets phyllo dough, thawed if frozen

1. Combine the pears, apricots, prunes, port wine, orange zest, orange juice, sugar, and cinnamon stick in a heavy medium saucepan. Bring to a simmer over medium heat, stirring once or twice. Cover the pan, reduce the heat to low, and simmer slowly, stirring occasionally, until the fruit is tender and all the liquid has been absorbed, about 35 minutes. Remove the pan from the heat and cool, uncovered, to room temperature; then discard the cinnamon stick and stir in the apples.

2. Adjust two oven racks to divide the oven into thirds and preheat the oven to 350°F. Coat two large baking sheets with vegetable cooking spray.

3. Melt the butter in a small saucepan over low heat. Stir in the oil and keep the mixture warm over very low heat. Combine the bread crumbs and nutmeg in a small bowl and set aside.

4. Work with 1 phyllo sheet at a time, keeping the remainder covered to keep them from drying out. Place the phyllo sheet on your work surface with a narrow end facing you. Brush the sheet lightly with

the butter mixture. Sprinkle 1½ teaspoons of the bread-crumb mixture down the center of the sheet of phyllo, covering a 4-inch band. Spoon ⅓ cup of the fruit mixture onto the bread crumbs about 2 inches from the end nearest you and spread it into a 4-inch strip running from left to right. Fold both long sides of the phyllo toward the center, overlapping them and covering the fruit mixture completely. Brush the phyllo very lightly with the butter mixture. Roll up the strudel, starting from the end nearest you; don't roll it tightly, or it may split during baking. Place the strudel seam side down on a baking sheet and brush it lightly with the butter mixture. Repeat the procedure with the remaining ingredients, placing 8 strudels on each baking sheet, spacing them 2 inches apart.

5. Bake for about 30 minutes, or until the strudels are a deep golden brown. Reverse the baking sheets top to bottom and front to back once or twice during baking to ensure even browning. Transfer the strudels to cooling racks and serve them warm or at room temperature.

Note: If you wish to make turnovers in the traditional triangular shape, use 2 sheets of phyllo for each pastry (32 sheets in all) and increase the butter to 8 tablespoons (1 stick) and the oil to 3 tablespoons. For each turnover, brush 2 sheets of phyllo lightly with the butter mixture and overlap them at the shorter ends by 2 inches. You will have a sheet of phyllo about 12 inches wide and 32 inches long.

Fold the long sides of phyllo over so that they meet in the center without overlapping, and brush the pastry again with the butter mixture. Sprinkle with 1 tablespoon of the crumb mixture. Place ⅓ cup of the apple mixture in the lower left corner of the strip of phyllo and flip it over to the right side to form a triangular shape. Continue this flip-flop folding, maintaining the triangular shape, all the way to the end of the strip. Brush the entire surface of the shaped triangle lightly with the butter mixture and place it on a prepared baking sheet. Repeat with remaining ingredients, placing 8 triangles on each baking sheet. Bake as directed above.

Hot Apple Soufflés

Individual hot soufflés always make an exciting and dramatic dessert. The apple base can be prepared ahead. In fact, you must make the Thick Apple Purée in advance. When you're ready to serve, simply whip the egg whites, fold them in, and pop the soufflés into the oven for twelve minutes. *Et voilà!* Serve these as soon as they come out of the oven. The tops will be lightly crusted with sugar and their interiors soft, buttery, and creamy. You'll need individual ceramic soufflé molds or ramekins with about a 1-cup capacity. (The dimensions are 4 inches across and 2½ inches deep. See page 261 for Mail-Order Sources.)

MAKES 6 SERVINGS

**3 tablespoons sugar, plus more for coating
the molds and dusting**
¾ cup Thick Apple Purée (page 18)
2 tablespoons unsalted butter, melted
2 tablespoons Calvados or Applejack
4 large eggs, separated
4 large egg whites
Pinch of salt

1. Adjust an oven rack to the lower third position and set a heavy baking sheet on the rack. Preheat the oven to 400°F. Lightly butter six 4 × 2½-inch-deep soufflé molds, including their rims, and coat them lightly with sugar. Tap out the excess sugar and set the molds aside. (The molds can be prepared hours ahead of time.)

2. In a medium bowl, whisk together the apple purée, melted butter, Calvados, and egg yolks until smooth. Set aside. (The apple base can be prepared hours ahead. Cover and refrigerate, but bring to room temperature before finishing the soufflés).

3. Beat the 8 egg whites with the salt in a large bowl until they form soft peaks. Gradually add the 3 tablespoons sugar, beating on medium speed. When all the sugar has been added, beat at high speed until the whites are shiny and hold a point but are not dry.

4. Stir a large spoonful of the whites into the yolk mixture. In two additions, fold half the remaining whites into the yolk mixture, then fold the yolk mixture into the remaining whites. Fold only until incorporated. Divide the mixture among the molds, filling them to the top. Sprinkle the soufflés very lightly with sugar. Grasp the rim of a mold between your thumb and index finger (your thumb should be on the inside) and rotate the mold one complete revolution. This disengages the soufflé mixture from the side and helps it to rise. Quickly repeat with the remaining molds.

5. Immediately place the molds on the baking sheet in the oven. Bake for 10 to 12 minutes, until the soufflés are puffed and browned but still soft in the center. Serve immediately on napkin-lined plates.

Apple Clafouti

A clafouti (sometimes spelled with an "s" in both singular and plural forms) is an eggy crêpe batter baked with fruit. The dessert originated in the Limousin region of southern central France, where it was traditionally made with sweet cherries. The word is derived from the dialect word *clafir,* which means "to fill." In our version, the apples are sautéed in butter to caramelize them slightly before baking. Use any crisp, tart apple, but avoid the sweet varieties such as Fuji and Gala.

Clafouti makes a wonderful brunch dish. You can cook the apples and make the batter the night before. Refrigerate them separately and bake the next morning.

MAKES 6 SERVINGS

**3 medium crisp, tart apples (about 1¼ pounds),
    quartered, cored, and peeled**
6 tablespoons (¾ stick) unsalted butter
1¼ cups milk
2 tablespoons Calvados or Applejack
1 tablespoon pure vanilla extract
5 large eggs
⅓ cup granulated sugar
⅛ teaspoon salt
**¾ cup (3 ounces) sifted unbleached
    all-purpose flour**
Confectioners' sugar for dusting

1. Adjust an oven rack to the center position and preheat the oven to 425°F. If you have a baking stone, set it on the rack and preheat for 45 minutes.

2. Slice each apple quarter lengthwise into 3 wedges. Melt 2 tablespoons of the butter in a 10-inch cast-iron skillet over medium-high heat. When hot, add about half the apple slices in a single layer and brown them lightly on both sides, about 2 minutes total. Remove the apples and add another 2 tablespoons butter to the skillet. Lightly brown the remaining apples and add them to the first batch. Add the remaining 2 tablespoons butter to the hot skillet off the heat and set it aside.

3. Combine the milk, Calvados, vanilla, eggs, sugar, salt, and flour in a blender jar and blend for 10 seconds at top speed. Scrape the sides of the jar and blend for 1 minute more.

4. Tilt the skillet to spread the butter evenly over the bottom and side, and pour in the batter. Distribute the apple slices over the batter and place the pan in the oven.

5. Bake for about 30 minutes, or until the clafouti has puffed majestically and is golden brown on top. A toothpick inserted into the batter will come out clean. Cool for 10 minutes (the clafouti will have settled by then).

6. Dust the clafouti with confectioners' sugar, cut into wedges, and serve warm.

honeycrisp is a surprising variety that shows that trying to predict the outcomes of nature can be perilous. This large apple with a wonderful crispness is the offspring of two varieties with medium-sized fruit of unremarkable texture, Macoun and Honey Gold. Bred in Minnesota, Honeycrisp can tolerate cold northern winters well. Applesource calls it the "best very hardy cultivar [variety] in the world today."

The cream-colored flesh is mild and sweet and has a delicate aroma. While Honeycrisp is delicious eaten out of hand, its special flavor can disappear upon cooking.

Apple Fritters

There's something very comforting about a delicate crispy batter cloaking hot, tender apple slices. The perfect batter is neither too thick nor too thin. It just coats the apple slices and turns an inviting deep brown color in the hot oil. Hard apple cider gives this batter an effervescence much as beer would, but the effect is more subtle. Cornmeal adds a welcome crunch. For maximum enjoyment, fritters should be eaten as soon as possible, but if they must wait, you can reheat and recrisp them. Be sure to use a crisp, firm apple, or use more than one kind of apple. It doesn't seem to matter if the apple is sweet or tart. Braeburn, Gala, Granny Smith, and Honeycrisp, among others, will all work.

MAKES 6 TO 8 SERVINGS

BATTER

3/4 cup unbleached all-purpose flour
   (scooped into the cups and leveled)
2 tablespoons white or yellow cornmeal
1/4 teaspoon salt
2 large eggs, separated
1/2 cup hard cider
1 teaspoon pure vanilla extract
2 teaspoons peanut or corn oil

1/3 cup sugar

½ teaspoon ground cinnamon
3 large crisp apples (about 1½ pounds),
   quartered, cored, and peeled
Peanut oil for deep-frying

1. To make the batter, place the flour, cornmeal, and salt in a medium bowl. In a small bowl, whisk the egg yolks, hard cider, vanilla, and oil to combine well. Add the egg yolk mixture to the flour mixture and whisk the two together gently but thoroughly.

2. Beat the 2 egg whites in a medium bowl until they are stiff but not dry. Fold them into the batter. The batter can stand safely at room temperature for 1 to 2 hours.

3. In a large bowl, combine the sugar and cinnamon. Remove and set aside 2 tablespoons of the mixture. Cut each apple quarter into 3 wedges. Add the apples to the sugar and cinnamon in the bowl and toss to combine well.

4. Place a large wire rack over a baking sheet for draining the cooked fritters. Heat 1 inch of oil in a deep wide saucepan or electric frying pan to 365°F. (If you don't have a deep-fry thermometer, you can estimate the temperature by tossing a cube of white bread into the oil; it should brown all over in about 45 seconds.)

5. When the oil is ready, add about 8 apple slices to the batter, first shaking off any juices that might have accumulated, and stir to coat them evenly. Remove the slices from the batter one at a time with your fingers, letting the excess batter drop back into the bowl, and carefully place the apples in the hot oil without crowding. Fry 2 to 3 minutes per side, until the apples are tender and the coating is well browned and crisp. Remove the fritters with a slotted spoon and set them on the wire rack to drain. Repeat with the remaining apples, returning the oil to 365°F before cooking each batch.

6. While the fritters are cooking, adjust an oven rack to the center position and preheat the oven to 400°F. When all the fritters are done and on the wire rack, transfer the rack on its baking sheet to the oven. Bake for about 5 minutes, until the fritters are very hot and crisp. Sprinkle them with the reserved cinnamon-sugar mixture, and serve immediately.

Beijing Apples

We ate this incredibly dramatic apple dessert in Beijing, China, where it is a specialty. Apple chunks are coated with a thin cornstarch-and-egg-white batter, deep-fried, and then tossed into a wok with a hot caramel syrup. The syrup-coated apples are piled onto a serving dish and hurried to the table before the caramel sets. Each diner picks up a chunk of apple with chopsticks and quickly dunks it into a bowl of cold water. The water sets the syrup into a thin shell of caramel candy. When you pop the chunk of apple into your mouth and bite down, the contrast of the hard crackly shell with the soft hot apple is extraordinary. Because the caramel syrup sets quickly, you must eat this as fast as you can. The experience is exquisite.

Be sure to use a crisp apple; it can be on the sweet side. Goldrush, Fuji, Braeburn, and Gala are all good choices. You can cook the apples hours ahead and set them aside at room temperature. Just before serving, make the caramel syrup and fry the apples quickly to recrisp and reheat them. Provide each diner with chopsticks and have two or three rice bowls with cold water ready on the table.

MAKES 6 TO 8 SERVINGS

BATTER

1/3 cup cornstarch

I large egg white

1/4 teaspoon salt

4 medium crisp sweet or tart apples
    (1 1/4 to 1 1/2 pounds), quartered, cored,
    peeled, and each quarter cut crosswise in
    half

Peanut oil for deep-frying

SYRUP

3 tablespoons oil

I cup sugar

1. To make the batter, whisk together the cornstarch, egg white, salt, and 2 tablespoons water in a large bowl until smooth. Add the apples and stir well with a large rubber spatula to coat.

2. Heat I inch of oil in an electric skillet or heavy medium saucepan to 350°F. Have ready a large wire rack set over a baking sheet.

3. Before adding the apples to the oil, stir them with the spatula again to be sure each piece has a thin coating of batter. Add about one third of the apple chunks one by one to the oil. Stir the apples with a fork and cook until golden brown, about 2 minutes. Remove the apples with a slotted spoon and set them on the wire rack to drain. Cook the remaining apples in two batches, bringing the oil back to 350°F each time. Set the apples aside at room temperature until

serving time. Strain the oil, discarding any bits of batter, and return it to the pan.

4. When you're ready to serve the dessert, place an ovenproof dessert platter in a warm oven (200°F), and reheat the oil to 375°F. While the oil reheats, prepare the caramel syrup: Place the 3 tablespoons oil in a large heavy skillet or wok and set the pan over medium heat. When the oil is warm, add the sugar and stir with a wooden spoon until the sugar melts and the mixture becomes foamy. Cook, stirring constantly, until the syrup becomes a rich caramel color.

5. Just before the caramel is ready, fry the apples in the reheated oil for about 1 minute, or until they are a deep brown.

6. Immediately remove the apples with a large slotted spoon or strainer and add them to the hot caramel syrup. Don't dawdle; you must work quickly here. Stir and fold the apples and syrup together with a slotted metal spatula or spoon, quickly pour the mixture onto the warmed dessert platter, and take it to the table right away.

Apple Cider Ice Cream

While working on the Lemony Apple Cider Caramel Cake (page 104), I wondered if a cider caramel syrup would work in ice cream. I wanted a creamy ice cream with a decided apple taste. Well, this is it. A scoop of this ice cream with a crisp cookie makes a wonderful dessert.

MAKES ABOUT 5 CUPS

2 cups apple cider
1 cup sugar
One 3-inch cinnamon stick
2 cups heavy cream
2 cups milk
6 large egg yolks
1/4 teaspoon salt

1. Combine the cider, sugar, and cinnamon stick in a heavy medium saucepan and bring to a boil over high heat, swirling the pan occasionally by its handle. Boil until the cider is as thick as maple syrup and the sugar has caramelized, about 15 minutes. As the cider reduces in volume, it will bubble up to the top of the pan. When this happens, lift the pan off the heat, swirl it until the bubbles subside, and then continue cooking; reduce the heat slightly if the mixture refuses to simmer down. When it is the right consistency, the bubbles will be very thick, large, and foamy and you'll have between 1/2 and

$^2/_3$ cup of syrup. A sure test that the syrup is ready is an instant-read thermometer. Remove the pan from the heat, tip it at an angle so that the syrup collects at one side, and insert the thermometer—the temperature should be 240°F. Remove the cinnamon stick.

2. While the syrup is cooking, scald the cream and milk in a large heavy saucepan over medium heat. (The mixture is ready when you see small bubbles around the edge of the pan and steam rising from the surface.) A wrinkled "skin" may also be present; just leave it alone. Keep hot over low heat.

3. As soon as the syrup is ready, pour it into the hot cream and milk while whisking vigorously. Cook over low heat, whisking constantly, until the syrup is thoroughly incorporated into the cream mixture. Remove the pan from the heat.

4. In a medium bowl, whisk the yolks and salt just to combine. Very gradually, whisk in the hot cider syrup mixture. Scrape the mixture into the saucepan and set the pan over medium-low heat. Cook, stirring constantly but gently with a heatproof rubber spatula, going all around the side and bottom of the pan, until the custard thickens enough to coat a metal spoon, about 10 minutes. An instant-read thermometer will register 180°F. Do not allow the mixture to boil, or it will curdle.

5. Immediately remove the pan from the heat and strain it into a bowl. Cool the custard, uncovered, stirring occasionally, until it reaches room temper-ature, then cover and refrigerate. It must be very cold when churned. If you want to speed this process, cool the custard in a bath of ice and water, stirring it from time to time until it is very cold.

6. Freeze in an ice cream maker following the man-ufacturer's instructions. Transfer the ice cream to an airtight container and store in the freezer for at least a few hours before serving. (The ice cream keeps well for about 2 weeks.)

Note: This caramel custard base makes a delicious sauce in its own right, but it will probably be a bit too thick after it has chilled. Thin it with a little milk and serve it with berries, cobblers, or fruit pies.

Pink Apple Sorbet

This recipe uses the peels and cores (and seeds) left over from a cake, cookie, pie, or other apple dessert you happen to be making. Pectin prepared from red-skinned apple trimmings gives the sorbet a lovely shade of pink. Any red apple will do. The pectin and the Calvados help to keep the texture smooth and velvety by preventing the formation of ice crystals. Because the sorbet doesn't freeze rock-hard, you can serve it straight from the freezer. Apple chips (see page 21) and sprigs of mint make attractive garnishes.

MAKES ABOUT 5 CUPS

Peels and cores from 2 pounds apples
I cup sugar
$^1/_2$ cup apple juice
3 tablespoons fresh lemon juice
2 tablespoons Calvados or Applejack

I. Combine the apple peels and cores with 4 cups water in a large saucepan. Bring the mixture to a boil over medium-high heat, stirring occasionally. Boil, uncovered, for 15 minutes. Strain the mixture into a bowl, pressing on the pulp to extract the maximum amount of pectin. You should have about $2^1/_2$ cups.

2. Add the sugar and stir until it is dissolved. Then stir in the apple juice, lemon juice, and Calvados. Refrigerate the mixture until it is very cold.

3. Freeze in an ice cream maker following the manufacturer's directions. Transfer the sorbet to an airtight container and freeze for at least 3 hours before serving. (The sorbet keeps well for a week.)

the big apple

how did New York City get its nickname, The Big Apple? We wish we had a definitive answer, but no one seems to know. It may have something to do with jazz. Or maybe with racetracks, or jazz by way of the racetracks.

The Encyclopedia of New York City says the nickname was first popularized by a reporter for the *Morning Telegraph* in the 1920s. He had picked up the term from black stablehands in New Orleans and in turn used it to refer to New York's racetracks. He is claimed to have written in 1924, "There's only one Big Apple. That's New York." The term faded into disuse by the 1950s but was revived in 1971 by the New York Convention and Visitors Bureau.

Other theories abound. Some say a popular jazz club in Harlem was named The Big Apple. Since New York was a mecca for jazz, heading for The Big Apple soon came to mean being on the way to New York. Others claim the nickname once belonged to New Orleans and was simply transferred to New York by the jazz musicians who migrated there. And others say the name derives from the Depression, when wealthy families were driven to selling apples on street corners, which suspicious citizens dubbed the "Big Apple Scam."

Cakes

I will make an end of my dinner;

there's pippins and cheese to come.

—WILLIAM SHAKESPEARE,
THE MERRY WIVES OF WINDSOR

We've already commented on the duality of apple's nature in possessing sweet and tart qualities. Add to that a third aspect of apple's nature: chameleon-like. Apples, especially applesauce, can either be obviously present in a recipe (as in the Spicy Apple Cupcakes) or completely disguised (as in the Chocolate-Chocolate Chip Fudge Cake). In the former, the apple taste and spices give the cupcakes their character; in the latter, the applesauce serves as a substitute for eggs and also acts to tenderize the cake. You won't taste the apple, but it's there fulfilling a couple of vital roles.

Similarly, you'll be hard-pressed to tell that boiled apple cider is in the Apple Chiffon Cake, but if it weren't there, the cake would be dry and dull. In some cases, as in the Caramel Apple Layer Cake, we include apples in more than one form in a single recipe—applesauce in the cake layers for tenderness and shredded apples in the filling for texture and flavor.

Cinnamon Apple Cake

This cake was featured on the cover of the October 1996 issue of *Cooking Light* magazine. I made it for a story on Jewish holiday treats. The cake is usually served in December during Hanukkah, the Jewish festival of lights. I think it is so special it deserves to be eaten regularly throughout the year. Offer it either as a dessert after a meal or as a coffee cake with brunch. Be sure to use a firm, tart cooking apple, such as Rome Beauty, Granny Smith, or Newtown Pippin. But don't be limited by these suggestions. Just about any apple that will hold its shape during baking will work.

MAKES 10 SERVINGS

1½ cups (6¾ ounces) unbleached all-purpose
    flour (spooned into the cups and leveled)
1½ teaspoons baking powder
¼ teaspoon salt
8 tablespoons (1 stick) unsalted butter,
    at room temperature
6 ounces Neufchâtel cream cheese,
    at room temperature
1¾ cups sugar
1 teaspoon pure vanilla extract
2 teaspoons ground cinnamon
2 large apples, quartered, cored, peeled,
    and diced (3 cups)
2 large eggs

1. Adjust an oven rack to the center position and preheat the oven to 350°F. Coat a 9-inch springform pan lightly with vegetable cooking spray.

2. Sift together the flour, baking powder, and salt and set aside.

3. In the large bowl of an electric mixer, beat together the butter, cream cheese, 1½ cups of the sugar, and the vanilla on medium speed until the mixture is smooth and fluffy, about 3 to 5 minutes. Stop to scrape the side of the bowl occasionally.

4. Combine the remaining ¼ cup sugar with the cinnamon. Set aside half of this mixture. Combine the remaining sugar-cinnamon mixture with the apples in a large bowl, stirring to coat the apple pieces well. Set aside briefly.

5. Add the eggs one at a time to the butter mixture, beating well after each addition on medium-high speed. On the lowest speed, add the flour mixture and beat just until incorporated. Remove the bowl from the mixer, and stir the batter a few times with a rubber spatula. Add the apple mixture and stir to combine well. Spread the batter level in the prepared pan and sprinkle the remaining sugar-cinnamon mixture evenly over the top.

6. Bake for 60 to 70 minutes, until a toothpick inserted into the center of the cake comes out clean. Cool the cake in its pan on a wire rack.

7. To serve, remove the side of the pan and use a sharp knife to cut the cake.

Apple Crumb Cake

This makes a terrific cake to pack into lunches or for snacks. You have a lot of flexibility in your choice of apple, but select one on the tart side. Early-season Macouns are excellent. But Granny Smith, Northern Spy, and York Imperial, among others, are also good choices.

MAKES 8 SERVINGS

TOPPING

1/4 cup unbleached all-purpose flour
   (spooned into the cup and leveled)
1/3 cup sugar
1 teaspoon ground cinnamon
3 tablespoons chilled unsalted butter

BATTER

2 1/4 cups (10 1/4 ounces) unbleached
   all-purpose flour (spooned into the cups
   and leveled)
1 teaspoon baking soda
1/2 teaspoon salt
1/2 teaspoon ground cinnamon
5 tablespoons unsalted butter,
   at room temperature
3/4 cup firmly packed light brown sugar
1 large egg
1 teaspoon grated lemon zest
1 tablespoon fresh lemon juice
2 teaspoons pure vanilla extract

1 cup buttermilk
2 medium apples, quartered, cored, peeled,
   and diced (2 cups)

1. Adjust an oven rack to the center position and preheat the oven to 375°F. Butter a 9-inch square baking pan or coat it with cooking spray. Dust it lightly with flour and tap out the excess.

2. To prepare the crumb topping, combine the flour, sugar, and cinnamon in a small bowl. Cut in the butter with a pastry blender until the particles resemble coarse crumbs. Refrigerate while you prepare the batter.

3. Sift together the flour, baking soda, salt, and cinnamon; set aside. In a large bowl, beat the butter and brown sugar together with an electric mixer until creamy and light. Add the egg and beat until incorporated. Add the lemon zest, lemon juice, and vanilla and beat well. On the lowest speed, alternately add the dry ingredients in three additions and the buttermilk in two additions, beating only until the ingredients are thoroughly incorporated. Scrape the bowl as necessary to keep the mixture smooth. Stir in the apple.

4. Spread the batter evenly in the prepared pan and smooth the top. Sprinkle the crumb topping evenly over the batter. Bake for 50 to 55 minutes, or until a toothpick inserted into the center of the cake comes out clean. Cool the cake in its pan on a rack for 30 minutes.

5. Using a small sharp knife, cut around the cake to release it from the pan. Cover the cake with a rack and invert the two. Carefully remove the cake pan. Cover the cake with another rack and invert again so it is right side up. Let stand until completely cool. To serve, cut with a sharp knife.

Apple Chiffon Cake

Boiled apple cider gives a subtle and mysterious flavor to this light and airy cake. The cake is gorgeous and tall—about four inches high. It is easy and quick to make and is great to have on hand, since it keeps well at room temperature for several days. The most important point to remember is to not underbeat the egg whites. You will need a 10 × 4-inch two-piece tube pan (*not* nonstick). Be sure the pan is scrupulously clean and free of grease. Although most cakes are baked in preheated ovens, chiffon and angel food cakes rise better if started in a cold oven.

MAKES 12 TO 16 SERVINGS

2 cups apple cider
2 cups (8 ounces) sifted unbleached
   all-purpose flour
1¼ cups granulated sugar
1 tablespoon baking powder
½ teaspoon salt
½ cup vegetable oil, such as safflower
7 large eggs, separated
1 tablespoon finely grated orange zest
1 large egg white, if needed
½ teaspoon cream of tartar
Confectioners' sugar for dusting

1. Boil the cider in a heavy medium saucepan until it has reduced to ¾ cup, 10 to 15 minutes. Swirl the pan by its handle occasionally. Set aside to cool to room temperature.

2. Resift the flour with 1 cup of the sugar, the baking powder, and salt into a large bowl. Make a well in the dry ingredients and add in the following order, *without* mixing, the oil, egg yolks, orange zest, and cooled cider. Using a large sturdy whisk, stir (don't beat) everything together briskly to make a smooth mixture. Set aside.

3. Measure the egg whites. You should have 1 cup. If not, adjust the volume with more egg white. In a large, clean electric mixer bowl, beat the whites on medium speed until foamy. Add the cream of tartar and beat until the whites hold a soft shape. Gradually beat in the remaining ¼ cup sugar. When all the sugar has been added, beat on high speed until the whites are very stiff and shiny but not dry.

4. In two additions, using a large rubber spatula, fold half the whites gently into the yolk mixture. Do not be too thorough at this point. Add the yolk mixture to the remaining whites and fold them together gently and thoroughly only until no whites show. Spoon the batter carefully into an ungreased 10-inch tube pan with a removable bottom, and smooth the top.

5. Adjust an oven rack to the lower third position and place the pan in the oven. Set the oven temperature to 325°F. Bake for 50 to 55 minutes, until the cake is a deep brown. Raise the temperature to 350°F and bake for 10 to 15 minutes more, until the cake springs back when lightly pressed.

6. Remove the cake from the oven and immediately turn it upside down, placing the tube over a narrow-necked wine bottle or metal funnel spout. There must be plenty of air circulation around the cake as it cools, or the texture will be gummy. Cool the cake for several hours.

7. To remove the cake from its pan, use a sharp narrow serrated knife. Stick the blade down between the cake and the pan, going all the way to the bottom of the pan. Press firmly with the knife against the side of the pan as you rotate the pan slowly and make small up-and-down motions all around the cake. Detach the cake from the center tube the same way. Lift the cake out of the pan by its tube and carefully cut the cake away from the bottom of the pan. Cover the cake with a cake plate and invert the cake onto the plate. Remove the bottom of the cake pan. The cake should be left upside down. Dust it lightly with confectioners' sugar and cut into portions with the serrated knife.

Apple Macadamia Cake

This big, luxurious cake has a moist, firm, subtle texture that comes from ground macadamia nuts. It keeps well at room temperature for days. If you cannot find unsalted macadamia nuts, cut the amount of salt in half. Be sure to use a tart, firm apple, such as Granny Smith, Northern Spy, or Jonathan. Early-season Macouns will also work.

MAKES 12 TO 16 SERVINGS

1 cup (5 ounces) unsalted macadamia nuts
    (see headnote)
3 cups (13 1/2 ounces) unbleached
    all-purpose flour (spooned into the cup
    and leveled)
1 1/2 teaspoons baking powder
1/2 teaspoon salt
2 1/4 cups sugar
1 teaspoon ground cinnamon
1/2 teaspoon ground ginger
1 1/2 pounds tart, firm apples, quartered,
    cored, peeled, and thinly sliced crosswise
    (about 4 cups)
5 large eggs
1/3 cup walnut oil
2/3 cup corn oil
1/2 cup apple cider
1 tablespoon pure vanilla extract

1. Adjust an oven rack to the lower third position and preheat the oven to 350°F. Coat a 10 × 4-inch tube pan with cooking spray. Dust it all over, including the tube portion, with fine dry bread crumbs and tap out the excess.

2. In a food processor, pulse the macadamia nuts 6 times. Add 1 cup of the flour and process for 10 seconds, or until the mixture is a fine powder. Transfer to a medium bowl and stir in the remaining 2 cups flour, the baking powder, and salt. Set aside.

3. In a large bowl, mix together 1/4 cup of the sugar, the cinnamon, and ginger. Add the apples and toss to coat well. Set aside.

4. In the large bowl of an electric mixer, beat the remaining 2 cups sugar with the eggs at high speed until the mixture triples in volume and is pale yellow and very thick, 8 to 10 minutes. Combine the oils in a 1-cup glass measure. While beating on high speed, very gradually add the oil in a thin stream. Don't rush this process. (Pretend you're making a mayonnaise.) Once all the oil has been added, beat for 1 more minute. Still beating on high speed, gradually add the cider, then the vanilla. Scrape the bowl.

5. On the lowest speed, gradually add the flour mixture, beating only until incorporated. Scrape the batter over the apple mixture and fold everything together gently but thoroughly. Turn the batter into the prepared pan and smooth the top.

6. Bake for about 1½ hours, until the cake is a rich golden brown, the top has cracks and springs back when lightly pressed, and a cake tester comes out clean. The cake may look done before it actually is, so test it carefully; it's best to err on the side of a few minutes longer in the oven than taking it out too soon.

7. Cool the cake in its pan for 30 minutes, during which time it will settle. Carefully invert the cake onto a cooling rack. Remove the pan and invert again on another rack to finish cooling right side up.

8. When the cake is completely cool, use a sharp serrated knife to cut it into thin slices. Store any leftovers, covered, at room temperature for 3 to 4 days.

Apple-Pecan Spice Cake

Lots of apple, cinnamon, pecans, and orange—in the form of zest, juice, and Grand Marnier—conspire to make this jewel of a moist cake. Just about any sweet and tart apple will work here. Braeburn, Macoun, and Golden Delicious are good choices. You will need a 9-inch (8-cup) kugelhopf pan.

MAKES 12 SERVINGS

2 cups (9 ounces) unbleached all-purpose
    flour (spooned into the cup and leveled)
1 teaspoon baking powder
½ teaspoon baking soda
2 teaspoons ground cinnamon
¾ teaspoon ground ginger
¼ teaspoon freshly grated nutmeg
12 tablespoons (1½ sticks) unsalted butter,
    at room temperature
1½ cups granulated sugar
2 teaspoons pure vanilla extract
3 large eggs
¼ cup sour cream
Grated zest of 1 large orange
1 large apple (8 ounces), quartered, cored,
    peeled, and shredded (2 cups)
⅔ cup finely chopped pecans
¼ cup fresh orange juice
¼ cup Grand Marnier
Confectioners' sugar for dusting

1. Adjust an oven rack to the lower third position and preheat the oven to 350°F. Coat a 9-inch kugelhopf pan with cooking spray. Dust it all over, including the tube portion, with fine dry bread crumbs and tap out the excess.

2. Sift the flour with the baking powder, baking soda, cinnamon, ginger, and nutmeg; set aside.

3. In a large bowl, beat the butter with an electric mixer until smooth and creamy. Add the sugar and vanilla and beat well, about 3 minutes. Add the eggs one at a time, beating well after each addition. Beat in the sour cream and orange zest. The mixture will not look smooth; that's okay. On the lowest speed, add half the sifted dry ingredients, mixing only until incorporated. Scrape the bowl and add the apple and pecans. Beat on the lowest speed to mix them in. Add the remaining dry ingredients and mix just until incorporated.

4. Scrape the thick batter into the prepared pan and spread it level. Bake for about 1 hour, until a cake tester comes out clean and dry and the top of the cake is well browned and springs back when lightly pressed.

5. While the cake bakes, combine the orange juice and Grand Marnier in a small cup. As soon as the cake comes out of the oven, brush the top of the cake with half the orange juice mixture. Let the cake cool in its pan on a rack for 10 minutes. Invert it onto a wire rack and carefully remove the cake pan. Brush the remaining orange juice mixture all over the cake. Let stand until the cake is completely cool.

6. Dust the cake with confectioners' sugar and cut into thin slices with a serrated knife.

braeburn

despite the efforts of breeders to create scientifically engineered varieties, many of the best apples continue to arise from chance seedlings, as did both Red and Golden Delicious in the old days. Braeburn, which appeared in a New Zealand orchard in the 1940s and reached our shores in the 1980s, is described by apple expert Warren Manhart, in his 1995 book, *Apples for the Twenty-First Century,* as "one of the great new apples of the world." We agree, having found the complex sweet-tart flavor of this crisp variety wonderful both for eating fresh and cooking. And because it is grown both in New Zealand and here in North America, Braeburn is available in stores most of the year.

Home growers, however, will be disappointed to learn that this variety should only be planted where Granny Smith has enough time to ripen, as it is a late cropper, ripening in October or November. It doesn't grow well, however, where it really gets hot in the summer. Both home growers and store customers should watch out for the newer, brighter red Braeburn, which may also be available. Like other "improved," redder strains of other varieties, this type is not as flavorful as the original.

Spicy Applesauce Cupcakes

These are light and tender cupcakes, bursting with the flavors of apple and spices and crowned with a classic cream-cheese icing. Golden raisins and pecans add fruitiness and crunch. It's important to use a thick, smooth applesauce for this recipe. We like Eden brand organic applesauce. The cupcakes stay fresh for days if refrigerated in an airtight container.

MAKES 12 CUPCAKES

CUPCAKES

1½ cups (7½ ounces) unbleached all-purpose flour (scooped into the cups and leveled)

1 teaspoon ground cinnamon

½ teaspoon freshly grated nutmeg

¼ teaspoon ground mace

2 teaspoons baking powder

¼ teaspoon baking soda

¼ teaspoon salt

8 tablespoons (1 stick) unsalted butter, at room temperature

1 cup sugar

1 teaspoon pure vanilla extract

1 cup unsweetened smooth applesauce

½ cup golden raisins

½ cup chopped pecans

ICING

6 ounces cream cheese, at room temperature

3 tablespoons unsalted butter, at room temperature

1 teaspoon finely grated lemon zest

¾ cup confectioners' sugar (scooped into the cups and leveled)

1½ to 2 tablespoons fresh lemon juice

1. Adjust an oven rack to the lower third position and preheat the oven to 350°F. Line 12 standard-size muffin cups with paper cupcake liners; set aside.

2. To make the cupcakes, sift the flour with the cinnamon, nutmeg, mace, baking powder, baking soda, and salt; set aside.

3. In a large bowl, beat the butter, sugar, and vanilla with an electric mixer on medium speed until fluffy and light, 2 to 3 minutes. Add the applesauce and beat it in briefly on low speed. The mixture will look curdled, which is all right. Fold in the flour mixture, then the raisins and pecans. The batter will be stiff. Spoon the batter into the lined muffin cups. Don't bother to smooth the tops; baking will take care of that.

4. Bake for about 25 minutes, until the cupcakes spring back when gently pressed in the center. Cool the cupcakes in the muffin cups for 2 to 3 minutes, then carefully transfer them to cooling racks to cool

completely. Since the cupcakes are delicate, the best way to remove them from the muffin cups is to cover the muffin pan with a wire rack and invert the two. Remove the muffin pan, then stand the cupcakes upright on the rack to cool completely.

5. To prepare the icing, beat the cream cheese and butter in a medium bowl with an electric mixer until smooth. Add the lemon zest, confectioners' sugar, and $1^1/_2$ tablespoons lemon juice and beat until smooth and creamy. The icing should be firm but not so stiff that it's difficult to spread. Beat in the remaining lemon juice by droplets if necessary. Spread the icing over the cooled cupcakes. Let stand for about 1 hour, until the icing is set, before serving.

applespeak

apples are so popular that they pervade our daily speech with terms like "Adam's apple" and phrases such as "You're the apple of my eye." Perhaps long ago, someone decided that a man with a prominent larynx looked as if he had tried to swallow an apple and not succeeded. The origin of "the apple of my eye" comes from the Bible and is found throughout the Old Testament. In Deuteronomy, the Lord protects Jacob in the wilderness, keeping him "as the apple of his eye." In Proverbs, the Lord exhorts his people to "keep my commandments and live, keep my teachings as the apple of your eye; bind them on your fingers, write them on the tablet of your heart." Clearly, the apple referred to is very precious. But what, exactly *is* the apple of one's eye?

Alice Martin, in *All About Apples* (Houghton Mifflin, 1976), comes to an interesting conclusion—that the apple of one's eye refers to the pupil of the eye, that dark, round, vital sphere which allows us to see. What could express the importance of something than to compare it with this vital organ?

Some apple references may be familiar to older readers but not younger ones—"applesauce" as a dismissive comment; "apple polisher" for a flatterer; or "apple-pie order" for having things neatly arranged. These phrases hark back to days of colorful language that is perhaps dying out in the TV culture of our times.

Lemony Apple Cider Caramel Cake

For this unusual cake, you prepare a caramel syrup from apple cider and sugar and then poach apples in the syrup until tender. When cool, the apples are folded into the batter. You must use a firm cooking apple that will hold its shape during the caramelization process. My first choice is one of the russet varieties, but Jonamacs, Braeburns, and Granny Smiths are good too.

MAKES 12 TO 16 SERVINGS

CARAMEL APPLES

2 cups apple cider

I cup sugar

I tablespoon butter

1^1/$_4$ pounds crisp, tart apples, quartered,
    cored, peeled, and thinly sliced (3 cups)

CAKE

3 cups (13^1/$_2$ ounces) unbleached all-purpose
    flour (spooned into the cup and leveled)

^{1}/$_2$ teaspoon baking soda

^{1}/$_4$ teaspoon salt

2 cups sugar

8 tablespoons (I stick) unsalted butter,
    at room temperature

8 ounces Neufchâtel cream cheese,
    at room temperature

I tablespoon finely grated lemon zest
    (from 2 lemons)

3 large eggs

2 tablespoons fresh lemon juice

I cup buttermilk

GLAZE

^{1}/$_4$ cup fresh lemon juice

^{1}/$_4$ cup apple cider

^{1}/$_4$ cup sugar

I teaspoon pure vanilla extract

Confectioners' sugar for dusting

I. To prepare the apples, boil the apple cider in a heavy medium saucepan over high heat, swirling the pan occasionally, until reduced to ^{1}/$_2$ cup, about 15 minutes. Watch carefully toward the end of cooking to prevent burning.

2. Stir the sugar into the hot reduced cider, and cook and stir over medium-high heat until the sugar dissolves and the mixture boils. Continue cooking, stirring constantly, until the syrup is thick and foamy and a deep dark caramel color, about 5 minutes. Remove the pan from the heat and cool for I minute. Stir in the butter. Add the apples and stir well.

3. Return the pan to high heat and cook and stir constantly until the apples have absorbed almost all of the liquid and the sauce is very thick and syrupy. Transfer the mixture to a bowl to cool completely. There'll be about 1^1/$_4$ cups of apples.

4. Adjust an oven rack to the lower third position and preheat the oven to 325°F. Coat a 10-inch, 12-cup Bundt pan well with cooking spray; dust evenly with fine dry bread crumbs and tap out the excess crumbs.

5. To make the cake, sift the flour, soda, and salt together and set aside.

6. In a large mixing bowl, beat the sugar, butter, cream cheese, and lemon zest on medium speed for about 5 minutes, until the mixture is very smooth and creamy, stopping to scrape the bowl and beaters as necessary. Add the eggs one at a time on medium speed, beating after each addition until thoroughly incorporated. Scrape the bowl and beaters occasionally. Beat in the lemon juice. On low speed, alternately add the flour mixture in three additions and the buttermilk in two additions, beginning and ending with the dry ingredients. Beat only until the batter is smooth; stop frequently to scrape the bowl and beaters. Fold in the cooled caramel apples. Spread the batter in the prepared pan.

7. Bake for 1½ hours, or until the top of the cake is golden brown and springs back when gently pressed and a cake tester comes out clean and dry.

8. Meanwhile, combine all the glaze ingredients in a small bowl. Stir frequently until the sugar is dissolved.

9. When the cake is done, remove it from the oven and let it stand for 5 minutes. Carefully invert the cake onto a wire rack and remove the pan. Set the rack on a baking sheet and immediately brush the glaze all over the cake, including the tube portion. Keep brushing until all the glaze is used. Cool the cake completely on the wire rack, then transfer it to a cake plate and dust it with confectioners' sugar. Cut with a serrated knife.

CAKES

Caramel Apple Layer Cake

This is a party cake par excellence. Tender buttermilk cake layers are split and filled with an apple-cheese mixture and frosted with a scrumptious caramel icing. You make the caramel the old-fashioned way, by melting sugar—without any water—in a skillet.

MAKES 12 TO 16 SERVINGS

CAKE

3 cups (10^1/$_2$ ounces) sifted cake flour

1 tablespoon baking powder

^{1}/$_2$ teaspoon salt

8 tablespoons (1 stick) unsalted butter,
   at room temperature

^{1}/$_4$ cup vegetable shortening

1^1/$_2$ cups sugar

2 teaspoons pure vanilla extract

3 large eggs

1 cup buttermilk

^{1}/$_2$ cup smooth unsweetened applesauce

FILLING

1^1/$_2$ pounds (about 4 medium or 3 large)
   apples, quartered, cored, peeled, and
   coarsely shredded (4 packed cups)

2 tablespoons fresh lemon juice

^{1}/$_3$ cup apple cider

2 large egg yolks

1 cup sugar

^{1}/$_8$ teaspoon ground cinnamon

4 ounces cream cheese or
   ^{1}/$_2$ cup mascarpone cheese

FROSTING

^{1}/$_2$ cup granulated sugar

8 tablespoons (1 stick) unsalted butter

^{1}/$_3$ cup heavy cream

One 1-pound box confectioners' sugar

1. Adjust an oven rack to the center position and preheat the oven to 350°F. Butter two 9-inch round cake pans, or coat them with cooking spray, and dust them lightly with flour, tapping out the excess.

2. To make the cake, resift the flour with the baking powder and salt and set aside.

3. In a large bowl, with an electric mixer, beat the butter with the shortening on medium speed for about 30 seconds, until the mixture is soft and creamy. Gradually beat in the sugar. Scrape the bowl, add the vanilla, and beat until the mixture is light and fluffy. Add the eggs one at a time, beating after each addition until thoroughly incorporated. Stop to scrape the bowl as necessary.

4. Combine the buttermilk and applesauce. On the lowest speed, add the flour mixture to the butter mixture in three additions and the buttermilk mixture in two additions, beginning and ending with the dry ingredients. Stop to scrape the bowl as nec-

essary and beat only until the ingredients are well combined. Divide the batter between the two pans. Smooth the tops.

5. Bake for 30 to 35 minutes, until the layers are golden brown and spring back when lightly pressed and a toothpick inserted into the center comes out clean. Cool the pans on a wire rack for 10 minutes. Run a small sharp knife around the sides to release the layers. Invert onto cooling racks and remove the pans. Cover the layers with other cooling racks and reinvert to cool right side up. When the layers are completely cool, you will have to split them horizontally; it's easier to do this if the layers are chilled, so refrigerate the cakes for an hour before splitting them. Prepare the apple filling.

6. Combine the apples, lemon juice, cider, egg yolks, sugar, and cinnamon in a heavy medium saucepan. Bring the mixture to a boil over medium-high heat, stirring constantly. Continue cooking at a boil, stirring constantly, for 7 to 8 minutes. The mixture will be very thick. Cool slightly, then beat in the cream cheese. Cool completely before using.

7. Using a long, sharp serrated knife, split each cake layer horizontally in half. Place the top half of one of the layers upside down on a cake plate and spread it with one-third of the apple filling. Place the bottom half of the layer cut side down over the filling and spread it with half of the remaining filling. Place the bottom half of the remaining cake layer cut side up over the filling. Spread with

the remaining filling and set the remaining half-layer over the filling, top side up. Set aside.

8. To make the frosting, place the granulated sugar in a heavy medium skillet over medium heat. When you see the sugar beginning to melt, start stirring gently with a wooden spoon. The sugar will gradually become a caramel-colored syrup. Adjust the heat so that the sugar melts slowly; it must not burn. Some sugar will harden on the wooden spoon. Don't be concerned. When the sugar is ready, take the pan off the heat and slowly add 3 tablespoons boiling water. The mixture will bubble furiously and the caramel will harden. Return the pan to medium-low heat and stir constantly with the wooden spoon until the sugar has remelted into a thick caramel syrup. Set aside and keep warm.

9. In a heavy medium saucepan, melt the butter over low heat. Stir in the heavy cream and heat briefly until warm. Set the pan with the caramel syrup over low heat and add the butter and cream mixture. Whisk them together to combine well. Remove the pan from the heat and cool until tepid.

10. Place the confectioners' sugar in the bowl of an electric mixer and scrape in the caramel mixture. Beat on low speed to moisten the sugar, then beat on high speed until the frosting is of spreading consistency. With a narrow metal spatula, spread the icing over the sides and top of the cake. Allow the icing to set for an hour or two before serving. (The cake can be assembled hours ahead.)

apples are the most widely grown tree fruit on earth. According to *Compton's Encyclopedia,* apple production runs at thirty-nine million tons per year. Until recently, when China upped its apple orchard plantings to around seven million acres, the United States was the biggest apple-producing country, and Europe was the continent that grew the most apples. In Europe, most apples are turned into mildly alcoholic cider. France, Germany, Italy, and Spain are the major producers.

Americans consume about forty pounds (one box) of apples a year, half fresh and half in processed form, per person. The Belgians and Italians consume three times that amount, while the Dutch come close to the adage "an apple a day keeps the doctor away."

Cider and Calvados-Soaked Pound Cake

This is a special cake for the holidays. You can make it two or three months ahead and store it in the freezer, where it will improve with age. A fine-textured pound cake made with confectioners' sugar can imbibe copious quantities of cider and Calvados and still not fall apart. Though definitely not for the kiddies, it is sure to be appreciated by discerning adults. This cake tastes best when cut thin. Serve two or three slices to a portion.

MAKES 16 SERVINGS

CAKE

3 cups (10$^{1}/_{2}$ ounces) sifted cake flour

$^{1}/_{2}$ teaspoon salt

$^{3}/_{4}$ pound (3 sticks) unsalted butter,
    at room temperature

2 teaspoons pure vanilla extract

$^{1}/_{2}$ teaspoon ground mace

Finely grated zest of 1 lemon

3 cups confectioners' sugar (spooned into
    the cup and leveled)

6 large eggs

SYRUP

6 cups apple cider

$^{1}/_{4}$ cup sugar

$^{1}/_{2}$ cup Calvados or Applejack

1. Adjust an oven rack to the lower third position and preheat the oven to 325°F. Butter a 10-inch (12-cup) Bundt pan or coat it with cooking spray; dust it lightly with flour and tap out the excess.

2. To make the cake, resift the flour with the salt and set aside.

3. In a large bowl, with an electric mixer, beat the butter on medium speed for about 30 seconds, until it is smooth and creamy. Add the vanilla, mace, and lemon zest and beat briefly to combine well. Gradually add the confectioners' sugar while beating on low speed. (If you beat at a higher speed, the sugar will fly out of the bowl.) Once all of the sugar has been added, stop to scrape the bowl. Beat on medium to medium-high speed for 4 to 5 minutes, until the mixture is thick, fluffy, and almost white in color.

4. Add the eggs one at a time, beating on medium speed until each is thoroughly incorporated before adding the next. Scrape the bowl as necessary. Beat on medium-high speed for 1 minute after the last egg has been incorporated. On the lowest speed, gradually add the flour mixture, beating only until incorporated. The batter will be thick. Spoon it into the prepared pan. Rotate the pan briskly on the countertop to level the batter. (It's all right if the batter isn't completely smooth on top; it will smooth out during baking.)

5. Bake for 65 to 70 minutes, until the top is golden brown, the cake springs back when lightly pressed, and a toothpick comes out dry.

6. While the cake is baking, prepare the syrup. Boil the cider with the sugar in a large heavy saucepan until it is reduced to 1½ cups, about 15 minutes. Cool for 5 minutes and stir in the Calvados. The syrup should be warm when used. Reheat if necessary.

7. When the cake is done, set the pan on a rack on your countertop and slowly pour about half the syrup along the edge of it so that the syrup runs between the cake and the pan. With pot holders, grasp the pan and tilt it to make sure the syrup reaches the bottom of the cake. With a wooden skewer, poke holes about 1 inch apart in the top of the cake, going about halfway down. Pour the remaining syrup evenly over the top of the cake. Let the cake cool in its pan for 1 hour on a wire rack.

8. To unmold the cake, bang the pan lightly on the countertop to loosen the cake. Cover the pan with a wire rack and invert the two. Carefully remove the pan and let the cake cool completely. It's best if you let the cake stand overnight, wrapped in plastic wrap, before serving. Cut into thin slices.

Apple-Caramel-Swirl Cheesecake

Apples and caramel are a magic combination. In this cheesecake, apples are coated with a caramel syrup and baked under a yogurt and cream cheese batter swirled with more caramel. You will need to start this two days ahead so that the yogurt has ample time to drain and become yogurt cheese and the baked cake can chill overnight. Be sure to use a yogurt with no additives, or it won't drain properly. The caramel syrup and apples can also be prepared a day ahead. You can use just about any tart, firm cooking apple for this cheesecake. Braeburn, Granny Smith, Northern Spy, Jonathan, and similar apples are best. Avoid McIntosh and members of their family. The graham cracker crust for this cheesecake is low-fat and made in an unusual way.

MAKES 12 SERVINGS

One 2-pound container low-fat
   vanilla yogurt (see Note)

SYRUP
1 cup sugar
1 tablespoon unsalted butter,
   at room temperature

$^2/_3$ cup low-fat evaporated milk
   (not sweetened condensed milk)
1 teaspoon pure vanilla extract
$^1/_8$ teaspoon salt

CRUST
20 squares (5 ounces) graham crackers
1 teaspoon ground cinnamon
$^1/_4$ cup sugar
1 tablespoon unsalted butter, at room
   temperature
2 tablespoons egg white

APPLES
$^1/_4$ cup firmly packed light or dark brown sugar
$^1/_4$ cup fresh orange juice
$1^1/_4$ pounds firm cooking apples (3 to 4
   medium), quartered, cored, peeled, and
   cut into $^1/_2$-inch cubes (about 3 cups)

CHEESECAKE
Two 8-ounce packages Neufchâtel cheese
$^1/_2$ cup sugar
3 tablespoons cornstarch
$^1/_4$ teaspoon salt
1 tablespoon pure vanilla extract
2 large eggs

1. At least 1 day ahead, rinse a large square of cheesecloth and squeeze out the excess moisture. Line a large wire strainer with the cloth and set it over a bowl. Turn the yogurt into the strainer, cover it loosely with plastic wrap, and refrigerate for 24 hours to

drain thoroughly. (If not using the yogurt cheese right away, refrigerate it in a covered plastic container for up to 3 days. Drain off and discard any liquid before using.)

2. To make the caramel, put the sugar and $^1/_4$ cup water in a small heavy saucepan. *Do not stir.* Place the pan over medium-low heat, and cook, swirling the pan gently from time to time, for about 12 minutes, or until the sugar dissolves. Cover the pan, increase the heat to medium-high, and boil for 1 minute. (This will dissolve any sugar crystals clinging to the sides of the pan.) Uncover the pan and boil, swirling the pan occasionally, for an additional 10 minutes, or until the syrup is amber.

3. Remove the pan from the heat and let it stand for 1 minute. Add the butter and stir with a wooden spoon until it melts. Gradually add the evaporated milk, stirring constantly. (The caramel will harden and stick to the spoon.) Place the pan over medium heat and cook for 3 minutes, or until the caramel melts and the mixture is smooth, stirring constantly. Remove the pan from the heat and stir in the vanilla and salt. Pour the caramel into a bowl; cover and refrigerate. (You will need $^2/_3$ cup for this recipe.) Use leftovers to stir into milk.

4. Adjust an oven rack to the lower third position and preheat the oven to 350°F. Coat a 9-inch springform pan with cooking spray.

5. To make the crust, place the graham crackers in a large zip-top plastic bag and crush with a rolling pin to make fine crumbs. Add the cinnamon and combine well. In a medium bowl, beat together the sugar, butter, and egg white with a hand-held electric mixer until very creamy, about 1 minute. Add the crumb mixture and toss and stir thoroughly with a fork. Turn the crumbs into the prepared pan and press enough of them onto the pan side to make a crust $1^1/_2$ inches high. Press the remaining crumbs firmly onto the bottom. If the crumbs are sticky, dip your fingertips into granulated sugar as necessary.

6. Bake the crust for 10 minutes. Remove the pan from the oven and reduce the temperature to 300°F. Cool the crust completely.

7. To prepare the apples, combine the brown sugar and orange juice in a medium nonstick skillet and bring the mixture to a simmer over medium-high heat, stirring occasionally. Add the apples and cook, stirring frequently, until the fruit is tender and the liquid has been completely absorbed, 5 to 8 minutes. Set aside to cool. Before using, drain off any juices in a strainer.

8. To make the filling, in a large bowl, beat the yogurt cheese and cream cheese together with an electric mixer on medium speed until very smooth. Stop as necessary to scrape the bowl and beaters. Add the sugar, cornstarch, salt, and vanilla and beat until smooth. On medium speed, beat in the eggs one at a time just until each is throughly incorporated. Scrape the bowl and beat for another 30 seconds.

9. To assemble the cheesecake, combine the apples with ⅓ cup of the caramel syrup and about ½ cup of the cheesecake batter and spread the mixture on the bottom of the crumb crust. Carefully spoon the remaining cheesecake batter over the apples. (The batter may extend above the rim of the crust; do not be concerned.) Drizzle another ⅓ cup caramel syrup in thin lines over the batter and swirl it in with the blade of a table knife. Lay a square of aluminum foil loosely over the top of the pan.

10. Bake for 50 minutes. Turn off the oven and remove the foil. Let the cheesecake stand in the turned-off oven with the door closed for 45 minutes longer. Remove the cheesecake from the oven and cool it to room temperature. Cover the cheesecake loosely with a paper towel and refrigerate it overnight before serving.

11. To serve, carefully remove the side of the spring-form. If necessary, run a small sharp knife around the edge of the pan to release the cheesecake. Use a sharp knife rinsed in hot water before making each cut.

Note: Be sure to check the ingredients on the yogurt container. There should be no gelatin, gums, or starch. No artificial anything. Do not use yogurts called "extra creamy"; they do not drain well.

Chocolate-Chocolate Chip Fudge Cake

The recipe for this moist and very chocolaty cake comes from Kris and Larry Evans, who own The Black Dog Restaurant in Missoula, Montana. It is one of their most popular desserts, and it is "vegan," meaning that strict vegetarians can enjoy it because the cake contains no dairy products. The secret ingredient is a large amount of applesauce. If you wish to make this a vegan cake, be sure the chocolate chips and margarine you buy contain no dairy products (such as milk solids or whey). If making the cake vegan doesn't matter to you, feel free to use any chocolate chips—and you might as well go whole hog and put butter into the icing too. Kept covered, the cake stays moist and fresh for days at room temperature.

MAKES 12 TO 16 SERVINGS

CAKE

2½ cups (11¼ ounces) unbleached all-purpose flour (spooned into the cups and leveled)
1 cup (3½ ounces) Dutch-process cocoa (scooped into the cup and leveled)
2 teaspoons baking soda
½ teaspoon salt
¾ cup granulated sugar
¾ cup firmly packed light brown sugar

2 cups smooth unsweetened applesauce

²/₃ cup safflower or corn oil

2 tablespoons distilled white vinegar

2 teaspoons pure vanilla extract

1 cup chocolate chips or miniature chocolate
   chips (dairy-free if desired)

ICING

1 tablespoon instant espresso powder

4 tablespoons (¹/₂ stick) margarine or unsalted
   butter, at room temperature

¹/₂ cup Dutch-process cocoa (scooped into the
   cup and leveled)

1 cup confectioners' sugar (scooped into the
   cup and leveled), plus more if needed

1¹/₂ teaspoons pure vanilla extract

1. Adjust an oven rack to the lower third position and preheat the oven to 350°F. Coat a 10-inch (12-cup) Bundt pan, preferably nonstick, with cooking spray and dust it with flour. Tap out the excess flour.

2. To make the cake, sift together the flour, cocoa, baking soda, salt, and granulated sugar into a large bowl. Add the brown sugar and mix it in with your fingertips, breaking up any lumps; set aside.

3. In a medium bowl, whisk together the applesauce, 1 cup cold water, the oil, vinegar, and vanilla until the mixture is creamy. Pour the liquid over the dry ingredients and stir with a rubber spatula until the batter is smooth. Stir in the chocolate chips. Scrape the batter into the pan and smooth the top.

4. Bake for 50 to 60 minutes, or until a cake tester comes out dry with just a few chocolate crumbs sticking to it. Cool the cake in its pan for 20 minutes. Cover the pan with a rack and invert the two. Remove the pan and let the cake stand until it is completely cool.

5. To make the icing, dissolve the instant coffee in ¹/₄ cup hot water. Add 2 tablespoons cold water and set aside to cool.

6. Place the margarine, cocoa, confectioners' sugar, and vanilla in a medium bowl. Add the cooled coffee mixture. Beat with an electric mixer, on low speed at first, then on medium speed, until the icing is smooth and creamy. It should be pourable but not at all runny. Adjust the consistency with more water or confectioners' sugar if necessary.

7. Set the cake (on its cooling rack) on a rimmed baking sheet. Gradually pour the icing all over the top of the cake in a wide band. The icing will slowly make its way down the sides, cloaking the cake almost completely. Let the cake sit until the icing is set, at least 1 hour.

8. With a wide metal spatula or two large pastry scrapers, carefully transfer the cake to a cake plate. Cut portions with a sharp knife rinsed in hot water.

Cookies

As round as appil was his face.

—GEOFFREY CHAUCER,
THE HOUSE OF FAME,
BOOK III, LINE 819

Cookies are comfort food at its most intimate. You can hold a cookie in your hand, nibble on it or gobble it down, but the only thing between you and the cookie is your mouth. No plate or fork gets in the way. Cookies are also informal food, and they appeal to people of all ages. A plate full of these cookies would be welcome at celebrations or informal gatherings. And they're great to pack into lunches. Apples in cookies help to keep them fresh, so these store well at room temperature for a few days.

Apple Bars

These bars showcase a thick apple filling between two tender layers of buttery brown sugar pastry. Incorporating beaten egg whites into the fruit filling keeps the apples from oozing. Use a tart apple such as Liberty, Macoun, McIntosh, or a similar variety. The bars stay fresh for several days when stored airtight at room temperature.

MAKES 16 BARS

CRUST

1/2 pound (2 sticks) unsalted butter,
   at room temperature
1 cup firmly packed light brown sugar
2 large eggs
2 cups (9 ounces) unbleached all-purpose
   flour (spooned into the cup and leveled)
1/4 teaspoon salt

FILLING

3 pounds apples, quartered, cored, and
   thinly sliced crosswise
3/4 cup sugar
Grated zest of 1 lemon
2 tablespoons fresh lemon juice
2 large egg whites

1 large egg yolk
1 teaspoon milk
Confectioners' sugar for dusting

1. In a medium bowl, beat the butter until smooth. Add the brown sugar and beat well. Add the eggs one at a time, beating after each until smooth. On low speed, add the flour and salt and beat only until incorporated. Remove the dough from the bowl and wrap in plastic wrap. Refrigerate for 2 hours, until firm.

2. Adjust an oven rack to the center position and preheat the oven to 350°F. Lightly butter a 13 × 9 × 2-inch baking pan or coat it with vegetable cooking spray.

3. Divide the dough in half. Roll one piece on a lightly floured surface to fit the bottom of the prepared pan. Place the dough in the pan and bake for about 15 minutes, until golden brown. Set aside to cool completely. Leave the oven on.

4. To prepare the filling, combine the apples, sugar, lemon zest, and juice in a large bowl. Beat the egg whites until stiff but not dry and fold them into the apple mixture. Spread the filling over the cooled crust.

5. Roll the remaining piece of dough to fit the top of the pan and place it over the apples. Beat the egg yolk and milk with a fork to combine well and brush over the top crust. Prick the crust with a fork at 2-inch intervals all over the top.

6. Bake for about 50 minutes, or until the crust is golden brown and the apples are tender. Cool completely before cutting into bars. Dust with confectioners' sugar before serving.

Oatmeal-Apple-Nut Bars

A thick purée of orange-flavored dried apples is sandwiched between a crunchy, buttery crumb crust with oatmeal and macadamia nuts. The dried apples can either be homemade (see page 10) or store-bought. The crumb mixture is best made with a food processor. These bars make great lunchbox treats.

MAKES 16 BARS

FILLING

4 ounces dried apples
$^2/_3$ cup fresh orange juice
$^1/_4$ cup sugar
$^1/_4$ teaspoon apple-pie spice or ground cinnamon

CRUMB MIXTURE

$^1/_2$ cup (2$^1/_2$ ounces) macadamia nuts, preferably unsalted
1 cup (5 ounces) unbleached all-purpose flour (scooped into the cup and leveled)
$^1/_2$ teaspoon salt
$^1/_2$ cup granulated sugar
$^1/_2$ cup firmly packed light brown sugar
12 tablespoons (1$^1/_2$ sticks) chilled unsalted butter, cut into $^1/_2$-inch cubes
1$^1/_3$ cups old-fashioned or quick-cooking rolled oats (not instant)

1. To make the filling, combine the apples, orange juice, sugar, and spice in a heavy medium saucepan. Bring the mixture to the simmer, uncovered, over medium heat. Cover the pan and adjust the heat to medium-low so the apples simmer slowly in the orange juice. After 10 minutes, give the mixture a stir. Continue cooking, covered, until almost all the orange juice is absorbed. Add $^1/_2$ cup water, cover the pan, and continue cooking, checking the apples every 10 minutes and adding $^1/_2$ cup of water each time as the liquid gets absorbed, until the apples are very tender. The whole process may take 45 minutes to 1 hour, depending on the dryness of the apples.

2. When the apples are completely tender and there is almost no liquid left in the pan, remove from the heat and use a potato masher to mash the apples. You should have a very thick purée that holds its shape in a spoon. If it seems too wet, stir the apples constantly over medium heat for about 1 minute to drive off the excess moisture. Cool to room temperature. (The apple mixture can be made 2 or 3 days ahead and refrigerated.)

3. Adjust an oven rack to the lower third position and preheat the oven to 325°F.

4. In a food processor with the metal blade, pulse/chop the macadamia nuts until they are medium-fine; the pieces should be about $^1/_8$ inch. Remove the nuts and set them aside. Reinsert the metal blade. Add the flour, salt (use only $^1/_4$ teaspoon salt if the macadamia nuts were salted), granulated

sugar, and brown sugar to the work bowl. Pulse 5 or 6 times to combine. Add the butter pieces and pulse rapidly until the mixture resembles large granules, about ⅛ inch. Do this step carefully—don't over-process, or the mixture will gather into large clumps, which is not what you want. Dump the mixture into a large bowl and stir in the nuts and oatmeal.

5. Place 3 cups of the mixture in an ungreased 8-inch square baking pan and press it firmly and evenly onto the bottom with your fingertips to make a compact layer. Spread the cooled apple mixture over the crust. Sprinkle the remaining crumb mixture evenly over the filling and press it firmly into place. The pan will be about half full.

6. Bake for about 70 minutes, until the crust is golden brown and has a toasty aroma. Cool the pan on a rack for 20 to 30 minutes.

7. Run a small sharp knife around the edge of the pastry to release it from the sides of the pan. Cover with a wire rack and invert the two. Some oatmeal flakes may fall off; it's all right. Remove the pan, cover the pastry with another wire rack, and reinvert the two so that the pastry is right side up. Cool completely; then, for ease in cutting, refrigerate the pastry for about 1 hour.

8. Use a sharp serrated knife to cut the pastry into 2-inch squares. Store the bars in an airtight container; they keep well for several days.

apples and gravity

legend says that the great physicist Isaac Newton discovered the force of gravity when he saw an apple fall from a tree. This is one legend that seems to be true. In 1666, Newton had left his home in Cambridge, England, for the countryside, in order to escape the feared bubonic plague epidemic. As he later related, he had been sitting alone in a garden in a thoughtful mood when he saw an apple fall from a tree. Watching the fruit fall took him to thinking about what could cause this universal phenomenon. From the apple, his mind moved to the moon, theorizing that the same force that brought the apple down might hold the moon in orbit. He went on to consider the sun, and how its gravity might control the planets that circled around it, and so forth, resulting in a theory to explain one of the most important forces in nature.

Apple Biscotti

This recipe came about by accident: I wanted to make a moist bar cookie. What I ended up with was a cookie that had great flavor but was too moist. So I let the whole panful sit at room temperature for a day and turned it into biscotti. These are addictive, crisp, spicy cookies.

MAKES ABOUT 5 DOZEN COOKIES

2 cups (9 ounces) unbleached all-purpose flour (spooned into the cup and leveled)
I teaspoon baking powder
I teaspoon baking soda
3/4 teaspoon salt
I teaspoon pumpkin-pie spice
1/2 teaspoon freshly grated nutmeg
I cup old-fashioned rolled oats (not instant)
I cup (4 ounces) chopped walnuts
I cup (5 ounces) golden raisins
3 large eggs
3/4 cup maple syrup
1/4 cup vegetable oil
I teaspoon pure vanilla extract
1/4 cup sugar
2 pounds tart apples, quartered, cored, peeled, and thinly sliced crosswise

I. Adjust an oven rack to the center position and preheat the oven to 350°F. Coat a 15 × 10 × 1-inch jelly-roll pan with cooking spray and set it aside.

2. Sift the flour with the baking powder, baking soda, salt, pumpkin-pie spice, and nutmeg into a large bowl. Stir in the oats, walnuts, and raisins.

3. In a medium bowl, beat the eggs until foamy. Add the maple syrup, oil, vanilla, and sugar and beat to combine well. Stir in the apples. Add the mixture to the dry ingredients and fold together only until the dry ingredients are thoroughly moistened. Spread the batter evenly in the prepared pan.

4. Bake for 30 to 35 minutes, until the top is an even golden brown color and springs back when lightly pressed. Cool the "cookie" in its pan for 10 minutes. Invert onto a large cooling rack, remove the pan, cover with another rack, and invert again to finish cooling right side up. Let stand at room temperature, uncovered, for I to 2 days.

5. Adjust an oven rack to the center position and preheat the oven to 275°F.

6. Transfer the cookie to a cutting surface. With a serrated knife, cut it lengthwise in half. Cut each half crosswise into 1/2-inch-thick slices. Stand the slices upright, spacing them about 1/2 inch apart, on ungreased cookie sheets. Bake one sheet at a time for I hour, or until the biscotti are golden brown all over. Rotate the sheet back to front once halfway during baking. Transfer the cookies to cooling racks. When completely cool, store in airtight containers. These keep well at room temperature for up to two weeks. Freeze them for longer storage.

Giant Chocolate Applesauce Cookies

These dark and spicy cookies are soft, moist, and huge. Currants and pecans make them extra yummy. Baking the cookies on parchment or silicone baking pan liners gives them a lovely rounded shape. If you use cooking spray or grease the sheets instead of using liners, the cookies tend to spread more and will do so unevenly.

MAKES 1½ DOZEN VERY LARGE COOKIES

2 cups (9 ounces) unbleached
    all-purpose flour (spooned into the
    cup and leveled)
⅓ cup Dutch-process cocoa
1 teaspoon baking soda
½ teaspoon salt
1 teaspoon ground cinnamon
½ teaspoon ground cloves
½ teaspoon ground allspice
8 tablespoons (1 stick) unsalted butter,
    at room temperature
1 cup sugar
1 teaspoon pure vanilla extract
1 large egg
1½ cups unsweetened smooth applesauce
1 cup currants
¾ cup chopped pecans

1. Adjust two oven racks to divide the oven into thirds and preheat the oven to 350°F. Cut three sheets of parchment to line large heavy cookie sheets (14 × 17 inches), or use silicone baking pan liners. If you don't have three cookie sheets, you can shape the cookies on the parchment or pan liners and let them wait at room temperature while the first batch bakes.

2. Sift the flour twice with the cocoa, baking soda, salt, cinnamon, cloves, and allspice and set aside.

3. In a large bowl, beat the butter with an electric mixer on medium speed only until it is smooth. Add the sugar and vanilla and beat for 2 to 3 minutes on medium to medium-high speed. Scrape the bowl, add the egg, and beat for 2 to 3 minutes on medium speed. Add half the dry ingredients and beat on low speed only until incorporated. Add the applesauce and beat on low speed until the mixture is smooth. Add the remaining dry ingredients and mix on low speed only until thoroughly moistened. Stir in the currants and pecans.

4. Use a soupspoon to form the cookies. Place heaping spoonfuls of batter 3 to 4 inches apart on the parchment or silicone pan liners, 6 to a sheet; the mounds should be about 2½ inches in diameter and 1 inch high. Place two of the pans in the oven and bake for 15 to 18 minutes. Reverse the sheets top to bottom and front to back once to ensure even baking. Bake only until the cookies spring back when gently pressed in their centers; do not overbake.

With a wide metal spatula, transfer the cookies to wire racks to cool. Bake the third sheet of cookies on the upper oven rack. When the cookies are completely cool, store them airtight. These stay fresh for several days at room temperature.

Variations: Substitute dark or golden raisins or dried sour cherries or cranberries for the currants, or use a mixture of dried fruits. · Chopped candied ginger and golden raisins is another good combination. · Feel free to use walnuts instead of the pecans, or use a combination; you could also increase the nuts by 1/4 cup. · To make the cookies even more chocolaty, add 1 cup of semisweet mini morsels along with the nuts and dried fruit.

to soften brown sugar

if you have a container of brown sugar that's turned hard as a rock, cut an apple into quarters and put it in with the sugar. The next day, the sugar will be soft and moist once again.

Rocky Mountain Applesauce Rocks

These are big, moist, mildly spiced cookies loaded with dried fruit and walnuts. Their taste resembles the German lebkuchen. They are called "rocks" because of their bumpy appearance. When the cookies come out of the oven, they are brushed with a glaze that hardens into a thin white shell as they cool.

MAKES 2 DOZEN LARGE COOKIES

1³/₄ cups (8 ounces) unbleached all-purpose flour (spooned into the cups and leveled)
³/₄ teaspoon baking soda
¹/₂ teaspoon salt
1¹/₂ teaspoons pumpkin-pie spice
¹/₂ cup untoasted wheat germ
8 tablespoons (1 stick) unsalted butter, at room temperature
1 cup firmly packed light brown sugar
1 large egg
1 cup smooth unsweetened applesauce
Finely grated zest of 1 orange
1 pound mixed dried fruits (diced dates, prunes, cranberries, golden raisins, sweet or sour cherries, and/or packaged fruit bits; see Note)
1¹/₂ cups (6 ounces) coarsely chopped or broken walnuts

**1½ cups confectioners' sugar plus more if
  needed (scooped into the cups and leveled)**
**4 tablespoons (½ stick) unsalted butter, at
  room temperature**
2 tablespoons heavy cream or half-and-half
2 to 3 tablespoons apple juice or apple cider

1. Adjust two oven racks to divide the oven into thirds and preheat the oven to 350°F. Line two heavy 14 × 17-inch cookie sheets with parchment or silicone baking-pan liners.

2. Sift the flour, baking soda, salt, and pumpkin-pie spice into a medium bowl. Stir in the wheat germ and set aside.

3. In a large bowl, beat the butter with an electric mixer only until it is soft and creamy. Add the brown sugar and beat for 2 to 3 minutes on medium speed. Scrape the bowl, add the egg, and beat for 2 to 3 minutes. Add the applesauce and orange zest and beat to combine well. (The mixture will look curdled, which is all right.) Stir in the dry ingredients, dried fruits, then the walnuts.

4. Use a soupspoon to form the cookies. Place 12 large mounds of dough on each of the lined cookie sheets, spacing them 2 to 3 inches apart; each cookie will be 2 to 2½ inches in diameter and about 2 inches high.

5. Bake for 18 to 20 minutes, until the cookies are golden brown and the tops spring back when gently pressed. Rotate the sheets top to bottom and back to front once about halfway during baking to ensure even browning.

6. While the cookies bake, prepare the glaze: Place the confectioners' sugar, butter, cream, and 2 tablespoons apple juice in a medium bowl. Beat with an electric mixer until very smooth. The icing should be the consistency of very softly whipped cream, not at all runny. Adjust the thickness with more sugar or drops of apple juice. Set aside.

7. As soon as the cookies come out of the oven, slide the liners off the sheets onto your countertop. Immediately brush the glaze all over the hot cookies, using a generous blob of glaze for each. The heat of the cookies will cause the glaze to melt and run down the sides. When all the cookies have been glazed, use a wide metal spatula to transfer them to large cooling racks. Let stand until completely cool and the glaze has set. Store airtight at room temperature. The cookies keep well for several days.

Note: You can use almost any combination of dried fruits. Just be sure they're soft and moist, not dry and brittle. About ¼ pound each of cranberries, cherries, golden raisins, and dates makes a good combo. Dried apricots, raisins, prunes, and cherries are also good. Or you could use just two different fruits. Use scissors to cut pitted dates, prunes, and apricot halves into bite-sized pieces.

Breads

And pluck till time and times are done
The silver apples of the moon,
The golden apples of the sun.

—WILLIAM BUTLER YEATS,
THE SONG OF WANDERING AENGUS

Apples can be added to breads in more different forms than they are used in any other type of apple cookery. Shredded, sliced, chopped, or diced raw apples, dried apples, applesauce, apple jam, apple juice, and apple cider can all become part of a quick or yeast bread recipe. Furthermore, apple breads don't always have to be sweet. Because so many varieties of apples have both sweet and tart attributes, they can add lots of oomph to savory breads.

What this means is that apple's possibilities with breads are virtually limitless. The recipes in this chapter only begin to demonstrate this point. Apple's presence ranges from the savory and quick Apple Corn Bread with Bacon and Jalapeño and the yeasted Apple-Cider Polenta Cheese Bread to the sweet Applesauce Doughnuts and Apple Babka.

Apple Loaf

This is a moist bread loaded with the taste of apple from the Thick Apple Purée and tart dried cherries and blueberries. It's great for breakfast or a snack, or to serve with tea or coffee. The bread is wonderful cut into thick slices and slathered with cream cheese. Let the loaf stand for at least several hours or overnight before serving.

MAKES 1 LARGE LOAF

1²/₃ cups (8¹/₄ ounces) unbleached
    all-purpose flour (scooped into the cups
    and leveled)
1 teaspoon baking powder
³/₄ teaspoon salt
1 teaspoon ground cinnamon
6 tablespoons (³/₄ stick) unsalted butter, at
    room temperature
¹/₃ cup vegetable shortening
1¹/₃ cups sugar
1¹/₂ teaspoons pure vanilla extract
3 large eggs
1¹/₃ cups Thick Apple Purée (page 18)
¹/₂ cup dried sour cherries
¹/₂ cup dried blueberries

1. Adjust an oven rack to the lower third position and preheat the oven to 350°F. Butter an 8-cup loaf pan (see Note) or coat it with vegetable cooking spray and dust it lightly with fine dry bread crumbs. Tap out the excess crumbs.

2. Sift the flour, baking powder, salt, and cinnamon together and set aside.

3. In a large bowl, beat the butter and shortening together with an electric mixer until smooth. Add the sugar and vanilla and beat for several minutes, until the mixture is fluffy and almost white. Add the eggs one at a time, beating well after each. Stop to scrape the bowl as necessary. Beat in the apple purée. On the lowest speed, gradually add the dry ingredients, mixing only until incorporated. Stir in the dried fruits. The batter will be very thick.

4. Spread the batter level in the prepared pan and bake for 75 to 85 minutes, or until the loaf is well browned and a cake tester comes out clean and dry. Cool the loaf in its pan on a wire rack for 30 minutes.

5. Carefully remove the loaf from the pan and cool it completely on a wire rack, right side up. Wrapped airtight, the loaf keeps at room temperature for 3 or 4 days. Freeze for longer storage.

Note: A 9 × 5 × 3-inch pan is standard, but if you have one that measures 10 × 4¹/₂ × 3 inches, the loaf will have a higher, more appealing shape.

Variations: You can use any dried tart fruits you like. Apricots and cranberries are a nice combo; use ¹/₂ cup of each. Some chopped walnuts or pecans (about ¹/₂ cup) are a good addition. You can also play around with spices. But do try it this way first.

Banana-Apple Macadamia Bread

America's number one and number two fruits aren't squabbling over rank in this bread. Dried apples are used for their concentrated taste and chewy texture, and tart cranberries soften the sweetness of the banana. Macadamia nuts add richness and crunch.

MAKES 1 LARGE LOAF

1¾ cups unbleached all-purpose flour
   (spooned into the cups and leveled)
1 teaspoon baking powder
¼ teaspoon baking soda
½ teaspoon salt
¾ teaspoon freshly grated nutmeg
¾ cup dried apples, cut into ¼-inch pieces
½ cup dried cranberries
⅔ cup coarsely chopped macadamia nuts
1 pound ripe bananas
2 large eggs
2 teaspoons pure vanilla extract
8 tablespoons (1 stick) unsalted butter, melted
1 cup sugar

1. Adjust an oven rack to the lower third position and preheat the oven to 350°F. Butter an 8-cup loaf pan (see Note) or coat it with vegetable cooking spray and dust it lightly with fine dry bread crumbs. Tap out the excess crumbs and set the pan aside.

2. Sift the flour with the baking powder, baking soda, salt, and nutmeg into a large bowl. Add the apples, cranberries, and macadamia nuts and toss to coat well. Set aside.

3. Mash the bananas in a medium bowl (you should have about 1⅓ cups). Whisk in the eggs, vanilla, melted butter, and sugar. Add to the dry ingredients and fold together with a rubber spatula only until the flour mixture is thoroughly moistened. Scrape the batter into the prepared pan and smooth the top.

4. Bake for about 1 hour, until the loaf is golden brown and a cake tester comes out clean. The loaf may crack on top, which is all right. Cool the loaf in its pan for 10 minutes. Carefully remove the loaf from the pan and set it on a cooling rack right side up. Cool completely, at least several hours, before serving.

Note: A 9 × 5 × 3-inch pan is standard, but if you have one that measures 10 × 4½ × 3 inches, the loaf will have a higher, more appealing shape.

Big Apple-Rhubarb Swirl

This beautiful sweet yeast bread, looking like a large flower, is filled with a tart and spicy jam of apples, rhubarb, and freshly grated ginger. Serve it at an afternoon tea or for brunch. Make the jam a day ahead so that its flavor and texture have time to "compose" themselves. Be sure to use an apple that will make a thick sauce, such as Jonamac. You can make the dough in a heavy-duty mixer, in a food processor, or by hand.

MAKES 10 TO 12 SERVINGS

JAM

$^3/_4$ **pound rhubarb, trimmed and cut into**
$^1/_2$-inch pieces (3 cups)
I$^1/_2$ **pounds crisp, tart apples, quartered,**
cored, peeled, and cut into $^1/_2$-inch cubes
(4 cups)
I$^1/_2$ **cups sugar**
$^1/_2$ **teaspoon freshly grated nutmeg**
$^1/_4$ **teaspoon salt**
One I-inch piece fresh ginger, peeled and
grated
One 3-inch cinnamon stick
3 tablespoons fresh lemon juice

DOUGH

3 cups (15 ounces) unbleached all-purpose
flour (scooped into the cup and leveled)

I **tablespoon SAF-Instant yeast**
$^1/_3$ **cup sugar**
$^3/_4$ **teaspoon salt**
$^1/_2$ **cup hot milk (120° to 130°F)**
I **large egg**
4 tablespoons ($^1/_2$ stick) unsalted butter,
at room temperature

$^1/_2$ **cup chopped pecans**

GLAZE

I **large egg**
I **tablespoon milk**

ICING

I **cup confectioners' sugar**
I **teaspoon pure vanilla extract**
I **teaspoon fresh lemon juice**

I. A day ahead, combine all the jam ingredients in a heavy medium saucepan and set the pan, covered, over medium heat. Cook, stirring occasionally with a wooden spatula, until the mixture comes to a simmer. Uncover the pan and continue cooking, stirring occasionally, until the jam is sauce-like. Then, stirring frequently, cook until the jam is thick and holds its shape in a spoon, about I hour total. Stir constantly toward the end of cooking to prevent the jam from scorching. You can tell if the jam is the proper consistency by lifting some of it onto the spatula and quickly turning the spatula upside down: If the jam stays put and doesn't fall off, the mixture is ready. Remove the cinnamon stick. You will have about 2 cups of jam. Cool to room temperature, then transfer the jam to a covered container and refrigerate overnight. It will be very thick.

2. To make the dough using *a heavy-duty mixer,* combine 2 cups of the flour with the yeast, sugar, and salt in the mixer bowl. Add the hot milk, $1/4$ cup hot water (120° to 130°F), the egg, and butter. Beat with the flat beater on low speed just to moisten the ingredients, then beat on medium speed for 5 minutes. Attach the dough hook, add the remaining 1 cup flour, and knead on medium speed until the dough is smooth and elastic, about 5 minutes. Remove the dough from the mixer bowl and knead it briefly on a lightly floured surface.

To make the dough by hand, combine 2 cups of the flour, the yeast, sugar, and salt in a large bowl. Add the hot milk, $1/4$ cup hot water (120° to 130°F), the egg, and butter and beat well with a wooden spoon to make a soft dough. Add the remaining 1 cup flour and stir it in well. Turn the dough out onto a lightly floured surface and knead until smooth, elastic, and only slightly sticky, about 8 minutes. Add flour as necessary to make the dough workable, but don't overdo it, or the dough will be dry.

To make the dough in a food processor, use the plastic dough blade or the metal blade. Place all of the flour, the yeast, sugar, and salt in the work bowl. Add the egg and softened butter. Combine the hot milk with $1/4$ cup hot water (120° to 130°F) in a 1-cup glass measure. Start the motor and pour the liquid mixture

through the feed tube in a slow steady stream, taking about 20 seconds to do so. Once the dough gathers into a ball, process for 45 seconds to knead. The dough should clean the side of the work bowl. If the dough is too wet, add flour by the tablespoon with the machine running. If it's too dry, add milk (which does not have to be hot) by the teaspoonful. The dough should be soft, smooth, elastic, and slightly sticky. Remove the dough from the bowl and knead it briefly on a lightly floured work surface.

3. Shape the dough into a ball. Lightly oil a medium bowl or coat it with cooking spray. Add the dough and turn to coat all surfaces with the oil, or spray the top of the dough with cooking spray. Cover tightly with plastic wrap and let the dough rise at room temperature until it has doubled in bulk, about $1^1/2$ hours. Test the dough by pressing it with a fingertip: The depression should remain when you remove your finger.

4. Turn the risen dough out onto a lightly floured surface and pat or roll it into a 10 × 18-inch rectangle, with one of the long sides facing you. Combine the apple jam and pecans and spread evenly over the dough to within $1/2$ inch of the side farthest from you. Starting with the long side nearest you, roll the dough up tightly and pinch the seam securely to seal it. Turn the roll seam side down and use a very sharp knife to cut the roll lengthwise in two. Turn each half so that its cut surface faces up.

5. Butter a heavy 12-inch pizza pan or coat it with cooking spray. Coil one half of the roll (cut surface up) and place it in the center of the prepared pan. Attach the second roll to the end of the coil with its cut side up, pinching firmly to seal, and coil it around the first piece. Tuck the end under the coil. Cover loosely with plastic wrap and let the dough rise at room temperature until it is puffy and light, about 1 hour.

6. Adjust an oven rack to the center position and preheat the oven to 350°F.

7. For the glaze, beat the egg and milk together with a fork to combine well and brush evenly over the risen dough. Bake for 35 to 45 minutes, until the swirl is a rich golden brown color and a cake tester inserted into the thickest part comes out clean. Remove the pan from the oven and let cool for 15 minutes.

8. To prepare the icing, whisk together the confectioners' sugar, vanilla, lemon juice, and 1 tablespoon hot water in a small bowl until smooth. Brush the icing all over the warm pastry. Let stand until the icing is set before serving.

Variation: To make individual rolls, pat or roll the risen dough into a 10 × 15-inch rectangle. Spread the filling and roll up as described above. Turn the roll seam side down. Butter a 15½ × 10½ × 1-inch jelly-roll pan or coat with cooking spray. Use a very sharp knife to cut the roll into fifteen 1-inch slices. Place the slices in the prepared pan, cut sides up, leaving ½ to 1 inch space between them. Cover loosely with plastic wrap and let rise in a warm place (about 85°F) until the rolls are light and doubled in size, about 1 hour. The rolls should be touching one another.

Brush the rolls with the glaze and bake at 350°F until the rolls are golden brown and a toothpick inserted into the thickest part comes out clean and dry, 20 to 25 minutes. Cool as directed and brush with the icing. Serve the rolls warm or at room temperature.

Apple Babka

Babka is a fabulous Polish sweet yeast cake. This one rises about two inches above the pan rim during baking—a most impressive sight—and then it settles a bit once out of the oven. The reason for this babka is a play reading I attended. In *Fortune*, by Deborah Laufer, one of the characters likes to bake a cherry babka. I was intrigued. How would apples be in a babka? I looked through all my baking books, but I never found one for apple babka. Now there is.

A fresh, thick applesauce flavors the eggy and buttery babka. Babkas make great eating any time of day. Since it should stand overnight before serving, you can have it for breakfast. The dough is more like a batter, much too soft to be rolled and filled. It is not difficult to make, but you will need a heavy-duty mixer. You will also need a 9½-inch kugelhopf pan, with a 10-cup capacity. The apple filling can be made a day or more ahead and refrigerated. Be sure to use crisp, tart apples that cook down to a thick sauce that will hold its shape—Jonamac, Winesap, Northern Spy, Granny Smith, and Goldrush are all good choices; I like to use a mixture. The babka will keep fresh for days at room temperature.

MAKES 12 SERVINGS

FILLING

2¼ pounds apples, quartered, cored, and peeled

¼ teaspoon salt

¾ cup sugar

½ teaspoon ground cinnamon

¼ cup fresh orange juice (grate the zest before juicing and reserve it for the dough)

BATTER

3¼ cups (16¼ ounces) unbleached all-purpose flour (scooped into the cups and leveled)

½ cup plus 1 tablespoon sugar

½ teaspoon salt

1 tablespoon SAF-Instant yeast

1 cup hot milk (120° to 130°F)

1 large egg, at room temperature

1 tablespoon pure vanilla extract

4 large egg yolks

12 tablespoons (1½ sticks) unsalted butter, at room temperature

Finely grated zest of 1 orange

1. Cut each apple quarter lengthwise into two wedges, then crosswise into thirds. You will have about 7 cups. Combine all the filling ingredients in a heavy medium saucepan and set the pan over medium heat. Cover and cook, stirring occasionally with a wooden spatula, until the mixture comes to a simmer. Uncover the pan and continue cooking, stirring occasionally, until the apples are completely

tender, about 10 minutes. With a potato masher, mash the apples to make a purée with several small pieces of apple still visible.

2. Continue cooking, stirring frequently, until the apple mixture is thick and holds its shape in a spoon (it will resemble mashed potatoes in consistency), 30 minutes to 1 hour total. The length of time depends on the moisture content of the apples. Stir constantly toward the end of cooking to prevent scorching. You can tell if the apples are ready by lifting some of the mixture onto the spatula and quickly turning the spatula upside down: If the mass stays put and doesn't fall off, the mixture has cooked enough. When you swipe a path through the apples rapidly with the wide side of the spatula, the bottom of the pan should remain visible for 2 or 3 seconds. Cool the filling completely. (You will have about 2 cups. The apple mixture can be covered and refrigerated for several days. Bring it to room temperature before use.)

3. To make the dough, in the bowl of a heavy-duty mixer, stir together 1 1/2 cups of the flour, 1 tablespoon of the sugar, the salt, and yeast. Add the hot milk all at once and stir well with a rubber spatula to combine thoroughly. Add the egg and beat it in with the spatula. Scrape the bowl, sprinkle the remaining 1 3/4 cups flour evenly over the batter, and cover the bowl tightly with plastic wrap. Set aside at room temperature until the batter is very bubbly and has partially engulfed the flour on top, about 1 hour.

4. Thoroughly coat a 9 1/2-inch kugelhopf pan (including the tube) with cooking spray or brush it well with softened butter. Add the remaining 1/2 cup sugar and the vanilla to the batter and beat in with the flat beater on low speed for 1 minute. Increase the speed to medium and add the egg yolks one at a time, beating for about 30 seconds after each addition. Scrape the bowl. Add the butter 2 tablespoons at a time, beating until each addition is thoroughly incorporated before adding the next. Add the orange zest and beat for 1 minute. The batter will be thick and elastic.

5. Remove the bowl from the mixer and add 1 cup of the apple filling. Fold and cut the apples into the batter with a rubber or firm plastic spatula to give a streaked appearance; don't be too thorough with this step. The batter will be too thick to pour. Here's how to get it into the pan: Using a large metal spoon, cut into the batter and remove spoonfuls of it. Place the spoonfuls on the bottom of the prepared pan, using about half the babka dough. Don't bother trying to spread the batter level. With a regular teaspoon, spoon 1/2 cup of the remaining apple filling in a ring over the batter. (Save any leftover apple filling to eat as applesauce or stirred into yogurt.) Then carefully spoon the remaining babka dough over the apple ring, covering it completely. The top of the babka will look uneven; just leave it alone. Cover the pan loosely with plastic wrap coated with cooking spray (sprayed side down) and let rise until the dough has nearly doubled in size and is 1/2 inch from the top of the pan, about 1 hour.

6. Adjust an oven rack to the lower third position and preheat the oven to 375°F.

7. Remove the plastic wrap and place the pan in the oven. Bake until the babka is a dark brown color and a wooden skewer inserted into the center comes out dry, about 40 minutes. If the babka seems to be browning too much, cover it loosely with a square of aluminum foil during the last 10 minutes of baking. Cool the babka in its pan on a rack for 10 minutes, then cover the babka with a wire rack and invert the two. Remove the pan and let the babka stand upside down until it is completely cool.

8. Wrap the babka securely in plastic wrap, and leave at room temperature overnight before serving. Use a sharp serrated knife to cut the babka. Properly wrapped, the babka will stay fresh for days.

Apple Hot Cross Buns

These sweet yeast rolls are loaded with dried apples instead of the usual raisins and citron. We like dried apple nuggets (see page 261 for Mail-Order Sources) for their intense flavor and chewy texture, but top-quality chopped dried apples will work just fine. The buns are brushed with a sugar syrup to give them a nice shiny look, and the traditional cross on top is made with a thick lemon-flavored confectioners' sugar icing. Serve these when very fresh, even slightly warm.

MAKES 12 BUNS

DOUGH

3½ cups (17½ ounces) unbleached all-purpose
    flour (scooped into the cups and leveled),
    plus more if needed

⅓ cup sugar

1 tablespoon SAF-Instant yeast

1 teaspoon salt

1 teaspoon ground cinnamon

½ teaspoon ground ginger

1 cup hot milk (120° to 130°F), plus
    more if needed

6 tablespoons (¾ stick) unsalted butter,
    at room temperature

2 large eggs

1 cup (4 ounces) dried apple nuggets or
    chopped dried apples

¼ **cup sugar**

GLAZE
1 large egg
1 tablespoon milk

ICING
1 cup confectioners' sugar
2 to 3 teaspoons fresh lemon juice
1 teaspoon pure vanilla extract

1. *To make the dough in a heavy-duty mixer,* place 3 cups of the flour, the sugar, yeast, salt, cinnamon, and ginger in the large mixer bowl. Add the hot milk, butter, and eggs. Beat with the flat beater on low speed until the mixture is thoroughly moistened, then beat at medium speed for 5 minutes. Attach the dough hook and add the remaining ½ cup flour. Knead on medium speed until the dough is smooth and elastic and no longer sticky, about 5 minutes. Adjust the consistency of the dough with more milk (which does not have to be hot) or flour if necessary.

To make the dough by hand, combine 3 cups of the flour, the sugar, yeast, salt, cinnamon, and ginger in a large bowl. Add the hot milk, butter, and eggs and beat well with a wooden spoon to make a soft dough. Add the remaining ½ cup flour and stir it in well. Turn the dough out on a lightly floured surface and knead until it is smooth, elastic, and only slightly sticky, about 8 minutes. Add flour as necessary to make the dough workable, but don't overdo it, or the dough will be dry.

To make the dough in a food processor, use the plastic dough blade or metal blade. Place all of the flour, the sugar, yeast, salt, cinnamon, and ginger in the work bowl. Add the softened butter and eggs. Start the motor and pour the hot milk through the feed tube in a slow steady stream, taking about 20 seconds to do so. Once the dough gathers into a ball, process for 45 seconds to knead. The dough should clean the side of the work bowl. If the dough is too wet, add flour by the tablespoon, with the machine running. If it's too dry, add a little milk (which does not have to be hot) by the teaspoonful. The dough should be soft, smooth, elastic, and no longer sticky when the kneading is complete.

2. Transfer the dough to a lightly floured work surface (if necessary) and knead in the apple nuggets to distribute them evenly. Shape the dough into a ball. Lightly oil a 3-quart bowl or coat with cooking spray and place the dough in the bowl. Turn the dough to coat all surfaces with oil, or spray the top with cooking spray. Cover tightly with plastic wrap and let the dough rise at room temperature until it has doubled in bulk, about 1½ hours. Test the dough by pressing it with a fingertip: The depression should remain when you remove your finger.

3. Line two 15½ × 10½ × 1-inch jelly-roll pans with cooking parchment or coat the pans lightly with cooking spray. Turn the risen dough out onto your work surface and pat it gently to remove air bubbles. Divide the dough into 12 even pieces and cover loosely with a kitchen towel for 10 minutes.

4. Shape each piece of dough into a ball, pinching the seam securely. Place 6 balls on each prepared sheet, seam side down, spacing them about 3 inches apart. Cover the rolls loosely with kitchen towels and let them rise at room temperature for 30 minutes.

5. Meanwhile, prepare the simple syrup: Combine the sugar with $\frac{1}{4}$ cup cold water in a small saucepan. Bring the mixture to the boil over medium-high heat, stirring frequently, and boil for 2 minutes. Remove the pan from the heat and set it aside to cool. To prepare the glaze, beat the egg and milk together with a fork to combine them well. Set aside.

6. Adjust two oven racks to divide the oven into thirds and preheat the oven to 400°F.

7. When the buns have rested for 30 minutes (they will not have doubled in size), snip an X in the top of each with sharp scissors, making the cuts about 2 inches long and $\frac{1}{2}$ inch deep. Brush the buns with the egg glaze and let them rest, uncovered, for 15 minutes.

8. Place the pans in the oven and bake for about 20 minutes, until the buns are a rich brown color. Rotate the pans top to bottom and front to back once about halfway during baking. Remove the pans from the oven and immediately brush the buns with the cooled simple syrup. Transfer the buns to cooling racks. Their surfaces will remain slightly sticky from the sugar syrup.

9. When the buns are almost cool, prepare the icing: Combine the confectioners' sugar, 2 teaspoons lemon juice, and the vanilla in a small bowl, stirring to make a mixture thick enough to pipe through a pastry bag fitted with a $\frac{1}{8}$-inch opening. Add the remaining lemon juice by droplets if the icing is too thick. Transfer the icing to a small pastry bag and pipe a cross of icing onto each bun. Serve the buns once the icing has set.

Apple Corn Bread with Bacon and Jalapeño

This corn bread is delicious alone, spread with sweet butter, or served with chili, soup, or just about any kind of stew. Although you could bake it in a 9-inch square baking pan, I recommend the cast-iron skillet. Use any crisp, tart apple.

MAKES 8 SERVINGS

6 slices bacon
Vegetable oil, if needed
1 cup cornmeal, preferably stone-ground (regular grind)
1 cup (4½ ounces) unbleached all-purpose flour (spooned into the cup and leveled)
3 tablespoons sugar
1 tablespoon baking powder
¾ teaspoon salt
2 large eggs
¾ cup milk
1 jalapeño chile, seeded and minced
1 shallot, finely chopped
1 crisp apple (about 6 ounces), quartered, cored, peeled, and shredded (1 cup)
6 cherry tomatoes, halved through the stem end

1. Cook the bacon in a large skillet over medium heat until browned and crisp. Drain the bacon on paper towels and reserve the bacon grease. There should be ¼ cup. If necessary, add vegetable oil to make up the difference. When the bacon is cool, chop it and set it aside.

2. Adjust an oven rack to the center position and preheat the oven to 450°F. About 20 minutes before baking, grease a 10-inch cast-iron skillet or 9-inch baking pan heavily with vegetable shortening, and set the pan in the hot oven.

3. In a large bowl, combine the cornmeal, flour, sugar, baking powder, and salt. Set aside.

4. In a medium bowl, whisk the eggs just to combine the yolks with the whites. Stir in the milk, bacon fat, jalapeño, and shallot. Pour the egg mixture over the dry ingredients, add the chopped bacon and apple, and stir with a rubber spatula only to moisten. Carefully remove the hot skillet from the oven with a pot holder and set the pan on a heat-resistant surface. Immediately pour in the corn bread batter. (It will sizzle.) Arrange the cherry tomatoes cut side up on top of the batter.

5. Bake for 20 to 22 minutes, until the top is browned and a toothpick comes out clean. Let the corn bread stand for 5 minutes, then cut it into wedges and serve hot.

Apple-Cider Polenta Cheese Bread

This bread is almost a meal in itself. Chunks of extra-sharp Cheddar cheese are kneaded into a yeast dough made with cooked polenta and sweetened with apple cider. The round loaves have an inviting rustic look. They're great to take on a picnic. Accompany the bread with slices of crisp apples.

MAKES 2 ROUND LOAVES

3³/₄ cups apple cider
¹/₂ cup yellow cornmeal, plus more for
    sprinkling
4 tablespoons (¹/₂ stick) unsalted butter,
    at room temperature
6 cups (30 ounces) unbleached all-purpose
    flour (scooped into the cup and leveled),
    plus more if needed
1 tablespoon SAF-Instant yeast
1 tablespoon salt
1 pound extra-sharp Cheddar cheese,
    cut into ¹/₂-inch cubes

1. Boil 3 cups of the cider in a heavy medium saucepan over high heat until it is reduced to ¹/₂ cup, 10 to 15 minutes. Swirl the pan occasionally during the reduction, and watch it closely toward the end of cooking. The mixture will be syrupy and thick with bubbles. Pour the cider into a heatproof cup and set it aside.

2. Combine the remaining ³/₄ cup cider with ³/₄ cup water in a heavy medium saucepan. Whisk in the cornmeal and place the pan over high heat. Whisk constantly as the mixture comes to a boil. Reduce the heat to medium and continue cooking, whisking all the while, for 2 minutes more, or until the mixture is slightly thickened. Remove the pan from the heat and add the butter. Whisk until the butter is melted, then add the reduced cider. Set the mixture aside briefly. (The mixture must be hot to make the dough.)

3. *To make the dough using a heavy-duty mixer,* stir together 4 cups of the flour, the yeast, and salt in the large mixer bowl. Add ¹/₂ cup ice water to the cooling cornmeal mixture, then take the temperature of the mixture with an instant-read thermometer. It should be between 120° and 130°F. If it is too hot, set it aside until it reaches the proper temperature. Add the cornmeal mixture to the flour mixture and use the flat beater attachment to mix everything together well on low speed. Increase the speed to medium and beat for 3 minutes. Replace the flat beater with the dough hook and add 1 cup of the remaining flour. Knead on low speed for 3 minutes. Add the remaining 1 cup flour and knead on medium speed for 3 to 5 minutes more, until the dough is smooth and elastic and only slightly sticky. If the dough is very sticky, add more flour by the tablespoon. Turn the dough out onto a floured work surface and knead until no longer sticky.

To make the dough by hand, combine 4 cups of the flour, the yeast, and salt in a large bowl. Add ½ cup ice water to the cornmeal mixture and check the temperature as above. Add the hot cornmeal mixture to the flour mixture and beat with a wooden spoon to make a thick, sticky dough. Add 1 cup of the remaining flour and stir to make a stiff dough. Sprinkle the remaining 1 cup flour on your work surface, scrape the dough out onto it, and knead until the dough is smooth and elastic and the flour has been incorporated. Add more flour until no longer sticky.

To make the dough in a food processor, you will need a larger-than-standard-size machine. With the plastic dough blade in the work bowl, add all of the flour, the yeast, and salt. Add ½ cup ice water to the cornmeal mixture and check the temperature as above. Turn the motor on and slowly add the hot cornmeal mixture through the feed tube, taking about 20 seconds to do so. Process for 1 minute, or until the dough gathers into a ball and cleans the side of the work bowl. If the dough is very sticky, add more flour by the tablespoonful through the feed tube with the motor running. Flour your work surface and knead the dough briefly until it is smooth and no longer sticky.

4. Oil a large bowl or coat it lightly with cooking spray. Shape the dough into a ball and place it in the bowl. Turn to coat all surfaces with the oil, or spray the top of the dough with cooking spray. Cover tightly with plastic wrap and let the dough rise in a warm place (about 85°F) until it has doubled in bulk, about 1½ hours. Test the dough by pressing it with a fingertip: The depression should remain when you remove your finger.

5. Turn the dough out onto your work surface and pat the dough to remove air bubbles. Add the cheese and work it into the dough until it is evenly distributed. Divide the dough in half and shape each half into a 6-inch disk. Make sure the cheese cubes don't poke through the dough. Generously butter two 9-inch round cake pans or coat with cooking spray. Place the loaves in the pans, sprinkle the top of each lightly with cornmeal, and cover them loosely with kitchen towels. Set the loaves in a warm place and let them rise until they are puffy-looking and almost doubled in bulk, about 1 hour.

6. Adjust an oven rack to the lower third position and preheat the oven to 350°F.

7. Place the risen loaves in the oven and bake for 50 to 55 minutes, or until well browned. Rotate the pans back to front once during baking to ensure even browning. Cool the loaves in their pans for 10 minutes, then carefully remove them to wire racks to finish cooling right side up. Cut into wedges with a serrated knife to serve.

Variations: For a spicy bread, add 2 tablespoons of chopped fresh jalapeño chiles, or a small can of diced green chiles drained well, to the dough during kneading.

magic apples sure got around, for Scandinavian legend features golden apples of eternal youth, which sounds a lot like the life eternal conveyed by the Greek golden apples. Idun, the goddess of Spring, kept the apples in a box. The gods tasted them whenever they wanted in order to stay young. These apples, however, don't seem to be as powerful as the Greek ones, for they failed to persuade the frost giantess, Gerda, to marry Frey, the god of sunshine, rain, peace, and a lot of other good things. Fortunately for Frey, she ended up marrying him after further persuasions.

Cider Gingerbread with Cider Cream

This is a moist and mildly spicy gingerbread with the taste of cider and applesauce. Served plain, it makes a marvelous snack. When offered along with a spoonful of the cider cream, it would be a welcome dessert after a hearty meal.

MAKES 8 SERVINGS

6 cups apple cider
2 cups (9 ounces) unbleached
   all-purpose flour (spooned into the cup
   and leveled)
$^1/_2$ teaspoon baking soda
$^1/_4$ teaspoon salt
1 teaspoon ground ginger
$^3/_4$ teaspoon ground cinnamon
$^1/_4$ teaspoon ground cloves
$^1/_4$ teaspoon ground allspice
$^2/_3$ cup firmly packed light brown sugar
8 tablespoons (1 stick) unsalted butter,
   melted and still warm
1 large egg
$^1/_2$ cup smooth unsweetened applesauce
$^1/_4$ cup milk
Confectioners' sugar
1 cup heavy cream
1 teaspoon pure vanilla extract

1. Place the cider in a large heavy saucepan and set the pan over medium-high heat. Boil the cider, swirling the pan occasionally, until it has reduced to ³/₄ cup, 20 to 30 minutes. Watch carefully as the cider thickens toward the end of cooking, to prevent burning. (The cider is ready when you can see large bubbles that rise almost to the top of the pan.) Remove the pan from the heat. When the bubbles have subsided, measure the cider. (You can do this hours or days ahead. When cool, cover and refrigerate.)

2. Adjust an oven rack to the lower third position and preheat the oven to 350°F. Butter an 8-inch square baking pan or coat with cooking spray.

3. Sift the flour with the baking soda, salt, ground ginger, cinnamon, cloves, and allspice; set aside.

4. In a large bowl, whisk together the brown sugar and warm melted butter until the mixture is smooth. Add the egg and whisk it in until smooth. Whisk in ¹/₂ cup of the cooled boiled cider. Add the applesauce and milk and whisk to combine well. Add the dry ingredients and stir gently with the whisk only until the batter is smooth and the dry ingredients are thoroughly moistened. Turn the batter into the prepared pan and smooth the top.

5. Bake for about 40 minutes, or until the gingerbread is golden brown, the top springs back when pressed lightly in the center, and the cake just begins to pull away from the sides of the pan. Cool the gingerbread in its pan for 15 minutes, then cover it with a cooling rack and invert the two. Remove the pan and cover the gingerbread with another rack. Reinvert and allow the gingerbread to cool right side up. When warm or completely cool, dust the top of the gingerbread with confectioners' sugar.

6. To make the cider cream, in a medium bowl, beat the cream with the remaining ¹/₄ cup cooled boiled cider and the vanilla until only barely thickened. Taste and add confectioners' sugar if necessary. Continue beating the cream until it holds a soft shape. Spoon a dollop of cream alongside each serving of gingerbread.

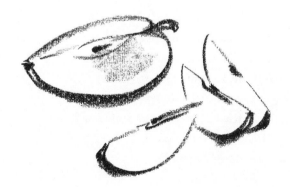

Apple-Ricotta Coffee Cake

This makes a great cake to serve for brunch or with afternoon tea or coffee. Ricotta cheese adds moistness and a rich flavor, and there actually is coffee in this coffee cake! You can prepare the crumb topping, the dry ingredients for the batter, and the ricotta mixture the night before and refrigerate them. In the morning, all you have left to do is to prepare the apples and bake the cake. You can use any crisp, tart apple, but if Macouns or their McIntosh relatives are in season, by all means use them.

MAKES 9 SERVINGS

1½ cups (6¾ ounces) unbleached all-purpose
    flour (spooned into the cups and leveled)
¾ cup sugar
1 teaspoon ground cinnamon
½ teaspoon salt
8 tablespoons (1 stick) chilled unsalted butter,
    cut into tablespoon-sized pieces
½ cup chopped pecans
2 teaspoons instant espresso powder
    (such as Medaglia d'Oro)
½ cup quick-cooking or old-fashioned
    rolled oats (not instant)
1 teaspoon baking powder
¼ teaspoon baking soda

Finely grated zest of 1 lemon
2 medium crisp, tart apples (10 to 12 ounces
    total), quartered, cored, peeled, and diced
    (about 2 cups)
½ cup whole-milk or part-skim ricotta cheese
2 large eggs
¼ cup milk
2 teaspoons pure vanilla extract

1. Adjust an oven rack to the center position and preheat the oven to 350°F. Grease a 9-inch square baking pan or coat with cooking spray.

2. Combine the flour, sugar, cinnamon, and salt well in a medium bowl. Remove ½ cup of the mixture and place it in a small bowl. Divide the butter pieces in half and add half to each bowl. Cut the butter in with a pastry blender until the particles in the larger bowl resemble coarse crumbs and in the smaller bowl, largish flakes.

3. Add the pecans and instant coffee to the small bowl; stir to combine well and refrigerate.

4. Add the oats, baking powder, and baking soda to the larger bowl and stir well. Add the lemon zest and apples and toss to combine well. In a small bowl, whisk together the ricotta cheese, eggs, milk, and vanilla. Add to the apple mixture and stir just until the batter is thoroughly moistened. Spread half the mixture over the bottom of the prepared pan. It will be a thin layer. Sprinkle on half the pecan mixture.

Because the batter is thick, it's easiest to make an even top layer by placing the remaining batter by spoonfuls over the pecan mixture and spreading them together with the back of the spoon. Sprinkle with the remaining nut mixture.

5. Bake for 45 to 50 minutes, or until the coffee cake springs back when lightly pressed and a tooth-pick comes out clean. Cool the cake in its pan on a rack for 20 minutes, then cover the cake with a square of wax paper and a cooling rack, invert the two, and carefully remove the pan. Cover the cake with another rack and invert again. Remove the wax paper and let the cake stand until warm or completely cool. Cut into squares and serve.

gala

new zealanders love apples, and their breeding program has created some wonderful fruit. When Gala began to show up in American supermarkets, people snapped it up as soon as they'd tried its crisp, sweet flesh. American apple growers were surprised, for this variety tends to be small, with red-marked yellow skin. So much for the idea that we only want large, solidly colored bright fruit! It took American growers some time to catch on. When Stark Brothers nursery first began offering the trees around 1980, orchardists wouldn't buy. Then the New Zealanders shipped fruit to the West Coast in 1981, and consumers showed with their cash that they want flavorful apples. The success of Gala was part of the beginning of the revolution in apple super-market availability. Before 1980, an American buyer was lucky to find anything other than Red and Golden Delicious in the produce department. Occasionally an old standard like Rome Beauty or Winesap would show up, but that was about all.

Now, we have much wider choice in apples, both for eating and cooking, and we have Gala partially to thank.

For best flavor, Gala needs warm summer temperatures, and it stands really hot weather better than most varieties. It can be grown a bit farther north and south of the usual apple-growing region. Gala is best eaten fresh or dried, but it is also a good addition to cider blends.

Apple-Rhubarb Muffins

I pluck first-of-the-season rhubarb from our garden in late April or early May to make these big, moist, and tangy muffins. Use a crisp, tart apple, such as Granny Smith, Greening, or Cortland. The batter for these muffins is very stiff, and you will think some liquid has been left out, but it's not so. Serve the muffins warm with butter or apricot preserves. They also make great snacks when cooled.

MAKES 12 MUFFINS

1 cup diced ($^1/_4$-inch) rhubarb
1 medium crisp, tart apple (6 ounces),
    quartered, cored, peeled, and diced (1 cup)
2 cups (9 ounces) unbleached all-purpose
    flour (spooned into the cup and leveled)
1 cup sugar
1 tablespoon baking powder
$^1/_2$ teaspoon salt
$^1/_2$ teaspoon freshly grated nutmeg
6 tablespoons ($^3/_4$ stick) chilled unsalted
    butter, cut into tablespoon-sized pieces
$^1/_2$ cup chopped pecans
$^1/_2$ cup whole-milk or part-skim ricotta cheese
$^1/_2$ cup milk
1 large or extra-large egg
1 teaspoon pure vanilla extract

1. Adjust an oven rack to the center position and preheat the oven to 400°F. Line 12 standard-size muffin cups with paper liners or coat them with cooking spray.

2. Combine the rhubarb and apple in a small bowl; set aside.

3. Sift the flour, sugar, baking powder, salt, and nutmeg into a large bowl. Cut in the butter with a pastry blender until the mixture resembles coarse crumbs. Add the pecans and the rhubarb and apple and toss to coat well.

4. In a small bowl, whisk together the ricotta, milk, egg, and vanilla until smooth. Add the ricotta mixture to the dry ingredients and fold and stir together gently only until the batter is completely moistened. It will be very stiff. Divide the batter among the muffin cups; do not smooth the tops. The cups will be very full.

5. Bake until the muffins are well browned and the tops spring back when lightly pressed, about 20 minutes. Let them cool for 5 minutes in the pan, then carefully remove them and serve warm.

Applesauce Doughnuts

These big, light-textured doughnuts are full of apple flavor with a hint of spice. The dough is quite soft, and you may think it is too soft to work with, but it isn't. Chilling the dough makes it manageable. You will need a doughnut cutter 3½ inches in diameter with a ¾-inch hole, or you can cut the doughnuts with a 3½-inch round cutter and use a 1-inch cutter for the holes.

Be sure to use fresh vegetable oil for the deep-frying. Peanut oil is my first choice because it has a higher smoking point than most oils. If you follow the cooking instructions closely (see Keys to Deep-fat Frying, page 142), you'll be rewarded with greaseless (not fat-free, mind you!) and delicious doughnuts. These doughnuts are at their best within two to three hours of frying. However, you can rejuvenate day-old doughnuts this way: Split the doughnuts in half like a bagel. Mix together some softened butter, sugar, and cinnamon and spread each cut side of a doughnut with a couple of teaspoons of the mixture. Arrange the doughnuts in a shallow pan, buttered sides up, and pop them under a broiler for a minute or two to melt the butter and caramelize the sugar. Watch them carefully to prevent burning.

MAKES ABOUT 12 LARGE DOUGHNUTS

½ cup firmly packed light brown sugar
⅓ cup buttermilk
4 tablespoons (½ stick) unsalted butter, melted
1 large egg
2 teaspoons pure vanilla extract
1 cup smooth unsweetened applesauce
3 cups (15 ounces) unbleached all-purpose flour (scooped into the cups and leveled)
½ teaspoon salt
2 teaspoons baking powder
½ teaspoon baking soda
½ teaspoon ground cinnamon
½ teaspoon freshly grated nutmeg
Vegetable oil for deep-frying (about 3 quarts)

OPTIONAL COATING
½ cup granulated sugar
2 teaspoons ground cinnamon

1. In a large bowl, whisk together the brown sugar, buttermilk, melted butter, egg, vanilla, and applesauce to combine well.

2. Sift the flour with the salt, baking powder, baking soda, cinnamon, and nutmeg. Add the flour mixture to the applesauce mixture and stir very gently with a rubber spatula only until the ingredients are well combined. It is important not to beat the batter, or the doughnuts will be tough. The dough will be quite soft. Scrape down the side of the bowl and cover tightly with plastic wrap. Refrigerate for 30 to 60 minutes.

keys to deep-fat frying

much of the bad rap deep-fat frying has gotten is related to improper technique. Soggy, greasy, fried foods are what happen. If you follow the points outlined here, you'll have excellent results every time. If you do a lot of deep-fat frying, see *The Fearless Frying Cookbook* by Hoppin' John Martin Taylor (Workman, 1997).

1. Always use fresh oil, and choose an oil with a high smoking point. Peanut oil is my first choice, although corn oil also works well.

2. Use plenty of oil when deep-fat frying. One cause of greasy fried foods is cooking too much food in too little oil. Have about 3 inches of oil in your fryer for best results.

3. Choose a deep heavy pot for deep-fat frying. A 6- to 7-quart cast-iron Dutch oven about 6 inches tall is ideal. Cast iron is a good conductor of heat, and it is able to maintain the oil at a relatively constant temperature.

4. Fill the pot half-full with oil (about 3 quarts). Attach a deep-fry thermometer to the side of the pan to monitor the temperature. Heat the oil over medium-high heat. In a 6-quart cast-iron pot, it takes 20 to 30 minutes to reach 365°F, the ideal temperature for most deep-fat frying.

5. Cook only a few pieces of food at a time, so that the oil temperature never falls below 360°F. The food should swim in the oil. Move the food around in the oil to ensure thorough cooking, and turn the food frequently for even browning. Wooden chopsticks are handy tools for turning doughnuts and fritters.

6. Remove the food from the oil with a slotted spatula, letting the excess oil drain back into the pot. Place the food on a wire rack set on a baking sheet to allow any remaining oil to drain off the food. If you set the food on paper towels or crumpled brown paper, it's more likely any oil still on the food will be absorbed by the food rather than the paper. (After draining on the rack, however, you can set the food on paper towels to absorb any remaining oil.) Try it both ways if you like to see which you prefer.

7. Make sure to return the oil temperature to 365°F before adding each batch to the pot. When finished cooking, let the oil cool, then strain it through a coffee filter. Store the oil in the refrigerator. You'll be able to use it once or twice more. Every time you reheat cooking oil, however, the smoking point goes down, which means there's a greater likelihood of the oil burning and ruining whatever you're cooking.

3. Generously dust your work surface with flour and scrape the chilled dough onto the flour. Sprinkle with additional flour and gently pat the dough to a ½-inch thickness. Check frequently to be sure the dough isn't sticking to your surface. With a floured doughnut cutter or two floured round cutters (see headnote), cut out doughnuts and holes; reserve the holes. Gently gather the scraps together, flour lightly, and repeat the patting and cutting of the dough. You should have about 12 large doughnuts.

4. Line a large baking sheet with parchment or a silicon baking pan liner and place the doughnuts and holes about 1 inch apart on the pan. Cover loosely with a kitchen towel and let the doughnuts rest at room temperature while the oil heats up. (If you're not going to cook the doughnuts within the hour, you can refrigerate them for up to 3 hours. Bring them to room temperature before frying.)

5. Place about 3 inches of oil in a heavy pot; a cast-iron Dutch oven is ideal. Attach a deep-fry thermometer to the side of the pan and heat the oil to 365°F over medium-high heat. Place a large cooling rack on a large baking sheet with a rim and set aside.

6. When the oil is ready, add 3 or 4 doughnuts and cook them for 2 to 3 minutes, turning them over every 30 seconds or so (wooden chopsticks work well), until they are puffed, cooked through, and a deep brown. Remove them from the oil with a slotted spatula, allowing the excess oil to drain back into the pot. Place the doughnuts on the rack to drain. Be sure the temperature of the oil does not drop below 360°F during frying, or the doughnuts will become soaked with oil. Return the temperature of the oil to 365°F before continuing with the cooking. Fry the doughnut holes last.

7. You can serve the doughnuts warm, or wait until they've cooled to room temperature. Although delicious plain, the doughnuts are even better when coated with a mixture of sugar and cinnamon. Combine the granulated sugar and cinnamon. Place the mixture in a large paper bag and add 4 doughnuts at a time. Close the top of the bag and shake it gently in all directions for a few seconds to coat the doughnuts with the sugar mixture. Remove the doughnuts from the bag, and they're ready to eat.

German Apple Pancakes

When I (Dorothy) lived in Germany for a summer many years ago, the mother in the family I stayed with made fabulous apple pancakes. The batter was wonderfully eggy and the apples delightfully tart, and I always looked forward to those special occasions when Frau Hack cooked them. One thing that made the pancakes so special was that they were "sandwiched" between two layers of apple.

MAKES 4 SERVINGS

1 pound crisp, tart apples, quartered, cored, peeled, and very thinly sliced
2 tablespoons plus 2 teaspoons granulated sugar
$\frac{1}{2}$ teaspoon ground cinnamon
$\frac{1}{2}$ cup ($2\frac{1}{2}$ ounces) unbleached all-purpose flour (scooped into the cup and leveled)
$\frac{1}{2}$ teaspoon salt
4 large eggs
$1\frac{1}{4}$ cups milk
$\frac{1}{2}$ teaspoon pure vanilla extract
4 tablespoons ($\frac{1}{2}$ stick) unsalted butter
Confectioners' sugar for dusting

1. Adjust rack to a position 3 inches below the broiler and preheat the broiler.

2. Combine the apples with 2 tablespoons of the sugar and the cinnamon in a medium bowl and set aside.

3. Stir the flour, the remaining 2 teaspoons sugar, and salt together in a medium bowl. Beat the eggs lightly to blend and combine them with the milk and vanilla. Add the egg mixture to the flour mixture and stir until well blended.

4. Melt 1 tablespoon of the butter in a 10-inch non-stick skillet over medium-high heat. Tip the pan as the butter melts to coat the bottom and partway up the sides. When the butter foams, arrange one quarter of the apple slices in a single layer in the pan and cook for 30 seconds. Add $\frac{1}{2}$ cup of the batter and tilt the pan to make an even layer. When the batter begins to firm up around the edges, place the skillet under the preheated broiler. Watch carefully, and cook only until the batter is set but not browned, about 1 minute.

5. Remove the skillet with a pot holder. Loosen the edges of the pancake with a spatula, slip the spatula under the pancake, and use the spatula to fold the pancake in half. Gently slide the pancake onto a plate, dust with confectioners' sugar, and serve hot. Repeat with the remaining butter, apples, and batter to make 4 pancakes in all.

Soups and Salads

Apples are an emblem of beginnings and endings.

—MOLLY O'NEILL,
A WELL-SEASONED APPETITE

Apples are like first-rate character actors, because they can assume just about any role in soups and salads. They are natural companions to onions, potatoes, fennel, and beets; carrots and other root vegetables; spices, especially curry mixtures and chiles; cheese; and tomatoes. But choosing the right apple can often determine the success of a recipe. Early-season tart apples are best to use as soup and sauce bases, since they have silky-smooth textures. Sweet apples, on the whole, are not as desirable in soups, though there are exceptions, such as the Curried Apple Soup.

In all of these soups, apple is a central ingredient, yet it may wind up playing a supporting role. Nevertheless, if it weren't there, you'd be missing a key element.

The same thing can be said of the salads. Apples add crunch, texture, aroma, tartness, and/or sweetness, bringing new dimensions to salads. Pungent ingredients such as ginger, sharp blue-veined cheeses, beets, mustard, horseradish, and smoked meats all interact with apples in their own unique ways. Nuts, too, are excellent in apple salads, both for taste and texture.

Curried Apple Soup

This spicy soup is welcome on a cold fall or winter evening. Use a crisp, sweet apple, such as Fuji or Gala, rather than one of the tart types. If the apple skin is tender, peeling is unnecessary; the flecks will look pretty in the soup. If you like your soup spicier, increase the amount of jalapeño and use a hot, rather than mild, curry powder. You can make this soup one day ahead and refrigerate it; reheat it gently before serving. Pass a basket of crisp pappadums at the table.

MAKES 8 SERVINGS

2 tablespoons unsalted butter
1 large sweet onion (8 ounces), coarsely
    chopped
1 cup chopped celery
1 jalapeño chile, seeded and finely chopped
1 to 2 teaspoons curry powder
2 to 3 large sweet apples, quartered, cored,
    peeled if desired, and coarsely chopped
    (5 cups)
1 medium boiling potato, such as Yukon Gold,
    peeled and coarsely chopped
Salt
1 cup milk or half-and-half
2 tablespoons dry sherry
2 tablespoons chopped flat-leaf parsley

1. Melt the butter in a heavy medium saucepan over medium heat. Add the onion and celery, cover the pan, and cook for about 5 minutes, until the vegetables are tender but not browned. Add the jalapeño and curry powder and cook, stirring, for 1 to 2 minutes. Add the apples, potato, 4 cups water, and 2 teaspoons salt. Bring the soup to a boil, uncovered, over high heat. Cover the pan, reduce the heat to medium-low, and simmer slowly until the apples and potato are almost falling apart, about 30 minutes.

2. Purée the soup with an immersion blender or in batches in a blender until very smooth. Return the soup to the pan and add the milk and sherry. Taste and add salt if desired. Heat slowly, stirring occasionally, until the soup is piping hot but not boiling. Ladle into bowls, sprinkle with the parsley, and serve.

Beer and Cheese Soup

This is a creamy, tangy, and smooth soup, but with some texture from the diced apples. Use a tart, crisp apple, such as Granny Smith. A light-tasting beer, Corona, for example, complements the apple and cheese flavors without overwhelming the soup.

MAKES 6 SERVINGS

4 tablespoons (1/2 stick) unsalted butter
I cup finely chopped onions
2 medium apples, quartered, cored, peeled, and diced (about 2 cups)
I cup beer
2 cups low-fat or whole milk
1/4 cup unbleached all-purpose flour, spooned into the cup and leveled
Salt
1/2 teaspoon Tabasco, or more to taste
2 cups (8 ounces) shredded extra-sharp or sharp Cheddar cheese
Sweet paprika

I. Melt the butter in a heavy saucepan over medium heat. Stir in the onions, cover the pan, and cook for about 5 minutes, until the onions are almost tender but not browned. Add the apples and cook, covered, until the apples are tender but still have a bit of crunch to them, 5 to 8 minutes.

2. Meanwhile, combine the beer and milk in a heavy saucepan and bring the mixture almost to a boil over medium-high heat. Set aside.

3. Add the flour, I teaspoon salt, and the Tabasco to the apple mixture and stir almost constantly over medium-high heat for 2 minutes to cook the flour. Remove the pan from the heat and add the beer mixture all at once. Stir gently with a wooden spoon, scraping the bottom of the pan to release any cooked flour.

4. Return the pan to medium-high heat and bring the soup to the simmer, stirring frequently. Simmer for 2 minutes, then lower the heat to medium and gradually add the cheese. Stir until it is melted and the soup is smooth and creamy. Taste and adjust the seasoning with more salt or Tabasco if necessary. Ladle into bowls and sprinkle lightly with paprika. Serve immediately.

Pasta Fagioli e Mele

Beans, pasta, pancetta, and *mele* (Italian for apples) make a satisfying soup to serve on a nippy fall or winter day. The apples add a lively freshness to perk up one's spirits. Although there are several steps in the recipe, each can be done ahead. The final assembly takes only a few minutes. Use a mixture of firm, sweet (Fuji) and tart (Granny Smith) apples. Tortiglioni is a short tubular twisted pasta. If you can't find it, use any twisted pasta, such as fusilli or bow-tie pasta (farfalle).

MAKES 6 SERVINGS

1 cup dried cannellini beans,
    picked over and rinsed
2 medium onions, 1 halved, 1 chopped
3 bay leaves
1 celery stalk with leaves, cut into
    2-inch pieces
1 tablespoon olive oil
1/4 pound pancetta, cut into 1/4 × 1/4 × 1/2-inch
    pieces
1 large carrot, halved lengthwise and
    thinly sliced
2 medium apples, quartered, cored,
    peeled, and diced (2 cups)
Salt and freshly milled black pepper
4 ounces dried tortiglioni pasta

6 cups chicken stock
1 tablespoon minced fresh thyme

1. Bring the beans and 6 cups water to the boil, uncovered, in a medium saucepan. Remove the pan from the heat; cover and let stand for 1 hour.

2. Drain the beans and return them to the pan. Add 6 cups fresh water, the halved onion, the bay leaves, and celery. Bring the mixture to a boil, then reduce the heat and simmer slowly, partially covered, for about 1 hour, until the beans are tender. Drain the beans and discard the vegetables and bay leaves. (The beans can be prepared several hours or up to 1 day ahead and refrigerated.)

3. Heat the olive oil in a medium skillet over medium-low heat. Add the pancetta and cook slowly, stirring occasionally, until it is browned but not crisp. Remove the pancetta with a slotted spoon and set it aside on paper towels to drain. Replace the skillet over medium heat. When the fat is hot, add the carrot and cook, stirring, for 2 minutes. Add the chopped onion, stir well, cover the pan, and cook for 3 to 5 minutes, until the vegetables are crisp-tender. Add the apples and salt and pepper to taste; cover, and cook for another 5 minutes. Remove the pan from the heat and set it aside. May be made 1 or 2 hours ahead.

4. Cook the pasta in 2 quarts boiling salted (1 teaspoon) water until al dente. Drain and transfer to a large bowl of cold water. When cool, drain well and set aside. May be made 1 or 2 hours ahead.

5. When ready to serve, bring the chicken stock to a simmer in a large saucepan. Season with salt and pepper. Add the pasta, apple mixture, pancetta, and beans and cook briefly, stirring, just until piping hot. Ladle into warmed soup bowls, sprinkle with the thyme, and serve.

fuji

fuji is a truly international apple, born in Japan of American parents. This crisp, sweet apple with a special anise bouquet is a product of a cross between the familiar Red Delicious and a once-popular variety named Ralls Janet. The origin of Ralls Janet is controversial. The official myth says that Thomas Jefferson named the apple in 1793 for two people—Edmond Charles Genet, a French minister to the United States, and Caleb Ralls, a Virginia orchardist. Supposedly, Genet gave Jefferson a cutting from a French apple tree that was then passed along to Ralls. The story didn't surface until a hundred years later, so no one knows if it is true or not. But whatever its origins, Ralls Janet thrived in the mild climate of Southern orchards for decades, then faded into obscurity.

The Japanese, however, discovered this fine, sweet apple, and it became a popular variety in Japan. In 1939, experimenters at a Japanese research station crossed Ralls Janet with Red Delicious and came up with a promising hybrid. As time went by, it became clear that, with its unique flavor and aroma, this was no ordinary apple, and it was honored with the name Fuji, after Japan's tallest and most sacred mountain.

Today, Fuji is the most popular apple in Japan. The Japanese are very particular about their fruit, doing everything they can to help the harvest approach perfection. A Japanese orchardist pays attention not just to each tree, but to each individual apple. One such orchardist describes on his Web site how he hand-thins the apples on his one thousand trees so that each tree bears just 120 fruits. Then, after the apples have sized up, he turns each apple so that the previously shaded side faces the sun, and he picks off any leaves that block the rays that will evenly color the fruit. Such attention to detail results in beautiful, sweet apples that bring a premium price.

Fuji is a tricky variety for home growers. It ripens late and is normally harvested toward the end of October or in November. If enough sugar doesn't develop in the fruit before harvest, woody, flavorless apples can result. If Fuji is grown in a hot climate, its color can end up a dirty, ugly yellow brown instead of delicate pink over soft green. But where it thrives, Fuji is one of the finest late-maturing varieties, and it's the best keeper of all the sweet apples. It will maintain its quality for up to a year in the refrigerator or several weeks displayed in a fruit bowl.

Apple and Fennel Soup

This beautiful coral-colored soup is slightly tart, with a faint taste of anise from the fennel. Some say they taste tomato, others shrimp, though neither is present. This is definitely a fall or winter soup, when apples and fennel are at their best. You can use just about any apple that is both sweet and tart, such as Grimes Golden, Golden Delicious, Macoun, or other McIntosh-type varieties. If Sweet Sixteen is available, that's also a good choice, since its anise overtones will complement those of the fennel. Don't stint on the white pepper. It makes things lively.

MAKES 8 SERVINGS

2 large fennel bulbs with stalks and
    feathery tops
3 bay leaves
6 parsley sprigs
2 large apples (1 pound), quartered, cored,
    peeled, and thinly sliced
2 medium carrots, thinly sliced (1 cup)
3 cups chicken stock
Salt and freshly milled white pepper
3/4 cup half-and-half

1. Cut the stalks from the fennel bulbs. Chop enough of the feathery tops to make about 3 tablespoons and reserve to sprinkle over the finished soup. Discard the outer layers of the bulbs if bruised. Cut each bulb lengthwise in half, remove the cores, and thinly slice the fennel. You'll have about 3½ cups. Put the fennel into a medium saucepan.

2. Tie the bay leaves and parsley sprigs together with kitchen twine and add them to the pan. Add the apples, carrots, chicken stock, 2 cups water, 1 teaspoon salt, and ½ teaspoon white pepper. Bring the mixture to a boil over medium-high heat, stirring occasionally. Reduce the heat to medium-low, partially cover the pan, and simmer slowly until the vegetables and apples are completely tender, about 30 minutes.

3. Remove and discard the bay leaves and parsley. Purée the soup with an immersion blender or in batches in a blender until very smooth. Return the soup to the saucepan and add the half-and-half. Taste and add salt and white pepper to taste (½ teaspoon of pepper spices things up nicely). (The soup can be made up to 1 day ahead; when cool, cover and refrigerate.)

4. Heat the soup over medium heat until it is piping hot but not boiling. Ladle into bowls, sprinkle with the reserved chopped fennel, and serve.

Gingered Carrot and Apple Soup

Tart apples contrast with the sweetness of carrots in this brilliant orange soup, and the ginger adds bite. The full amount will give the soup a pronounced ginger flavor; add enough to suit your own taste. Be sure to use a tart apple variety, such as Cortland, Winesap, Arlet, Sunrise, Newtown Pippin, or Granny Smith. A food processor will make quick work of all the slicing. If you have a thin slicing disc for your machine (2-mm), use it.

MAKES 8 SERVINGS

1½ pounds carrots (about 5 large), thinly
   sliced
2 medium-to-large tart apples
   (12 to 14 ounces), quartered, cored,
   peeled, and thinly sliced
1 large yellow onion (8 ounces), thinly sliced
1 to 2 tablespoons peeled and
   coarsely chopped fresh ginger
2 cups chicken stock
½ cup heavy cream
Salt and freshly milled black pepper
Chervil sprigs for garnish

1. Combine the carrots, apples, onion, and ginger, with 4 cups water in a heavy medium saucepan. Cover the pan and bring the mixture to the boil over high heat. Reduce the heat to medium and cook, covered, stirring occasionally, until the carrots, onion, and apples are very tender, about 30 minutes.

2. Either use an immersion blender to purée the soup and stir in the chicken stock, or purée half the mixture in a blender and, while the machine is running, add 1 cup of the chicken stock. Continue puréeing until very smooth. Transfer the purée to a clean saucepan. Repeat the procedure with the remaining soup mixture and chicken stock and add it to the first batch. Stir in the cream and add 1 teaspoon salt and ½ teaspoon pepper. Taste and add more salt and pepper if necessary. (The soup can be made 1 to 2 days ahead, cooled, covered, and refrigerated.)

3. Heat the soup until it is piping hot (do not allow it to boil, or it might curdle), ladle into bowls, and garnish with the chervil sprigs. Serve immediately.

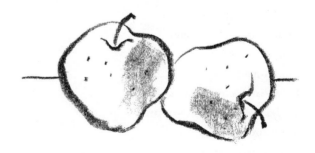

Latvian Pumpernickel and Fruit Soup

The inspiration for this delicious and unusual dessert soup comes from "Food Traditions of Jews from the Soviet Union," a booklet of recipes published in 1982 by the Federation of Jewish Philanthropies. Maria Ravena, the contributor of this recipe, says it is Latvian. I use dried apricots, prunes, dried cranberries, and lots of fresh apple in the soup. The combination of tastes with pumpernickel bread is astonishing. Be sure to use a tart apple here. Cortlands and Greenings are excellent, as are Macouns or other McIntosh-type apples.

MAKES 8 SERVINGS

12 slices (about 4 ounces) cocktail
    pumpernickel bread
2 medium tart apples (12 ounces), quartered,
    cored, peeled, and shredded
$^1/_2$ cup pitted prunes, halved
$^1/_2$ cup dried apricots
$^1/_2$ cup dried cranberries
$^1/_2$ cup hard cider
$^1/_2$ cup sugar
One 3-inch cinnamon stick
1 tablespoon fresh lemon juice
$^3/_4$ cup sour cream
Ground cinnamon

1. Tear the bread into small pieces and put them into a large bowl. Add 4 cups boiling water. Let stand until completely cool. Purée with an immersion blender or in a blender until smooth.

2. Combine the apples, prunes, apricots, cranberries, $^1/_2$ cup water, the hard cider, sugar, cinnamon stick, and lemon juice in a medium saucepan. Cover the pan and bring the mixture to a boil over medium heat. Reduce the heat and simmer until the dried fruits are tender but not falling apart, about 20 minutes. Remove the pan from the heat and set aside to cool, covered. Discard the cinnamon stick.

3. Add the pumpernickel mixture to the fruit mixture. Stir well, cover, and refrigerate until very cold.

4. Ladle the soup into bowls. Stir the sour cream to soften and top each portion of soup with some sour cream. Dust lightly with ground cinnamon and serve.

Sun-Dried Tomato and Apple Cream Soup

Chef Christine D. Seitz regularly serves this creamy, indulgent soup at her restaurant, Red-Bird, in Missoula. I have loved this from my first spoonful. The apple taste is definitely there, as is the sun-dried tomato, but they harmonize beautifully. The magic is achieved by first making a spicy apple chutney (it can be prepared well ahead), then combining it with the other soup ingredients. Mango slices can be found packed in a light sugar syrup in the refrigerated section of many supermarkets. When fresh mangoes are in season, use them instead.

MAKES 6 SERVINGS

CHUTNEY

1 large Granny Smith apple, quartered, cored, peeled, and coarsely chopped
8 ounces sliced mango, or 1 pound fresh, peeled and cut into 1/2-inch pieces
1 medium onion, coarsely chopped
1 small red bell pepper, cored, seeded, and finely chopped
4 small jalapeño chiles, seeded and finely chopped
1/2 cup cider vinegar
1/2 cup sugar
1/4 cup golden raisins
1 teaspoon dry mustard
Salt

SOUP

1 tablespoon olive oil
1 medium onion, coarsely chopped
2 garlic cloves, chopped
Salt and freshly milled white pepper
1 slice firm-textured sandwich bread, trimmed of crusts and torn into 1-inch pieces
1 cup chicken stock
2 cups milk
2 cups heavy cream
1/2 cup sun-dried tomatoes packed in oil, drained

Snipped fresh chives

1. Combine all the chutney ingredients except the salt in a medium saucepan and bring the mixture to a boil, stirring occasionally. Reduce the heat to medium-low and simmer, stirring occasionally, until thickened, 30 to 40 minutes. Add salt to taste. Cool, cover, and refrigerate. (The chutney will keep in the refrigerator for at least 2 weeks.)

2. To make the soup, heat the olive oil in a medium saucepan over medium heat. Add the onion and garlic. Cook, stirring occasionally, until the vegetables are tender but not browned, 6 to 8 minutes. Add 1/2 teaspoon salt, 1/2 teaspoon white pepper, and

the remaining ingredients except the chives. Bring the soup to a boil, then reduce the heat and simmer for 20 minutes, stirring occasionally.

3. Add ¾ cup of the chutney to the soup. (Store remaining chutney in the refrigerator for another use). Purée the soup with an immersion blender or in batches in a blender until smooth. Taste and add salt and white pepper if needed. If using a regular blender, reheat the soup so it is piping hot. Ladle into soup bowls and sprinkle with the chives.

Savoy Cabbage Apple Coleslaw

Apple and savoy cabbage are natural partners as in this low-fat slaw. The cabbage is sliced thin and then roughly chopped for interesting texture. If savoy cabbage is not available, substitute regular green cabbage. Be sure to use a tart, crisp apple such as Cortland or Greening. Granny Smith will also work. If you want more apple in the coleslaw, feel free to add it.

MAKES 6 SERVINGS

¾ cup low-fat mayonnaise
⅓ cup low-fat sour cream
1 tablespoon cider vinegar
2 tablespoons apple cider
¼ to ½ teaspoon Tabasco
½ teaspoon celery seed
Salt and freshly milled black pepper
1 pound savoy cabbage, cored, thinly sliced,
    and roughly chopped
1 large tart apple (8 ounces), quartered,
    cored, peeled, and shredded

In a large bowl, whisk together the mayonnaise, sour cream, cider vinegar, cider, Tabasco, celery seed, and salt and pepper to taste. Fold in the cabbage and apple, and refrigerate until chilled or up to 3 hours. Serve cold.

how can apples, a fall crop, be available in the supermarket year-round? Some of these off-season apples are imported from Australia or New Zealand, but most are grown right here in the United States. How are they kept crisp and fresh for months and months? The answer is Controlled Atmosphere Storage, abbreviated CA by the industry. Throughout the apple-growing parts of Washington state stand big rectangular-shaped buildings with no windows. These are CA rooms. Inside, millions of apples rest comfortably in a state of suspended animation, waiting to be awakened and taken to market.

Apples are alive. Like all living things, apples metabolize, constantly interacting with their environment by taking in oxygen, using it to change the starches in their flesh into sugars, and releasing carbon dioxide. When apples are left at room temperature, they metabolize quite rapidly, ripening and then quickly becoming overripe. We've all done it— bought some firm, shiny apples at the store and arranged them artfully in an attractive bowl, only to bite into one a few days later and find cottony mush. Keeping apples in the refrigerator slows down the process, but CA storage brings it almost to a standstill.

The principle behind CA storage was discovered in England before World War II. Farmers found that their produce stayed fresh longer in airtight rooms than in rooms where the air was allowed to circulate. We now know that in an airtight room the oxygen gets used up by the fruits or vegetables, so the metabolism of the stored produce is forced to slow down. Scientists have studied this phenomenon for years and have perfected formulas for the gases and air temperatures for CA, customized for each apple variety. Thanks to CA, an apple bought in August can be just as crisp and juicy as one eaten straight from the tree in October.

A CA room can hold from ten thousand to a hundred thousand boxes of apples. Once the apples have been put in the room, nitrogen gas is added and oxygen levels are reduced. The air we breathe contains about 21 percent oxygen. A CA room has only 1 or 2 percent, just enough to keep the apples alive but asleep. In addition, the carbon dioxide content of the atmosphere is controlled, the humidity is kept at about 95 percent, and the temperature is kept constant, just above freezing. If we entered such a room, we'd become unconscious within seconds, then die from lack of oxygen. But the apples stay right on the edge of life in CA.

In order for the apples to keep well in CA storage, the harvest must be perfectly timed. The apples should be mature but not too ripe. They are tested for a number of qualities, including sugar content and firmness, to make sure they are right for CA storage. The fruit that passes the test is then transported to CA rooms that are sealed and marked with the date they will be opened to provide us with harvest-ripe fruit.

The Original Waldorf Salad

Oscar Tschirky was New York's Waldorf-Astoria Hotel's famous maître d'hôtel for half a century, from the hotel's opening in 1893 until his retirement in 1943. Among the many recipes included in his *Cook Book by "Oscar" of the Waldorf,* is the ubiquitous Waldorf salad. Why this particular recipe should have captured the public's imagination is anybody's guess. Possibly at the time he created it in 1893, it was considered quite sophisticated— or it became so because it was served at a special supper for fifteen hundred of society's luminaries who had traveled to New York from Boston, Baltimore, and Philadelphia to celebrate the hotel's opening. At the time, sweet salads were all the rage.

Whatever the reason, by today's standards of culinary adventurousness it is rather out of sync. Why, then, for more than one hundred years, has the Waldorf salad remained such an American culinary icon? Versions of the recipe have appeared in cookbooks throughout this century. In *Betty Crocker's Picture Cookbook* (1950), the salad is served in a lettuce cup and garnished with a maraschino cherry. Recent editions of *The Fannie Farmer Cookbook* call for the salad to be dressed with a honey-and-lemon-flavored mayonnaise.

But what was Chef Tschirky's original recipe? This is how it appeared in a 1908 printing of his cookbook: "Peel two raw apples and cut them into small pieces, say about half an inch square, also cut some celery the same way, and mix it with the apple. Be very careful not to let any seeds of the apples be mixed with it. The salad must be dressed with a good mayonnaise." That's it. Just three ingredients. No specified amounts, except for the apple. And no walnuts, which had become a staple part of the recipe in other cookbooks. In his book, Chef Oscar lists various foods by their seasonal availability. For apples, he says, "All the year," which means he used the best of what was available, probably a mixture of crisp, all-purpose apples—some sweet, some tart. New York State was then the premier apple-growing region in the country, so many varieties would have satisfied those criteria. Celery, the second ingredient, is plain old celery and not celery root. So the remaining question is, what did he use for mayonnaise? In his book, mayonnaise comes into play many times, and his recipe for Sauce Mayonnaise does give proportions: "Place in an earthen bowl a couple of fresh egg-yolks and half a teaspoonful of ground English mustard, half a pinch of salt, half a saltspoonful of red pepper, and stir well for about three minutes without stopping, then pour in, a drop at a time, one and a half cupfuls of the best olive oil, and should it become too thick, add a little at a time, some good vinegar, stirring constantly." This is clear and direct. A saltspoon is just that—a spoon with which to take salt at the table. Half a saltspoonful probably means a big pinch. When the instructions say to "stir well . . . without stopping," it likely means doing so with a wire whisk. "Some good vinegar" is open to question. Was it distilled white vinegar or some sort of wine vinegar? Although we can't be sure, we favor the distilled white vinegar. It adds acidity without complication. White vinegar will complement the apple's taste, not interfere with it. One to two tablespoons should be sufficient. Finally, although the original recipe says to peel the apples, we prefer not to, providing the skin is tender. So, making some minor concessions, and with a tip of our humble hat, here is Chef Oscar's classic recipe.

MAKES 4 TO 6 SERVINGS

2 large egg yolks
$^1\!/_2$ teaspoon dry mustard
Salt
Big pinch of cayenne pepper
$1^1\!/_2$ cups extra virgin olive oil
Distilled white vinegar
2 crisp apples, 1 sweet, 1 on the tart side
    (about 1 pound total), quartered, cored,
    and diced ($^1\!/_2$-inch)
2 large celery stalks, diced ($^1\!/_2$-inch)
Lettuce leaves, optional

1. To make the mayonnaise, in a warmed medium-size heavy bowl (earthenware if you have one), whisk together the egg yolks, mustard, $^1\!/_4$ teaspoon salt, and the cayenne until thick and creamy, about 2 minutes. Set the bowl on a folded dampened towel. (This will keep it from sliding all over your counter as you beat in the oil.) Very gradually, whisk in the oil by driblets, making sure each is incorporated before adding more. When you've whisked in about 1 cup of oil, you can add the remaining oil in larger dollops, whisking each addition in thoroughly before adding the next. Taste and add more salt and cayenne if necessary. If you feel the mayonnaise needs tartness, whisk in vinegar a little at a time until it tastes right.

2. Combine the apples and celery with enough of the mayonnaise to bind them together. (You will have about half the mayonnaise left. Transfer it to an airtight container and refrigerate it. It will keep for at least 10 days.) Serve right away on plates lined with lettuce leaves, if you wish, or in small bowls, or chill the salad and serve it within an hour or two.

Twenty-first Century Waldorf Salad

2 cups apple cider
1 cup low-fat yogurt
1 teaspoon celery seed
$1/4$ teaspoon freshly milled black pepper
4 cups diced unpeeled apples (use a mixture
    of sweet and tart fruit with green, yellow, and
    red skins)
2 cups diced celery root
$1/2$ cup finely chopped toasted walnuts
8 butter lettuce leaves

Slightly more than one century after the creation of the original Waldorf salad comes this calorie-streamlined version. Low-fat yogurt replaces the traditional mayonnaise, and celery root stands in for the usual celery. The celery root gives the salad a "bouncy" texture. Buy a celery root that weighs one pound or more, since half will be waste. Put it on its side on your work surface and cut off the root and stem ends with a heavy chef's knife. Stand the celery root on a cut surface and slice away the peel with a small sharp knife, moving in a downward curve as though you were peeling an orange. Be sure to work quickly, as celery root oxidizes readily and will begin to turn brown shortly after peeling. To prevent this, rub the peeled celery root with a cut lemon and continue rubbing with the lemon as you dice. Pat the celery root dry on paper towels after cutting it. For the apples, use a mixture of three different kinds with different-colored skins, tastes, and textures for variety. Serve the salad well chilled, but don't make it any more than two or three hours ahead, as the color and texture change.

1. Boil the apple cider in a heavy medium saucepan over medium-high to high heat, swirling the pan occasionally, until the cider is reduced to $1/3$ cup, about 15 minutes. Watch carefully during the last minutes of cooking to prevent burning. Cool completely.

2. In a large mixing bowl, whisk together the yogurt, cooled cider, celery seed, and pepper. Fold in the apples, celery root, and walnuts. Refrigerate until chilled, or up to 3 hours.

3. Serve cold on the lettuce leaves.

MAKES 8 SMALL SERVINGS

Beet, Apple, and Ginger Salad

This is a stunning-looking salad with strips of deep red-colored beets that tint the unpeeled julienned apples a shocking reddish pink. Choose a crisp apple with both sweet and tart flavors, such as Braeburn, Elstar, McIntosh, or Cortland. The salad can be made several hours ahead.

MAKES 6 SERVINGS

6 medium beets (about 1¹/₂ pounds)
3 tablespoons corn oil
2 tablespoons sherry vinegar
¹/₄ teaspoon salt
¹/₄ teaspoon freshly milled black pepper
One 1-inch piece fresh ginger, peeled and
    finely grated
1 medium apple (about 5 ounces), quartered,
    cored, and cut into julienne strips
2 tablespoons snipped fresh chives

1. Adjust an oven rack to the center position and preheat the oven to 350°F.

2. Wash the beets and wrap them securely in a double thickness of aluminum foil. Bake for about 1¹/₂ hours, or until tender when pierced with the tip of a sharp knife. Cool in the foil until warm, then peel. When completely cool, cut the beets into julienne strips.

3. In a large mixing bowl, whisk together the oil, vinegar, salt, pepper, and ginger. Add the apple and beets and toss gently to coat evenly with the dressing. Cover and refrigerate for at least 1 hour.

4. Just before serving, sprinkle with the chives.

gravenstein

gravenstein has been a popular apple variety for so long no one knows where it came from. The first certain record comes from what is now Denmark in around 1670. This apple, with its rich, tangy flavor, is grown extensively in northern California, where it arrived by 1820. It's one of the best varieties for sauce and pie. Unfortunately, Gravenstein is not easy to grow. It isn't very hardy, and it is susceptible to just about every disease apples can get. Another problem that can develop with a number of varieties is especially common with Gravenstein—biennial bearing. That means that the trees easily get in the habit of blooming and fruiting every other year. Another problem for home growers is pollination. Gravenstein needs another variety to pollinate it, but it blooms earlier than most other high-quality varieties. In addition, its pollen isn't much good at pollinating other varieties. In favorable areas, however, such as around Portland, Oregon, old backyard Gravenstein trees have been growing happily and producing bushels and bushels of fruit for their owners for almost a hundred years.

Beet, Apple, and Gorgonzola Salad with Walnuts

This salad is easy to put together and can be made several hours ahead and refrigerated. Bring it to room temperature before serving. Serve it with crusty bread for a luncheon or as a side salad at dinner. Use a tart, crisp apple, such as Cortland, Granny Smith, or a similar variety.

MAKES 6 SERVINGS

6 medium beets (about 1^{1}/$_{2}$ pounds)
3 tablespoons olive oil
3 tablespoons sherry vinegar
^{1}/$_{4}$ cup mayonnaise
1 teaspoon prepared horseradish
1 tablespoon Dijon mustard
1 large tart, crisp apple (about 8 ounces), quartered, cored, and cut into ^{1}/$_{2}$-inch cubes
^{1}/$_{2}$ cup (2 ounces) crumbled Gorgonzola or other blue cheese
^{1}/$_{2}$ cup toasted walnuts

1. Adjust an oven rack to the center position and preheat the oven to 350°F.

2. Wash the beets and wrap them securely in a double thickness of aluminum foil. Bake for about 1^{1}/$_{2}$ hours, or until tender when pierced with the tip of a sharp knife. Cool in the foil until warm, then peel. When completely cool, cut the beets into ^{1}/$_{2}$-inch cubes.

3. In a large mixing bowl, whisk together the olive oil, vinegar, mayonnaise, horseradish, and mustard. Add the beets and apple to the dressing and toss to coat well. Fold in the cheese and walnuts and serve at room temperature. The salad can be made 2 or 3 hours ahead and refrigerated. Bring to room temperature before serving.

Smoked Turkey and Apple Salad

It's essential to use high-quality smoked turkey in this salad. Or you could substitute smoked chicken or duck. Choose a sweet, crisp apple, such as Fuji or Honeycrisp, or use a mixture of sweet and tart apples. For an elegant presentation, arrange the salad on a bed of mixed baby lettuces. Include a bit of arugula for some sharpness.

MAKES 4 SERVINGS

¹/₂ cup mayonnaise
¹/₂ cup yogurt
¹/₄ teaspoon salt
¹/₄ teaspoon freshly milled black pepper
1 teaspoon ground ginger
2 tablespoons minced flat-leaf parsley
2 tablespoons minced shallot
2 cups (10 ounces) diced smoked turkey
1 medium Fuji apple (6 ounces), quartered, cored, and diced
¹/₂ cup thinly sliced celery
¹/₂ cup halved seedless red grapes or ¹/₃ cup diced dried figs

In a medium bowl, whisk together the mayonnaise, yogurt, salt, pepper, ginger, parsley, and shallot. Stir in the remaining ingredients. Refrigerate for 1 to 3 hours before serving.

Apple-Cheese Purses

This isn't a soup or a salad, but it is a terrific appetizer we couldn't find any other place for in the book. So here it is. A cheese and apple mixture is wrapped in phyllo and baked until crisp and golden brown. We've adapted it from a recipe by Judith Benn Hurley in *Organic Gardening* magazine. Use a crisp, tart apple variety, such as Sunrise, Arlet, Newtown Pippin, or Granny Smith. You can assemble the purses hours ahead and refrigerate them until ready to bake. They're great with predinner drinks.

MAKES 16 PURSES

2 medium apples, quartered, cored, peeled, and finely diced (about 2 cups)
2 teaspoons fresh lemon juice
¹/₂ cup grated extra-sharp Cheddar cheese or freshly grated Parmesan cheese
2 tablespoons minced shallot, scallion, or fresh chives
8 sheets phyllo dough, thawed if frozen
5 tablespoons unsalted butter, melted
Olive oil cooking spray

1. Combine the apples, lemon juice, Cheddar cheese, and shallot in a bowl.

2. Place 1 of the phyllo sheets on your work surface, keeping the other sheets covered with plastic wrap. Brush the phyllo lightly with some of the butter and cover with a second sheet of phyllo. Repeat the buttering and stacking to make a stack of 4 sheets. Make a second stack with the remaining sheets of phyllo, buttering them the same way.

3. Using a sharp chef's knife, cut each stack of phyllo lengthwise in half, then crosswise into quarters, making 16 stacks in all. Divide the apple-cheese mixture among the phyllo stacks. Bring the corners of each rectangle up over the filling and pinch together to form purses, enclosing the filling completely. Set the purses on a large nonstick baking sheet, leaving about 1 inch between them. Bake right away or refrigerate the purses until ready to bake.

4. Adjust an oven rack to the center position and preheat the oven to 375°F.

5. Lightly coat each pastry with olive oil cooking spray and place the pan in the oven. Bake for 20 minutes, or until the purses are crisp and golden. Serve warm.

Bacon-and-Swiss Apple Purses: Cook 4 strips of bacon until crisp. Drain well and chop them medium-fine. Substitute grated Jarlsberg or Gruyère cheese for the Cheddar or Parmesan, and substitute chopped yellow onion for the shallot. Add the bacon to the apple-cheese mixture.

Pancetta and Provolone Apple Purses: Cut 2 ounces of pancetta into $1/4$-inch strips and cook it in 2 tablespoons olive oil in a small skillet over medium heat until crisp. Drain well and chop medium-fine. Substitute shredded provolone cheese for the grated cheese, omit the shallot, and add 1 tablespoon chopped fresh oregano, along with the pancetta, to the apple-cheese mixture.

Seafood and Game

As the apple tree among the trees of the wood,

so is my beloved among the sons.

—SONG OF SOLOMON

Fish and game have been eaten by humans since time immemorial, and we suspect that these foods might have been paired with apples once they came on the scene because the union is such a compatible one. Game is typically hunted in the fall, when apples come into their own, yet most recipes for game with fruit tend to include berries or cherries instead of apples. Similarly, tomatoes and wine make great foils for fish and seafood, but how about apples and cider?

Although our recipe selection is limited in this chapter, it shows off apples' compatibility and versatility with these foods. Bearing in mind that apples and products made from them (such as ciders, vinegar, and brandy) may have pronounced sweet or tart flavors, they are ideal partners for the inherent sweetness of fish and game.

Vietnamese Imperial Rolls

Shortly after moving to Montana, we met a delightful Vietnamese woman named Chu Chu Pham. She taught me several recipes and even demonstrated a few on my television show, "Big Sky Cooking." One of our favorites is called cha-gio (pronounced j-eye yaw). The filling she made included jicama. We decided to substitute apples, and it is even better that way. Braeburns are extremely good in this, but other sweet-tart, firm apples, such as Sunrise or Arlet, would work as well. Although many supermarkets now carry a wide variety of Asian ingredients, you may need to shop at a specialty market for the wrappers.

MAKES 18 ROLLS; ABOUT 12 APPETIZER SERVINGS

FILLING

1 package (1.85 ounces) bean threads (cellophane noodles)
4 ounces fresh shiitake mushrooms, stems removed and caps chopped medium-fine
1 pound medium shrimp in the shell
1 cup finely chopped onions
1 pound apples, quartered, cored, and cut into julienne strips
1 cup bean sprouts
3 scallions, thinly sliced
1 large egg

1 teaspoon salt
1/2 teaspoon freshly milled black pepper
One 1-inch piece peeled fresh ginger, finely grated
18 round Vietnamese rice papers (8- to 9-inch) or 18 square (8-inch) lumpia wrappers
1 large egg, lightly beaten (if using lumpia wrappers)

DIPPING SAUCE

1/4 cup plus 2 tablespoons Vietnamese fish sauce (nuoc mam)
2 tablespoons rice vinegar
1/4 cup fresh lime juice
1/4 cup sugar

Oil for pan frying

Cilantro sprigs for garnish

1. To make the filling, place the bean threads in a bowl and cover with hot water. Let stand until soft, about 30 minutes. Drain well and chop into small pieces. Place in a large bowl and add the shiitake mushrooms.

2. Drop the shrimp into 2 quarts rapidly boiling water. Cover the pan and remove from the heat. Let stand for 10 minutes. Drain and cool the shrimp. Peel and chop them medium-fine.

3. Add the shrimp, onion, apples, bean sprouts, and scallions to the bean threads and toss to combine

well. Beat the egg, salt, pepper, and ginger together in a small bowl and combine it with the apple mixture.

4. *If using Vietnamese rice papers,* one at a time, brush them lightly with water and let stand a few seconds until pliable. Place ½ cup of the filling about 2 inches from the edge nearest you, shaping it into a 4-inch-long horizontal cylinder. Fold the near edge of the rice paper over the filling, then fold over the sides. Roll up tightly and set on a baking sheet, seam side down. Repeat with the remaining rice papers and filling.

If using lumpia wrappers, place one on the work surface with a corner facing you. Place ½ cup of the filling about 3 inches from the corner of the wrapper, shaping it into a 4-inch-long horizontal cylinder. Fold the corner of wrapper nearest you up over the filling and tuck it under the filling. Brush the exposed edges of the wrapper lightly with the egg. Fold the sides of the wrapper toward the center and roll the package up tightly. Seal the seam with more egg, if necessary. Set aside on a baking sheet seam side down. Repeat with the remaining wrappers and filling.

(The rolls can be refrigerated for 2 to 3 hours before cooking.)

5. To prepare the dipping sauce, combine the fish sauce, rice vinegar, 2 tablespoons water, the lime juice, and sugar in a bowl. Stir until the sugar dissolves. (The sauce can be prepared hours ahead.)

6. When ready to cook the rolls, heat ½ inch of oil in a large skillet or electric frying pan to 375°F.

(To check the temperature, dip the tips of a pair of wooden chopsticks into the oil. If bubbles form around the chopsticks, the temperature is correct.) Cook the rolls 4 or 5 at a time, turning them occasionally with chopsticks, until a deep brown, about 5 minutes. Drain well on paper towels.

7. To serve, cut the rolls on the bias and arrange 3 halves on each plate, along with a small cup of the dipping sauce. Garnish with cilantro sprigs. Before eating, dip the cut ends of each roll into the sauce.

Note: The rolls can be cooked an hour or so ahead. Reheat on a baking sheet in a preheated 425°F oven for about 5 minutes.

what's in a name?

apples have inspired our more fanciful senses in a number of ways, including how we have named certain varieties. Here are some of the more interesting names for apples we have come across: American Seek-No-Further, Arkansas Baptist, Evening Party, Yellow Gilliflower, Greasy Pippin, Ladies Favorite of Tennessee, Mumper Vandervere, Ne Plus Ultra, Pim's Beauty of the West, Sheepnose, Twitty's Paragon.

Salmon in Hard Cider Cream Sauce

About thirty years ago, we had a fabulous meal at Fernand Point's renowned restaurant, La Pyramide in Vienne, France. Monsieur Point had died a few years prior, but his wife was carrying on in his tradition. On our way to Italy with our two young sons, we had decided on a whim to eat at the legendary Michelin three-star restaurant.

We settled on the prix fixe menu of the night, and one of the most astonishing things we ate was salmon in Champagne sauce. We've thought about this recipe for years, and each time sighed at the memory of it, but we had never attempted to re-create this remarkable dish until recently. Hard cider substitutes for the Champagne in a most intriguing and delicious way. Serve this as its own course, with nothing else except a good French baguette and chilled hard cider.

MAKES 4 SERVINGS

**Four 6-ounce skinless salmon fillets,
    any bones removed
Salt and freshly milled black pepper
1 tablespoon unsalted butter
3/4 cup hard cider
4 Roma (plum) tomatoes, peeled, seeded,
    juiced, and diced**

**3/4 cup fish stock
1/3 cup heavy cream
1 tablespoon chopped fresh tarragon**

1. Adjust an oven rack to the center position and preheat the oven to 400°F.

2. Season the salmon on both sides with salt and pepper. Melt the butter in a large heavy ovenproof skillet over medium-high heat. When the butter foam subsides, add the salmon and cook for about 30 seconds on each side. Add 1/4 cup of the cider, cover the pan, and set the pan in the oven.

3. Bake until the salmon is just cooked through, about 5 to 6 minutes for 1-inch-thick fillets. Transfer the salmon to a plate. Cover and keep warm.

4. Set the skillet over medium-high heat and boil down the juices until reduced to a syrupy glaze. Add the tomatoes and cook, stirring, for 30 seconds. Add the remaining 1/2 cup hard cider and boil until reduced by half. Add the fish stock and boil, stirring frequently, until reduced by about half. Add the cream and boil for 1 to 2 minutes, just until the sauce is slightly thickened. (You'll end up with about 1 cup of sauce.) Stir in the tarragon and season with salt and pepper.

5. Add any juices from the salmon to the skillet and boil for a few seconds more. Place the salmon on heated plates, spoon the sauce over, and serve immediately.

Trout with Cider, Chanterelles, and Cream

Tangy hard cider and cream sauce complement trout's mild flavor, and chanterelle mushrooms add sweetness and texture. Make this in the spring or early fall, when the mushrooms are in season. If trout are unavailable, salmon can be substituted. Serve with steamed new potatoes and green beans.

MAKES 4 SERVINGS

8 small or 4 large skinless trout fillets
   (see Note)
Salt and freshly milled black pepper
4 tablespoons (½ stick) unsalted butter
I large shallot, finely chopped
½ pound chanterelle mushrooms, cleaned and
   thinly sliced
I tablespoon vegetable oil
Flour for dusting
One 12-ounce bottle hard cider
½ cup heavy cream
2 tablespoons chopped flat-leaf parsley

I. Check the trout fillets to make sure all the bones have been removed; if necessary, use tweezers to extract any you find. Season the trout with salt and pepper and set aside.

2. Heat 2 tablespoons of the butter in a large skillet over medium heat. Add the shallot and cook, stirring, for a few seconds. Add the chanterelles and salt and pepper to taste and cook, stirring occasionally, until tender, about 5 minutes. Remove the contents of the pan and set aside.

3. Heat the remaining 2 tablespoons butter and the oil in the skillet over medium-high heat. Dust the trout fillets lightly with flour and shake off the excess. When the butter foam begins to subside, add the trout and cook for I to 2 minutes per side, until lightly browned and cooked through. Transfer the trout to a plate and cover to keep warm.

4. Add the hard cider to the skillet and boil it down over high heat until it is reduced by about half. Add the cream and cook for I to 2 minutes, or until the sauce coats a spoon lightly. Season to taste with salt and pepper and stir in the parsley and mushrooms.

5. Place the trout on heated dinner plates, spoon the sauce over the fillets, and serve immediately.

Note: If you use small skinless trout fillets (2 to 3 ounces each), serve two for each portion; one large fillet (4 to 5 ounces) will be ample for a serving. If using salmon, skinless 5- to 6-ounce fillets are a good size. Because it's thicker, salmon will require longer cooking than the trout.

Baked Sea Bass with Apples and Vegetables

Julienned leeks, carrot, fresh fennel, and apples braised in hard cider act as a bed for sea bass fillets baked atop the mixture. This is a great dish for fall, when all these vegetables and apples are coming into their own. Use a crisp, tart apple variety, such as Cortland, Greening, Northern Spy, and the like. Early-season McIntosh varieties, such as Macoun, will also work. If sea bass is unavailable, substitute halibut, escolar, or other similar white firm-fleshed species. Parslied red-skinned potatoes are the ideal accompaniment.

MAKES 4 SERVINGS

I teaspoon finely grated lemon zest
2 tablespoons fresh lemon juice
$^{1}/_{4}$ cup olive oil
Salt and freshly milled black pepper
Four 1-inch-thick skinless sea bass fillets
   (about 1$^{3}/_{4}$ pounds)
3 large leeks
I large carrot
2 large fennel bulbs without tops
I tablespoon unsalted butter
$^{3}/_{4}$ cup hard cider or dry white French
   vermouth, plus more if needed
   (see Note)

I large crisp, tart apple (8 ounces), quartered,
   cored, and cut into julienne
$^{1}/_{4}$ cup heavy cream
2 tablespoons chopped flat-leaf parsley

1. Combine the lemon zest, lemon juice, 2 tablespoons of the olive oil, $^{1}/_{2}$ teaspoon salt, and $^{1}/_{4}$ teaspoon pepper in a shallow dish just large enough to hold the fish. Add the fish and turn to coat on both sides with the mixture. Set aside while you prepare the vegetables, or up to about 1 hour or so ahead. Don't prepare the fish more than 2 hours ahead, or it may start to "cook" in the lemon juice (see Note below).

2. Cut off and discard the tough dark green parts of the leeks, trim away the root ends, remove any tough outer layers, and cut the leeks lengthwise in half. Rinse under cool running water, fanning the leek layers to wash away hidden dirt. Cut the leeks crosswise in half, then slice them into julienne. You will have about 3 cups. Peel the carrot and cut it into 2$^{1}/_{2}$ to 3-inch lengths, then cut into julienne. You'll have a generous 1 cup. Remove the tough outer layers of the fennel bulbs and cut away any bruised areas. Cut each bulb vertically in half, then lengthwise into thin slices. You'll have about 2 cups.

3. Heat the remaining 2 tablespoons olive oil with the butter in a large ovenproof skillet over medium heat until bubbly. Add the leeks, carrot, fennel, 1 teaspoon salt, $^{1}/_{2}$ teaspoon pepper, and the cider.

Stir well, cover the pan, and simmer for 15 minutes, or until the vegetables are tender but still retain some crunch.

4. Adjust an oven rack to the lower third position and preheat the oven to 450°F.

5. Bring the vegetable mixture to a boil over high heat. There should be about $\frac{1}{2}$ cup of liquid in the pan. If not, add more hard cider or vermouth. Add the apple and cook for 1 minute, stirring. Add the cream. Set the sea bass fillets over the bubbling mixture, cover the pan, and place it in the oven. Bake until the fish is just cooked through, 10 to 20 minutes, depending on how heavy your skillet is and how thick the fillets are. Serve on warmed dinner plates, and sprinkle with the parsley.

Note: If you wish, the leeks, carrot, and fennel can be cooked hours ahead and refrigerated. In that case, marinate the fish once the vegetables are cooked, but no more than 1 to 2 hours before serving. You may find that vegetables cooked ahead will have absorbed most of the liquid in the pan; if so, add $\frac{1}{2}$ cup more hard cider, water, vermouth, or part water and part hard cider or vermouth before bringing the mixture to a boil.

newtown

newtown, often called Newtown Pippin, is another one of capricious nature's gifts to the apple lover. Found growing as a chance seedling near the village of Newtown on Long Island in the early 1700s, it has been popular ever since. Thomas Jefferson planted around 170 trees of this variety. Perhaps, like modern apple expert Warren Manhart, he considered it the best of the best. Newtown is not among the hardiest of varieties: It is grown commercially largely in Oregon and parts of California; it can, however, also be grown in the less brutal climates of the east, such as Pennsylvania.

If you are a true apple lover with room to grow trees, you should seriously consider this fine versatile variety. It is good for just about anything except salads (it darkens quickly after being cut). Unfortunately, some people may have developed a bad impression of Newtown. When Granny Smith came on the scene, some growers began picking their Newtowns early, while they were still green and tart, in hopes of competing with the new imported bright green competitor. Unfortunately, when Newtowns are picked too early, they can be hard insipid-tasting rocks. But if they are picked when ripe, they have a tender flesh with a wonderful sweet-tart balance and delightful complexity of flavor. A bonus for the home grower is that they store well, even in a garage.

Apple Venison Sausage

Apples help to moisten, tenderize, and flavor lean venison. Even so, you will have to add a bit of fat for flavor. Just about any variety of apple that is sweet/tart will work. McIntosh, Braeburns, and Galas are good choices. Avoid very tart apples, as they will overwhelm the venison. I have made this sausage with a meat grinder and with the food processor, but the meat grinder results in a smoother texture and practically purées the apple so that it mixes more evenly into the venison. The sausage mixture can be stuffed into casings or shaped into patties, sautéed, and served for breakfast or brunch.

MAKES ABOUT 1¾ POUNDS

1 pound fully trimmed lean venison
¼ pound beef suet or pork fatback
1 large apple (8 ounces), quartered and cored
1¼ teaspoons salt
½ teaspoon freshly milled black pepper
2 garlic cloves, minced
1 teaspoon olive oil
1 large shallot, finely chopped
1 tablespoon Calvados or Applejack

1. Cut the venison and fat into strips about 1 inch wide. Pass them through the fine holes of a meat grinder into a large bowl. Cut the apple quarters into pieces that will fit into the grinder and pass them through the grinder. Add the salt, pepper, and garlic to the mixture and beat them in with a wooden spoon.

2. Heat the oil in a small heavy skillet over medium-high heat. Add the shallot and cook, stirring constantly, for 30 seconds. Add the shallot to the venison mixture along with the Calvados and beat in well. If not ready to use immediately, wrap securely and refrigerate. Shape into patties and cook in a skillet with a little oil or coated with vegetable cooking spray over medium-high heat for 2 to 3 minutes on each side.

Apple Venison Meat Loaf: Preheat the oven to 325°F. In a shallow roasting pan, shape the sausage mixture into a loaf that measures 8 × 3 × 3 inches. Lay 4 strips of bacon lengthwise over the loaf. Bake for about 1¼ hours, until the juices run clear when the loaf is pierced with a fork.

Pizza Topping: Venison sausage makes a delicious pizza topping. Simply dab generous pinches of sausage over pizza dough that has been spread with a thin layer of cooked sweet onion and peppers, and sprinkle with some crumbled feta cheese. Bake at 450°F for 12 to 15 minutes, until the sausage is cooked and pizza crust is done.

Buffalo Meatballs in Sweet-and-Sour Sauce

Buffalo's sweet, mild taste shines in this dish. I have adapted the recipe from my book *New Cooking from the Old West* (Ten Speed Press, 1996). The meatballs and sauce can be made ahead and reheated just before serving. Use any crisp/tart apple, such as Braeburn, Granny Smith, Cortland, or the like. Well-stocked supermarkets or Asian grocery stores will have light soy sauce (not a low-sodium product), chili paste with garlic, and Asian sesame oil. Ground buffalo meat can be ordered by mail (see page 261).

MAKES ABOUT 40 MEATBALLS

MEATBALLS

1 1/2 pounds ground buffalo

1 cup peeled and finely diced apple

1 1/2 tablespoons peeled and minced fresh ginger

1 garlic clove, minced

2 tablespoons light soy sauce

1 tablespoon Calvados or dry sherry

1 teaspoon salt

1/4 teaspoon freshly milled black pepper

1 large egg

2 tablespoons apple juice

1 tablespoon cornstarch

2 tablespoons vegetable oil

SAUCE

3 tablespoons cornstarch

1 cup sugar

1/3 cup dry sherry

1/2 cup light soy sauce

1 tablespoon dark soy sauce

1 teaspoon chili paste with garlic

1/2 cup apple juice

1/2 cup distilled white vinegar

1/2 cup ketchup

1 1/2 teaspoons salt

2 tablespoons Asian sesame oil

1/2 cup chopped flat-leaf parsley

1. Adjust an oven rack to the center position and preheat the oven to 350°F. Coat an 18 × 12 × 1-inch baking sheet lightly with cooking spray.

2. To make the meatballs, place the buffalo, apple, ginger, garlic, soy sauce, Calvados, salt, and pepper in a large bowl. Toss with a fork to combine well. In a small bowl, beat together the egg, apple juice, and cornstarch. Stir in the oil. Add to the buffalo mixture and mix well with the fork.

3. Shape the buffalo mixture into 1-inch balls, rolling them between the palms of your hands, and place 1 inch apart on the baking sheet. Bake for 20 minutes. Remove the pan from the oven and set aside to cool. (If making ahead, transfer the cooled meatballs to a plate, cover, and refrigerate. They will keep for 1 to 2 days.)

4. To make the sauce, combine $1/2$ cup water with the cornstarch in a small bowl and set aside. Combine the sugar, sherry, soy sauces, chili paste, apple juice, vinegar, ketchup, and salt, in a large nonreactive saucepan. Bring to a boil over medium-high heat, stirring occasionally with a heatproof rubber spatula. Stir the cornstarch mixture well and pour it all at once into the boiling liquid. Cook, stirring constantly but gently, for 1 to 2 minutes, or until the sauce is clear and slightly thickened. Remove the pan from the heat and stir in the sesame oil. Add the meatballs to the sauce and set aside until serving time. (May be made a few hours ahead and refrigerated).

5. When ready to serve, set the pan, uncovered, over low to medium heat. Bring the mixture to a simmer, stirring occasionally. When the meatballs and sauce are piping hot, stir in the parsley. Transfer the meatballs and sauce to a heated serving dish. Serve with toothpicks.

Poultry

All human history attests
That happiness for man—the hungry sinner!—
Since Eve ate apples, much depends on dinner.

—LORD BYRON, *BEPPO*

Whether you're cooking chicken, duck, turkey, or goose, apples can make them all taste better. Perhaps it's because, as with meat, seafood, and game, the sweet/tart duality of apples complements the inherent sweetness of these foods. In any event, these recipes show off apple's astonishing versatility and distinctiveness in cooking. Whether diced and used in an Anglicized curry-based sauce for Country Captain, for example, or puréed with onions and ginger for a more authentic Indian chicken curry, the results are amazingly different.

Hard cider cooked in sauces to serve with poultry adds a subtle tang and effervescence that is not possible to achieve in other ways. It's like Champagne, only better.

Most of these chicken recipes call for leg-thigh combinations or thighs because these are juicier and more flavorful than breasts. But if you prefer breasts, by all means use them.

Roast Chicken with Pork and Apple Stuffing

Stuff a chicken with a mixture of pork and apples, roast it, and you'll have some mighty fine eating. You will need a large roasting chicken, one weighing from four to four and a half pounds. The stuffing recipe makes more than enough for one chicken. You could stuff and roast two chickens, make only half the stuffing recipe, or place the extra stuffing in a baking dish, cover it, and bake it alongside the chicken.

MAKES 4 TO 6 SERVINGS

One (4 to 4¹/₂-pound) roasting chicken
Salt and freshly milled black pepper
Pork and Apple Stuffing (recipe follows; see
  headnote above)
1 tablespoon olive oil, plus more if needed
1 shallot, minced
³/₄ cup hard cider
³/₄ cup chicken stock
1 garlic clove, minced
1 tablespoon unsalted butter
1 tablespoon minced flat-leaf parsley or 1 tea-
  spoon minced fresh thyme

1. Adjust an oven rack to the lower third position and preheat the oven to 450°F. Have ready a shallow roasting pan with a rack.

2. Remove the giblets and pieces of fat from the chicken's body cavity. Rinse the chicken under cool running water and pat it dry inside and out. Lightly salt and pepper the inside of the chicken and spoon in about 2¹/₂ cups stuffing, without packing it tightly. Truss the bird and rub the skin all over with the olive oil.

3. Set the chicken breast side down on the rack in the roasting pan and place the pan in the oven. After 10 minutes, turn the chicken on its side and roast for another 10 minutes. Baste the chicken with any fat in the pan or with additional olive oil and turn it on its other side. Roast for another 10 minutes. Reduce the oven temperature to 350°F, baste the chicken again, and turn it breast side up. Sprinkle the skin lightly with salt. Continue roasting for about 45 minutes longer, until the legs move easily in their sockets when jiggled and the juices run a clear yellow from the tail opening when you tip the chicken upright. Transfer the chicken to a carving board, tent it loosely with foil, and let it rest for 15 minutes before carving. Meanwhile, prepare the sauce.

4. Pour off any fat from the roasting pan. Set the pan over medium-high heat and stir in the shallot. Add the hard cider and chicken stock and boil until the liquid is reduced by about two-thirds. Add the garlic and remove the pan from the heat. Stir in the butter and parsley, and taste for salt and pepper. Transfer to a small heated dish or sauceboat. There will be just enough sauce to moisten each serving.

5. Carve the bird and serve, spooning some of the stuffing alongside each portion.

Roasted Stuffed Duck: Duck is delicious when stuffed and cooked this way. Rinse and dry a 5-pound duckling as directed above, and prick the skin all over with a fork. Do not bother rubbing the duck with olive oil, since there is plenty of fat under the skin. Season and stuff the duck, but don't bother trussing it. Follow the directions for roasting, but pour 2 tablespoons Calvados over the duck during the last 30 minutes. Prepare the sauce using duck stock instead of chicken stock, if you have it. Save the rendered duck fat to use in cooking.

northern spy

northern spy is 100 percent American, an apple that appeared mysteriously from seeds planted in East Bloomfield, New York, between 1790 and 1800. Like some other especially popular apples, Northern Spy almost didn't survive. The original seedling died, but not before a Mr. R. Humphrey planted some suckers from the young tree.

We can all thank Humphrey, for Northern Spy is one of the tastiest apples around. Apple expert Fred Lape says, "To bite into the tender flesh of a well-ripened Spy and have its juice ooze around the teeth and its rich tart flavor fill the mouth and its aroma rise up into the nostrils is one of the outstanding experiences of all fruit eating." And to top it off, the apple is just as good cooked as it is raw and is especially fine in pies.

Unfortunately, Northern Spy is one of those wonderful varieties that is fast disappearing from stores, for both the tree and its fruit have several disadvantages for commercial growers. Northern Spy does not have the bright red color commercial growers think their customers want. A bright red type does exist, but its flavor is vastly inferior to the classic Northern Spy. The fruit also bruises easily (which is not a problem for the careful home orchardist). The trees tend to take several years to bear and may become quite large. They also have a tendency to bear a good crop only every other year.

Home gardeners can solve these problems by planting this variety on M.9 rootstock (see Growing Your Own Apples, page 249). The resulting small trees will begin to bear after only three years and will tend to give a crop every year. In the far north, however, a more hardy rootstock is needed. Furthermore, if ripened properly on the tree, Northern Spy stores well. This variety thrives farther north than many others, growing best from slightly north of Chicago and north and east from there. As long as winter temperatures stay consistently above minus 30°F, the trees should thrive.

Pork and Apple Stuffing

You can double the recipe for a large turkey. Use a crisp, tart apple such as Granny Smith, Cortland, Pippin, or Winesap.

MAKES ABOUT 5 CUPS

1 pound unseasoned ground pork
$^1/_4$ cup Calvados or Applejack
$^1/_2$ cup beef stock
Salt and freshly milled black pepper
1 tablespoon chopped fresh sage
1 teaspoon chopped fresh thyme
1 tablespoon sugar
$^1/_4$ teaspoon ground cinnamon
2 tablespoons unsalted butter
4 large tart apples (2 pounds), quartered, cored, peeled, and sliced crosswise $^1/_4$ inch thick

1. Sauté the pork in a large skillet over medium heat, breaking up the meat with a wooden spoon, until it is lightly browned and cooked. Remove the pork with a slotted spoon, drain it on paper towels, and set it aside in a bowl. Discard the pork fat.

2. Add the Calvados and beef stock to the skillet and boil rapidly over high heat, scraping up any browned bits of pork, until the liquid is reduced to about 3 tablespoons. Pour the syrupy mixture over the pork (set the skillet aside) and add 1 teaspoon salt, $^1/_2$ teaspoon pepper, the sage, and thyme. Stir well and set aside.

3. Combine the sugar with the cinnamon and set aside. Melt the butter in the skillet over medium-high heat. When sizzling, add the apples and the sugar mixture. Cook, stirring occasionally, until the apples are lightly browned and almost tender, but not mushy. Add the apples to the pork mixture and fold together gently. Cook a test patty, then taste and adjust the seasoning with salt and pepper, if necessary. (You can make the stuffing a day or two ahead and refrigerate it, covered. Bring it to room temperature before stuffing the chicken).

Herbed Chicken Thighs with Cider Red Cabbage

This dish is just right for a nippy fall or winter evening. The chicken is massaged with a dry rub for added flavor. Serve with parsleyed potatoes.

MAKES 6 SERVINGS

Salt and freshly milled black pepper
³/₄ teaspoon ground thyme
³/₄ teaspoon dried oregano
¹/₂ teaspoon ground coriander
6 skinless bone-in chicken thighs (about
  5 ounces each)
1 tablespoon olive oil
1 medium red onion, thinly sliced
1¹/₂ pounds red cabbage, cored and sliced
  ¹/₂-inch thick (about 8 cups)
2 tablespoons red wine vinegar
1 tablespoon sugar
³/₄ cup apple cider, preferably pasteurized
  fresh

1. Combine ¹/₂ teaspoon salt, ¹/₂ teaspoon pepper, the thyme, oregano, and coriander and rub into the chicken thighs. Let stand for 30 minutes to 1 hour.

2. Heat the olive oil in a large heavy nonstick skillet over medium-high heat. Add the chicken and brown it well on both sides. Remove from the pan and set aside.

3. Add the onion, cabbage, red wine vinegar, and sugar to the skillet, stir well, and bring the mixture to a boil over medium-high heat. Cover the pan, reduce the heat to medium, and cook for 5 minutes, or until the cabbage begins to wilt. Stir in the cider. Place the chicken on top of the cabbage and cover the skillet. Cook over low to medium-low heat at a gentle simmer until the chicken is tender, about 30 minutes. Taste and adjust the seasoning with salt and pepper, if necessary. Serve hot.

Chicken Scaloppine with Tomatoes and Raisins

Chicken thighs can be turned into delicious scaloppine. Here they are served in a sauce made with hard cider, apples, tomatoes, and raisins. Use any firm, tart apple. This goes together very quickly and it is a terrific dish for friends or family. Serve with buttered noodles.

MAKES 4 SERVINGS

6 boneless skinless chicken thighs
   (about 1¹/₂ pounds)
Salt and freshly milled pepper
2 tablespoons unsalted butter
2 tablespoons olive oil
Flour for dusting
²/₃ cup hard cider
²/₃ cup chicken stock
2 medium Roma (plum) tomatoes, peeled,
   seeded, juiced, and diced
1 medium tart apple (about 6 ounces),
   quartered, cored, peeled, and diced
¹/₄ cup raisins
2 tablespoons finely chopped flat-leaf parsley

1. Pound the chicken thighs between sheets of wax paper to a ¹/₄-inch thickness. Cut each thigh into two pieces and season both sides lightly with salt and pepper.

2. Heat 1 tablespoon each of the butter and oil in a large heavy skillet over medium-high heat. Dust half the chicken pieces with flour, add to the pan, and sauté on both sides until golden brown and cooked through, 4 to 5 minutes total. Transfer the chicken to a plate and add the remaining butter and oil to the pan. When hot, flour the remaining chicken and sauté the same way. Add to the first batch; cover and keep warm.

3. Pour the fat out of the skillet. Replace the pan over medium-high heat and add the hard cider. Cook, scraping up the browned bits from the bottom of the pan, until the cider is reduced and syrupy. Add the chicken stock, tomatoes, apple, and raisins. Cook, stirring, until the sauce is slightly thickened, about 2 minutes. Taste and adjust the seasoning with salt and pepper. Return the chicken to the pan, baste with the sauce, and cook briefly just to reheat. Sprinkle with the parsley and serve at once, 3 scaloppine per serving.

Chicken Breasts Stuffed with Apple and Goat Cheese

Apples and goat cheese add moistness, sweetness and tang to chicken breasts. Use any firm, sweet/tart apple, such as Braeburn or Golden Delicious. Serve with puréed butternut squash, scalloped potatoes, or fried potatoes.

MAKES 6 SERVINGS

6 large boneless skinless chicken breast halves
     (about 2 pounds)
Salt and freshly milled black pepper
1/4 cup plus 2 tablespoons (3 ounces) goat
     cheese (chèvre)
1 teaspoon finely grated lemon zest
1 large firm apple (8 ounces), quartered,
     cored, peeled, and shredded
Flour for dusting
1 large egg
1 1/3 cups fine fresh bread crumbs
1/2 cup freshly grated Parmesan cheese
2 tablespoons unsalted butter
2 tablespoons olive oil

1. Place the chicken breasts on a large sheet of wax paper, skinned sides down. Cover with another sheet of wax paper. Pound the chicken to a 1/4-inch thickness. Remove the top sheet of wax paper and season the side of the chicken facing up lightly with salt and pepper.

2. In a small bowl, combine the goat cheese, lemon zest, and apple. Spread the mixture evenly over half the surface of each breast. Fold each breast in half and press the edges together to form a packet.

3. Sprinkle the flour onto a sheet of wax paper. Beat the egg with 1 tablespoon water in a pie plate. Combine the bread crumbs and Parmesan cheese in a shallow dish. Dust each breast lightly with flour, dip into the egg mixture to moisten all surfaces, and coat with the crumbs, patting the crumbs gently in place. (The chicken can be prepared to this point several hours ahead; cover and refrigerate. When ready to cook, bring the chicken to room temperature.)

4. Heat the butter and oil in a large heavy skillet over medium heat. Add the chicken packets and cook for 5 to 6 minutes on each side, until nicely browned and cooked through. Drain on paper towels and serve immediately.

Chicken-Apple Curry

The sauce for this curry is a thick purée of onions, garlic, ginger, and spices. The cider and apples add both sweetness and tang. Use a firm, tart apple, such as Granny Smith. You can make this a day or two ahead if you wish, and reheat it slowly on top of the stove or in the oven. Serve with basmati rice.

MAKES 6 SERVINGS

6 skinless bone-in chicken breast halves
    (about 2 pounds)
Salt and freshly milled black pepper
1/4 cup plus 2 tablespoons vegetable oil
One 12-ounce bottle hard cider
2 large onions, cut into 1-inch pieces
6 garlic cloves
Two 1-inch cubes peeled fresh ginger
1 tablespoon ground cumin
2 teaspoons ground coriander
1/2 teaspoon ground turmeric
1/4 teaspoon cayenne
1 large tart apple (8 ounces), quartered, cored,
    peeled, and thinly sliced crosswise
2 Roma (plum) tomatoes, peeled, seeded, and
    diced
1/4 cup chopped fresh cilantro

1. Season the chicken lightly with salt and pepper. Heat the oil in a large heavy skillet over medium-high heat. Add the chicken and cook until lightly browned on both sides, about 5 minutes total. Remove the chicken and set it aside.

2. Meanwhile, place 3/4 cup of the cider, the onions, garlic, and ginger in a blender jar. Blend until smooth and thick, about 30 seconds. Stop to scrape the side of the container as necessary.

3. Pour the cider mixture into the hot oil in the skillet. Stir and cook over medium-high heat until the sauce thickens and begins to stick to the bottom of the pan, 2 to 3 minutes. Add the cumin, coriander, turmeric, and cayenne and cook for 1 minute longer. Stir in the remaining cider and the apple. Taste and add salt and pepper if necessary.

4. Return the chicken to the pan and spoon the sauce over the pieces to cover them completely. Scatter the tomatoes over the chicken and sprinkle with the cilantro. Cover the pan and cook at a simmer over medium-low heat until the chicken is cooked through and very tender, 25 to 30 minutes. Serve hot.

Apple Country Captain

Some Georgians claim that Country Captain is a dish that originated in Savannah when spice traders put into port there. We've added hard cider and McIntosh apples for tartness and fruitiness. Macouns or other McIntosh-type apples will also work, but avoid sweet apple varieties such as Fuji or Golden Delicious. Although we call for chicken leg-thigh pieces, you can use two whole chickens cut into quarters or bone-in chicken breasts. This dish is best when made a day ahead and reheated. Serve with basmati rice.

MAKES 6 SERVINGS

I cup all-purpose flour
Salt
$^{1}/_{2}$ teaspoon cayenne
6 large skinless chicken leg-thigh pieces
$^{1}/_{2}$ cup vegetable oil
3 tablespoons olive oil
2 large onions, chopped
I large red bell pepper, cored, seeded, and diced
I cup diced celery
3 garlic cloves, finely chopped
I pound McIntosh apples, quartered, cored, peeled, and diced
I tablespoon curry powder (see Note)

I teaspoon dried oregano, preferably Greek, crumbled
Freshly milled black pepper
Two 14$^{1}/_{2}$-ounce cans diced peeled tomatoes in juice, well drained
One 12-ounce bottle hard cider
$^{1}/_{3}$ cup currants
I tablespoon fresh lemon juice
$^{1}/_{2}$ cup chopped flat-leaf parsley

1. Adjust an oven rack to the lower third position and preheat the oven to 350°F.

2. Combine the flour, I teaspoon salt, and the cayenne in a large plastic bag. Add half the chicken and shake to coat evenly with the flour mixture. Remove the chicken and shake off the excess flour.

3. Heat the vegetable oil in a large ovenproof skillet over medium-high heat. Fry the floured chicken until golden brown all over, adjusting the heat as necessary to prevent burning. Remove the chicken and set it aside. Coat and fry the remaining chicken. Discard the oil and wipe out the pan.

4. Add the olive oil to the skillet and set the pan over medium heat. Stir in the onions, bell pepper, and celery. Cook, stirring occasionally, until the vegetables are tender, 8 to 10 minutes. Add the garlic and apples. Stir and cook for 2 to 3 minutes. Add the curry powder, oregano, I$^{1}/_{2}$ teaspoons salt, and I teaspoon pepper and cook, stirring for I to 2 minutes. Add the tomatoes, cider, and currants and stir well.

5. Add the chicken to the pan and spoon the sauce over it to cover it completely. Bring the sauce to a simmer, cover the pan, and place it in the oven. Bake for 45 minutes, or until the chicken is very tender.

6. Remove the pan from the oven and uncover it carefully. Sprinkle with the lemon juice and parsley and serve hot. (If making this ahead, don't add the lemon juice and parsley. Allow the chicken to cool in the skillet, then refrigerate. Reheat in a preheated 350°F oven until hot, about 30 minutes. Sprinkle with the lemon juice and parsley just before serving.)

Note: For the curry powder, you can substitute 1 teaspoon ground cumin, 1 teaspoon ground coriander, $^1/_2$ teaspoon ground fennel, and $^1/_2$ teaspoon ground turmeric.

Chicken-Apple Sausage

This low-fat sausage is versatile and can be used in many ways. To use it as a pizza topping, incorporate it into a pasta sauce, cook it as cutlets for dinner, or serve as patties for breakfast or brunch, see the recipes that follow. A meat grinder does the best job of grinding the chicken, but a food processor will also work. Use any tart apple for the sausage.

MAKES ABOUT $2^1/_2$ POUNDS

$1^1/_4$ **cups apple cider**
1 pound boneless skinless chicken breasts
1 pound boneless skinless chicken thighs
1 large apple (8 ounces), quartered, cored, and peeled
2 teaspoons rubbed sage
$^1/_2$ **teaspoon crumbled dried thyme**
1 tablespoon kosher salt
1 teaspoon freshly milled black pepper
$^1/_4$ **teaspoon freshly grated nutmeg**
vegetable oil

1. Boil the cider in a medium saucepan until it has reduced to 3 to 4 tablespoons. Swirl the pan occasionally and watch it carefully toward the end of cooking to prevent scorching. Transfer the reduced cider to a small bowl and cool to room temperature.

2. Pass the chicken and apple through the small holes of a food grinder into a medium bowl. Add the reduced cider and the remaining ingredients except the vegetable oil and beat the mixture briefly with a wooden spoon to combine well.

If you don't have a food grinder, cut the chicken into 1-inch pieces, arrange them on a wax paper–lined baking sheet, and freeze them until firm, about 30 minutes. The pieces should not be frozen solid; if they are firm but the tip of a sharp knife can penetrate them, they're ready for processing. With the metal blade in place, add half the breasts and thighs to the work bowl. Pulse the machine quickly 5 or 6 times, scrape the work bowl, and continue pulsing until the chicken is finely chopped. Transfer to a bowl and repeat the procedure with the remaining chicken. Pulse the apple pieces until very finely chopped and add to the chicken, then proceed as above.

3. To test the sausage for flavor, wet your hands and shape a small amount of the mixture into a small patty about ½ inch thick. Heat a little vegetable oil in a small skillet over medium heat. Add the patty and cook until done, about 2 minutes on each side. Cool slightly and taste for seasoning.

Chicken Sausage Patties

MAKES ABOUT 12 PATTIES

Chicken-Apple Sausage
Rubbed sage, optional
Freshly milled black pepper, optional
Fresh sage leaves
Vegetable oil

Season the sausage mixture with more sage and pepper if desired. Wet your hands and shape the mixture into 3-inch patties about ½ inch thick. Press 1 or 2 sage leaves onto the top of each patty. Add enough vegetable oil to a heavy skillet to film the bottom lightly and set the pan over medium heat. When hot, add the patties. Cook for 2 to 3 minutes per side, until browned and completely cooked. Drain on paper towels and serve hot.

Note: You can shape the mixture into patties and place them on baking sheets lined with plastic wrap. Set the pans in the freezer. When the patties are frozen solid, transfer them to airtight freezer bags and store frozen for up to 1 month. To use, remove the number of patties you need and let them thaw at room temperature before cooking.

Chicken Sausage Cutlets
with Shallot-Mustard Sauce

MAKES 4 SERVINGS

1¼ pounds Chicken-Apple Sausage
Flour for dusting
3 tablespoons olive oil
1 large shallot, finely chopped
½ cup beef stock
½ cup dry white French vermouth
1 tablespoon Dijon mustard
Salt and freshly milled black pepper

1. Wet your hands and divide the sausage mixture into four equal parts. Shape each into an oval cutlet about 1 inch thick, setting them onto a sheet of plastic wrap as you go. Spread the flour on a sheet of wax paper.

2. Heat the olive oil in a large skillet over medium heat. Coat each cutlet lightly with the flour, dusting off the excess. When the oil is hot, add the cutlets and cook for 3 to 4 minutes per side, until nicely browned and cooked through. Cover the pan during the last minute of cooking. Remove the cutlets to a plate; cover and keep warm.

3. Pour the cooking fat out of the skillet, add the shallot to the pan, and return the pan to medium-high heat. Cook the shallot, scraping up the browned bits in the pan, for 1 minute. Add the beef stock, vermouth, and mustard, whisking until smooth, and boil, stirring constantly, until the sauce is reduced by about half. Taste and adjust seasoning with salt and pepper. Pour the sauce over the cutlets and serve.

william tell

This feat of Tell, the archer, will be told
While yonder mountains stand upon their base.
By heaven! The apple's cleft right through the core.
Wilhelm Tell

we've all heard that William Tell shot an apple off his son's head with an arrow. But who, other than opera buffs, knows any more than that about this peculiar event? Turns out William Tell was a native of Uri, Switzerland, at the beginning of the fourteenth century. At the time, Austrian bailiffs ruled the land, and Tell refused to honor Gessler, the local bailiff. As a punishment, he was commanded to shoot an apple off his son's head. Fortunately, Tell was a good shot, and he succeeded in this nerve-wracking task. But he was angry enough afterward to kill Gessler in revenge, setting off a revolt against the bailiffs. The revolt succeeded, and the bailiffs were ousted on January 1, 1308. The legend has embellished on the facts, but it all makes a great story.

Chicken Sausage Pasta Sauce

MAKES 6 SERVINGS

2 tablespoons olive oil
1 medium onion, coarsely chopped
2 garlic cloves, finely chopped
1 pound Chicken-Apple Sausage (page 182)
½ cup dry white French vermouth
1 (14½-ounce) can crushed tomatoes, drained
2 tablespoons capers, drained and rinsed
Salt and freshly milled black pepper
1½ pounds fettuccine or spaghetti
¾ cup freshly grated Parmesan

1. Heat the olive oil in a medium skillet over medium heat. Add the onion and garlic and cook, stirring occasionally, until the onion is tender but not browned, 6 to 8 minutes. Add the Chicken Apple Sausage. Break the meat up with a wooden spoon, and cook, stirring, until lightly browned. Add the vermouth and cook until it is almost evaporated. Add the tomatoes and capers and cook, stirring occasionally, until slightly thickened, about 20 minutes. Add salt and pepper to taste. Set aside. Reheat, if necessary, just before serving.

2. Cook the pasta in a large pot of lightly salted water until al dente. Drain well and toss with the pasta sauce. Serve immediately, passing the Parmesan at the table.

Chicken Sausage Pizza Topping

To use the chicken sausage as a pizza topping, break off 1-inch nuggets of the mixture and sauté until browned in hot olive oil. Drain on paper towels and scatter the sausage over the pizza before popping it into the oven.

Cider-Braised Duck Legs

Use any crisp, tart in-season apple. For best results, allow the duck to marinate overnight. Fresh Muscovy ducks can be special-ordered (see page 261). Use the legs for this recipe and the breasts for the following one. Turn the carcasses into a brown duck stock, following the recipe below (be sure to reserve the necks and giblets). Follow the instructions on page 194 for how to cut up a pheasant.

MAKES 4 SERVINGS

1 teaspoon juniper berries
Salt and freshly milled black pepper
1 teaspoon dried oregano, preferably Greek
4 Muscovy duck legs (about 1½ pounds), excess
    fat removed (see Note)
2 large yellow onions (1½ pounds), sliced
    ¼ inch thick
1½ pounds red cabbage, cored and sliced
    ½ inch thick (about 8 cups)
One 12-ounce bottle hard cider
2 tablespoons sherry vinegar
1 large firm, tart apple (8 ounces), quartered,
    cored, peeled, and thinly sliced
Big pinch of ground allspice
6 bay leaves
2 cups Duck Stock (recipe follows)
½ cup chopped flat-leaf parsley

1. Crush the juniper berries in a mortar with a pestle. Add 1½ teaspoons salt, ½ teaspoon pepper, and the oregano. Grind briefly with the pestle to combine well. Sprinkle over both sides of the duck legs and massage the mixture in with your fingers. Place the duck in a zip-top plastic bag and refrigerate it for at least 2 hours, preferably overnight.

2. Place the duck legs skin side down in a large heavy skillet and set the pan over medium-low heat. (It isn't necessary to add any fat, because the skin will render its own.) Cook the duck, without turning it, until the skin is crisp and browned, about 20 minutes. If an excessive amount of fat is rendered, remove it with a bulb baster.

3. Adjust an oven rack to the lower third position and preheat the oven to 350°F.

4. Transfer the duck to a dish and set aside. Add the onions to the fat remaining in the pan (there should be 2 to 3 tablespoons) and cook over medium heat, stirring occasionally, until the onions start to soften and caramelize slightly, about 10 minutes. Add the cabbage, 1 cup of the cider, the sherry vinegar, and apple. Stir well, cover the pan, and cook until the cabbage is wilted, about 8 minutes. Uncover the pan, raise the heat to high, and boil until the liquid is reduced almost to a glaze, about 5 minutes. Stir frequently to prevent scorching.

5. Remove the pan from the heat and add ½ teaspoon salt, ¼ teaspoon pepper, and the allspice. Stir well. Bury the bay leaves in the cabbage mixture.

Set the duck legs on top, skin side up, and pour the stock and the remaining cider around the duck. The liquid should barely cover the cabbage and onions and just reach the duck; do not submerge the duck in the cooking liquid.

6. Cover the pan and bring the contents to a simmer over medium-high heat. Place the pan in the oven and bake until the duck is very tender, about 1½ hours.

7. Remove the duck to a platter; cover and keep warm in the turned-off oven. Transfer the cabbage mixture to a colander to drain, saving the liquid. Discard the bay leaves. Place the cabbage in a covered dish and set it in the oven with the duck.

8. Pour the cooking juices into a heavy medium saucepan and boil over high heat until reduced to about 1 cup. Taste and adjust the seasoning with salt and pepper. Stir the parsley into the cabbage mixture and spread it on a warmed serving platter. Place the duck pieces on top, skin side up, and spoon some of the sauce over the duck. Pass the remaining sauce at the table.

Note: The legs are leg-thigh combinations. Remove them from the ducks as units.

Duck Stock

MAKES ABOUT 4 QUARTS

2 duck carcasses plus the reserved necks and
    giblets
2 large carrots, scrubbed and cut into 1-inch
    pieces
1 large yellow onion, unpeeled, quartered
4 large celery stalks with leaves, cut into 3-inch
    pieces
1 large leek, washed well and cut into 2-inch
    pieces
1 garlic head, cut crosswise in half
1 cup dry white French vermouth
6 parsley sprigs
6 oregano sprigs
6 thyme sprigs
1 teaspoon black peppercorns
2 bay leaves

1. Adjust an oven rack to the center position and preheat the oven to 450°F.

2. Chop the duck carcasses into 3 or 4 pieces each. Put them in a roasting pan along with the reserved necks, hearts, and gizzards. (Save the liver for another use.) Roast for 1 hour. Reduce the temperature to 400°F, add the carrots, onion, celery, leek, and garlic, and stir well to coat the vegetables with some of the rendered fat. Roast for another 30 minutes.

3. Transfer the bones and vegetables (but not the fat) to a large stockpot. Add 5 quarts water and the remaining ingredients and set aside. Carefully pour off the fat from the roasting pan. Add 1 cup water to the roasting pan and set the pan over high heat. Scrape the pan with a wooden spoon to release the browned bits, and add the liquid to the stockpot.

4. Bring the stock to a simmer very slowly over medium-low heat and simmer, partly covered, for 3 to 4 hours. The stock should bubble very gently during cooking.

5. Strain the stock and refrigerate it. Once it's chilled, remove the solidified fat from the surface and the stock is ready to use. If you want a stronger stock, boil it down until it reaches the desired strength. If you reduce the stock by half, you will have duck demi-glace. (I usually use half the stock as is and boil down the rest to make demi-glace.) Both stock and demi-glace freeze well for up to 6 months.

Duck Breasts with Hard Cider, Orange, and Calvados Sauce

Muscovy duck breasts served with a sensational sauce made from brown duck stock, hard cider, orange juice, Calvados, and heavy cream are heady stuff, ideal for an intimate dinner. The method for preparing the duck is adapted from Paula Wolfert's *The Cooking of Southwest France.* The seasoned breasts should be refrigerated overnight before cooking. Serve with oven-roasted potatoes and butternut squash purée.

MAKES 4 SERVINGS

4 Muscovy duck breast halves
Salt and freshly ground milled pepper
3 cups Duck Stock (page 187)
1 cup hard cider
⅓ cup fresh orange juice
¼ cup Calvados
⅓ cup heavy cream

1. Using a small sharp knife, remove each breast half, with the attached skin, from the breastbone of the carcass in a single piece. Trim the excess fat from the duck breasts with kitchen shears. Sprinkle both sides of the breasts with 2 teaspoons salt and ½ teaspoon pepper. Rub the seasoning into the flesh and skin

gently with your fingers. Place the breasts in a zip-top bag and refrigerate overnight.

2. When ready to cook, adjust an oven rack to the center position and preheat the oven to 350°F.

3. Boil the duck stock until it is reduced to 1½ cups; set aside.

4. Remove the duck from the bag and blot dry with paper towels, rubbing off excess salt and pepper. To prevent the duck breasts from curling during cooking, score the skin in a crisscross pattern at ¾-inch intervals, being careful not to cut into the flesh. Place the duck skin side down in a large heavy skillet. Set the pan over medium to medium-high heat and cook until the skin is browned and crisp, about 5 minutes. Transfer the breasts to a heavy baking sheet, skin side down, and place them in the oven. Bake until the breasts feel firm but springy when pressed, 10 to 12 minutes. The flesh will still be pink.

5. While the duck is in the oven, pour the fat out of the pan and blot up any remaining fat in the pan with paper towels. Set the pan over high heat and add the hard cider, orange juice, and Calvados. Bring to a boil, scraping up the browned bits from the bottom of the pan. Then, stirring constantly, boil until the liquid is reduced to a syrupy glaze. There'll be only 2 to 3 tablespoons.

6. Add the reduced stock and boil, stirring occasionally, until the sauce is reduced by about half. You should have a scant 1 cup. Transfer the sauce to a medium heavy saucepan and set the pan over high heat. As soon as the sauce is at a rolling boil, immediately start adding the cream in a slow steady stream, adding it only as fast as the sauce can incorporate it. Do not stir during this process, or the sauce may "break" and become thin. Once all the cream has been added, continue to boil, swirling the pan by its handle occasionally, for 2 to 3 minutes, until the sauce coats a spoon. Remove the pan from the heat and season with salt and pepper if necessary. Keep warm.

7. Place the duck breasts skin side down on a cutting board. Cover them loosely with foil and let them rest for 2 to 3 minutes.

8. Cut each breast on the bias into ½-inch-thick slices with a sharp knife. Fan the slices out on warmed dinner plates, spoon some of the sauce over, and serve. Pass the remaining sauce at the table.

Turkey Scallops with Apple-Onion Confit

Turkey is a great impostor for veal. Their tastes and textures are remarkably similar; after turkey spends a full day in a marinade of sweet apple cider, you may not be able to tell the the difference. A whole turkey breast with bone provides you with enough meat for both this recipe and the kabobs (on page 192). And you'll have the trimmings to turn into stock if you like. Use any tart, crisp apple.

MAKES 4 SERVINGS

1 whole turkey breast with bone
(about 6 pounds)
About 4 cups apple cider
3 garlic cloves, thinly sliced

APPLE-ONION CONFIT
2 pounds red onions
2 tablespoons olive oil
¹/₄ cup cider vinegar
2 tablespoons red wine vinegar
2 tablespoons sugar
Salt and freshly milled black pepper
1 large tart, crisp apple, quartered, cored,
peeled, and diced
One 12-ounce bottle hard cider
2 tablespoons cassis

2 thyme sprigs
3 bay leaves

Salt and freshly milled black pepper
2 tablespoons unsalted butter
2 tablespoons vegetable oil
Flour for dusting
2 tablespoons minced flat-leaf parsley

1. Remove the skin from the turkey. Cut the breast meat off the bone with a sharp boning knife. You'll have two large breast halves. The underside of each breast half has a strip of meat (the fillet or tender) with a tendon running through it. Cut the tenders away from the breast and carefully remove the tendons. Reserve the tenders for the kabob recipe on page 192.

Each breast half has a thick end and a thin end. Cut a strip of meat about 1¹/₂ inches wide off each thick end. Wrap these pieces and the tenders and refrigerate them for use in the kabob recipe.

2. Place the remaining meat between sheets of wax paper and pound to about ³/₈ inches thick. Cut each flattened breast half into four squarish pieces. Place the turkey in a shallow dish and pour in enough sweet cider to just cover the turkey; add the sliced garlic. Wrap tightly and refrigerate overnight, or for up to 2 days.

3. Meanwhile, prepare the confit: Cut the onions in half through the stem ends. Set the onions cut side

down and slice them lengthwise about ¼ inch thick. Heat the olive oil in a large saucepan over medium heat. Add the onions, both vinegars, sugar, ¾ teaspoon salt, and ¼ teaspoon pepper, stir well, and cover the pan. When the mixture comes to the simmer, cook for 10 minutes longer, stirring occasionally.

4. Add the apple, hard cider, cassis, thyme, and bay leaves. Bring the mixture to a boil over high heat, partially cover the pan, and reduce the heat to low. Cook at a simmer, stirring occasionally, until the onions are very tender and the liquid is thick and syrupy and has been almost completely absorbed, about 1½ hours. Taste and add more salt or pepper if necessary. Discard the thyme and bay leaves. When cool, cover and refrigerate. When ready to serve, reheat until warm or hot. (There will be about 3 cups of confit. It will keep well for 1 week. Use leftovers to serve with burgers.)

5. To cook the scallops, remove them from the marinade and pat them dry on paper towels. Season them with salt and pepper. Heat the butter and oil in a large skillet over medium-high heat. When hot, coat the scallops lightly with flour, add to the pan, and sauté for about 3 minutes on each side, until nicely browned and cooked through. They should feel springy to the touch. Drain them on paper towels and place them on a heated serving platter or on dinner plates. Top each scallop with a spoonful of warm confit and sprinkle with the parsley. Serve immediately.

apples in song

when we read Carl Sandburg's line, "The classical American rural tune . . . steps around like an apple-faced farmhand . . . as American as Andrew Jackson, Johnny Appleseed, and Corn on the Cob" *(The American Songbag)*, we decided to see how many songs featured apples in their titles. After all, Sandburg managed two apple references in two lines. However, search as we might through our own memories and those of friends, we didn't manage to find a single song about apples themselves. We've been commanded, "Don't Sit Under the Apple Tree with Anyone Else But Me," and treated to reminiscences about what goes on "In the Shade of the Old Apple Tree." We know something about the flowers, from "Cherry Blossom Pink and Apple Blossom White" to "I'll Be with You in Apple Blossom Time." But what about the apples themselves? I dug out an old songbook that had belonged to my grandmother, called *Songs That Never Die*. The title belied the fact that I'd never heard of most of the songs, including yet another flower title, "Time of Apple Blossom," whose words and music both made me realize why it hadn't, in truth, lived.

Cider-Glazed Turkey Kabobs

For these kabobs, chunks of cider-marinated turkey are skewered with small red-skinned potatoes and brushed with a cider glaze as they grill to give them an appetizing sheen and marvelous flavor. Start this a day or two before, as the turkey must marinate for at least twenty-four hours for best results.

MAKES 4 TO 6 SERVINGS

1½ pounds reserved turkey tenders and
    thick breast meat (see previous recipe),
    cut into 1½-inch chunks
About 3 cups apple cider
3 garlic cloves, thinly sliced
18 small (about 1½ inches in diameter)
    red-skinned potatoes
¼ cup sherry vinegar
3 tablespoons sugar
1 tablespoon Dijon mustard
1 teaspoon finely grated fresh ginger
Salt and freshly milled black pepper

1. Place the turkey in a nonreactive pan and add apple cider to cover. Add the garlic, cover the pan, and refrigerate for at least 24 hours and up to 3 days.

2. Boil the potatoes in lightly salted water until just tender, 8 to 10 minutes. Drain well and cover with cold water to stop the cooking. When cool, drain the potatoes and pat dry. (Cover and refrigerate them if making a day ahead.)

3. In a small saucepan, combine 1 cup apple cider, the sherry vinegar, sugar, mustard, and ginger. Boil, stirring occasionally, until the mixture is reduced to between ⅓ and ½ cup. Set aside. (The glaze can be made ahead and refrigerated for up to 3 days.)

4. When ready to cook, prepare a hot fire in a charcoal grill.

5. Remove the turkey from the cider marinade (it's not necessary to pat the pieces dry). Thread the turkey and potatoes onto skewers, alternating them and beginning and ending with turkey. Brush lightly with some of the glaze and grill, brushing occasionally with the glaze and turning the skewers frequently, until the turkey is cooked through, about 15 minutes. Season with salt and pepper and serve hot.

Turkey Apple Burgers

Lean ground turkey breast combined with finely shredded apple makes juicy and delicious burgers. They are also low in fat. The mayonnaise-style sauce gets its sweet/sour tang from a reduction of cider vinegar and apple juice. Use any tart apple: Cortland, McIntosh, and Macoun are my first choices. At our house, when we say burger, this is what we're talking about.

MAKES 4 SERVINGS

1¼ pounds ground turkey breast
½ cup loosely packed and peeled, finely
    shredded tart apple
1 garlic clove, minced
1 teaspoon minced fresh thyme
¾ teaspoon salt
¼ teaspoon freshly milled black pepper
1 tablespoon Calvados or Applejack

SAUCE
¼ cup cider vinegar
¼ cup apple juice
1 teaspoon sugar
⅓ cup mayonnaise (regular, light, or
    mayonnaise dressing)
1 teaspoon Dijon mustard

2 tablespoons vegetable oil

4 kaiser rolls, split and toasted
Lettuce leaves
Sliced tomato
Sliced peeled English cucumber

1. Place the turkey, apple, garlic, thyme, salt, pepper, and Calvados in a large bowl and combine them gently with your hands. Avoid overworking the mixture, as this will make the burgers tough. Shape the mixture into four 4-inch patties and refrigerate them until needed. (The patties can be prepared up to 1 day ahead.)

2. To make the sauce, boil the cider vinegar, apple juice, and sugar in a small heavy saucepan until reduced to 1 to 2 tablespoons. Cool completely.

3. In a small bowl, stir together the mayonnaise, mustard, and reduced cider mixture. (The sauce can be prepared 1 to 2 days ahead and refrigerated.)

4. To cook the burgers, heat the oil in a large skillet over medium heat. Add the burgers and cook them about 3 minutes on each side, until lightly browned and cooked through. Set the burgers on paper towels to drain briefly. Spread the tops and bottoms of the kaiser rolls with the sauce and assemble the burgers, using the lettuce leaves, cucumbers, and tomatoes. Serve immediately.

Pheasant Breasts with Macadamia Nut Crust

The flavor of pheasant, like most game, benefits when paired with fruit. In this dish, cubes of crisp apple and dried apricots work their magic. Use a firm sweet/tart apple that will not fall apart when cooked, such as Jonagold or Braeburn. The macadamia nut crust adds crunch and sweetness. The key to this recipe is a rich pheasant stock. To make it, you'll need to start a day ahead. Order two pheasants (see Mail-Order Sources, page 261). Remove the breasts (for this recipe) and leg-thighs (for the following recipe).

Place the pheasant on a cutting board with the breastside up. With a sharp boning knife, make an incision to one side of the breastbone, cutting through the skin and into the flesh along the ridge of the breastbone. Always keeping the blade of the knife against the breastbone, scrape down the length of the breastbone to release the meat in one piece. Then detach the breast from the shoulder end where it is connected to the ball joint of the wing. Repeat the procedure on the other side of the bird and with the second pheasant. Each pheasant provides two boneless breast halves.

To remove the thighs, grasp one of the leg-thigh joints and bend it toward the backbone until you can hear a "snap." At this point the pheasant thigh bone (femur) should be detached from its ball joint and is connected to the carcass only by the skin. If not, use the tip of your boning knife to sever the connection of the thigh bone to its ball joint. Turn the pheasant on its side and cut the skin all around the thigh portion, making sure to include the "oyster," a small nugget of meat nesting in a depression on the pheasant's backbone.

To remove the thigh bone, place a leg-thigh piece flesh side up on your cutting board. Use the tip of the boning knife to cut the flesh on either side of the thigh bone. Grasping the thigh bone, slide your knife under it to separate it from the meat; detach the thigh bone from its connection to the leg bone by cutting through the ball joint. Repeat on the second side of the pheasant and with the second pheasant. If your pheasant came with the feet and neck attached, chop them off and use them to make pheasant stock.

Chop the carcass into pieces and use them with all the trimmings and giblets to prepare stock. Save the liver for another use.

Bone the thighs and refrigerate the pheasant pieces. Prepare the stock following the recipe for Duck Stock (page 187) and refrigerate overnight.

Chop the macadamia nuts with a heavy chef's knife. You'll get uneven-sized pieces, which adds interest to the dish. Or, pass the nuts through the shredding disk of the food processor. Whether you chop the nuts or use the food processor, be sure the macadamias are at room temperature. Use any tart apple.

4 boneless skinless pheasant breast halves

2 teaspoons fresh lemon juice

Flour for dusting

1 large egg

1 cup (5 ounces) finely chopped or shredded
    macadamia nuts

Salt and freshly milled black pepper

3 tablespoons unsalted butter

1 medium tart apple (6 ounces), quartered,
    cored, peeled, and diced

2 tablespoons diced moist dried apricots

2 tablespoons vegetable oil

1 large shallot, minced

1 cup dry white French vermouth

1/4 cup Calvados or Applejack

1 cup rich pheasant stock (see headnote)

1 tablespoon minced fresh rosemary

1. Place the pheasant breasts between sheets of wax
paper and flatten the thicker ends slightly with a
meat pounder so that they are of even thickness.
Rub both sides of the breasts with the lemon juice
and let stand for 10 minutes.

2. Spread the flour on a sheet of wax paper. Beat the
egg with 1 teaspoon water in a pie plate to combine
well. Put the macadamia nuts in a shallow bowl.
Season the breasts lightly with salt and pepper. Dust
them with a thin coating of flour and shake off the
excess. Dip the breasts one at a time into the egg

mixture, then coat them with the macadamia nuts.
Put the breasts on a wire rack set on a baking sheet
and refrigerate for at least 1 hour. (The breasts can
be prepared hours ahead to this point and refrigerated. Bring to room temperature before cooking.)

3. Melt 1 tablespoon of the butter in a medium
skillet over medium heat. Add the apple and cook,
stirring occasionally, until the pieces begin to brown
lightly, about 5 minutes. Stir in the apricots, transfer the mixture to a plate, and spread it out to cool.

4. Heat the vegetable oil in a large skillet over medium
heat. Add the pheasant breasts. Cook for 3 to 4
minutes per side, until golden brown and cooked
through. The pheasant should feel springy when
pressed. Watch carefully to prevent burning. Transfer the breasts to a dish; cover them and keep warm.

5. Discard the cooking fat. Place the skillet over
medium-high heat, add the shallot, and stir and
cook for about 30 seconds. Add the vermouth and
Calvados. Cook briskly, swirling the pan occasionally, until the liquid is reduced to about 1/2 cup. Add
the stock and cook until the sauce is thickened and
reduced to about 1 cup. Add the remaining 2 tablespoons butter and swirl the pan until the butter is
incorporated into the sauce. Taste and season with
salt and pepper. Add the rosemary and the apple
mixture and heat briefly to warm the fruit.

6. Arrange the pheasant on a warmed platter, spoon
on the sauce, and serve immediately.

pippins and russets

you may wonder about the words *pippin* and *russet* that keep appearing in the names of apple varieties. Originally, a pippin meant an apple grown from a pip, or seed, rather than from a graft. But apple seeds don't reproduce their parent tree reliably, so the term has lost its original meaning. Apple seeds do sometimes end up producing fine apples, however, such as the Newtown Pippin, now called simply the Newtown.

Russets have rough patches, or russeting, on their skin and are often old-fashioned varieties once popular with home growers. Russets have character. They tend to be spicier than other varieties. They generally store well, often becoming more flavorful as the winter wears on. You won't find russets in the supermarket, no matter how great their flavor — commercial growers and marketers think people will find them unappealing.

Stuffed Pheasant Legs

Boneless pheasant leg-thigh pieces are given a Middle Eastern–style treatment, stuffed with a cumin-and-cinnamon-scented mixture of onion, apples, rice, and pine nuts. You'll need a rich pheasant stock (see the headnote on page 194) for this dish to really work.

MAKES 4 SERVINGS

1 tablespoon unsalted butter
1 cup chopped yellow onions
2 garlic cloves, finely chopped
1 small crisp apple (4 ounces), quartered, cored, peeled, and diced (3/8-inch)
1/4 teaspoon ground cumin
Pinch of ground cinnamon
Salt and freshly milled black pepper
1/2 cup cooked white rice
1/2 cup rich pheasant stock (see page 194), plus more if needed
1/4 cup pine nuts
1/4 cup finely chopped flat-leaf parsley
4 pheasant leg-thighs boned (see page 194)
2 tablespoons olive oil
1/4 cup dry white French vermouth

1. Remove thigh bones and leg bones from the pheasant (see page 194) and set the pheasant aside. Melt the butter in a small skillet over medium-low

heat. Stir in the onions and garlic, cover the pan, and cook for 5 minutes. Add the apple, cumin, cinnamon, 1/2 teaspoon salt, and 1/4 teaspoon pepper; cover, and cook for another 5 minutes. Add the rice and 1/4 cup of the pheasant stock, cover, and cook for 5 minutes longer. Uncover the pan and raise the heat to medium-high. Cook, stirring constantly, until almost all the liquid has evaporated. Remove the pan from the heat and cool to room temperature.

2. Transfer the apple mixture to the work bowl of a food processor fitted with the metal blade and pulse 6 to 8 times. Scrape into a small bowl and set aside.

3. Place the pine nuts in a small heavy pan and cook over medium heat, stirring frequently, until toasted. Set aside to cool.

4. Stir the nuts and parsley into the apple mixture. Season the pheasant lightly with salt and pepper. Fill the drumstick cavities with some of the stuffing and spread the remaining stuffing evenly over the thigh meat, packing it into place. (The pheasant can be prepared several hours ahead to this point. Cover and refrigerate until ready to cook.)

5. Heat the olive oil in a heavy heavy skillet over medium heat. Add the pheasant pieces, stuffing side down, and cook for 2 to 3 minutes. Carefully turn the pieces over and cook for about 3 minutes longer, until well browned. Remove the pheasant from the pan.

6. Discard the cooking fat, increase the heat to medium-high, add the vermouth, and bring to a boil, scraping up the browned bits from the bottom of the pan. Add the remaining 1/4 cup stock and bring the liquid to a simmer. Return the pheasant to the pan, skin side down, cover tightly, and cook over low heat, so the liquid bubbles slowly, for about one hour, or until the pheasant is very tender.

7. There should be about 1/2 cup of a nice syrupy sauce in the pan; add more stock if necessary. Taste and adjust the seasoning with salt and pepper. Place the pheasant in a serving dish, spoon the sauce over, and serve immediately.

POULTRY

Beef, Pork, and Lamb

The best apple is taken by the pig.

—AMERICAN PROVERB

What is it about beef, pork, and lamb that makes them natural companions of the apple? Although we can't say for sure, what we can say is that there must be a sweet/sour principle at work. One of our happiest discoveries while working on these recipes was that apple ciders—both sweet and hard—aren't only for drinking. They make excellent marinades and sauce bases for beef, pork, and lamb. The acid in cider has a dual role in helping to tenderize and complement the sweetness of these meats.

For cider to work in a marinade, an overnight stint or longer is needed in order for the cider to fully penetrate the meat. For a sauce, however, a quick reduction will suffice to concentrate and accentuate cider's flavors. Calvados, or apple brandy, adds yet another dimension of apple taste to sauces.

Steak au Poivre with Cider Sauce

Dried apples, hard cider, and butter add a new twist on the French classic *steak au poivre*. This is a great company dish since much of the preparation can be done ahead. Then only the steaks need to be cooked and the sauce made just before serving.

MAKES 4 SERVINGS

One 12-ounce bottle hard cider
1/2 cup diced moist dried apple slices
2 tablespoons black peppercorns
Four 6-ounce fully trimmed beef tenderloin
    steaks
Salt
2 tablespoons corn or peanut oil
2 large shallots, minced
2 garlic cloves, minced
1/2 cup beef stock
1 teaspoon minced fresh thyme, plus whole
    sprigs for garnish
4 tablespoons (1/2 stick) unsalted butter, at
    room temperature
1 tablespoon minced flat-leaf parsley

1. Combine 3/4 cup of the cider with the apples in a small saucepan. Bring to a simmer over medium heat. Cover the pan and cook slowly until the apples are tender, about 10 minutes. Set aside. (The apples can be prepared hours ahead.)

2. Crush the peppercorns on your work surface with the bottom of a saucepan. Pat the steaks dry with paper towels and press the crushed pepper onto both sides of them. Refrigerate the steaks, covered, until ready to use. (You can do this step several hours ahead. Bring the steaks to room temperature before cooking.)

3. Lightly season the steaks with salt. Heat the oil in a large skillet over medium-high heat. Add the steaks and cook for 2 to 3 minutes per side for rare to medium-rare. Transfer the steaks to a platter; cover and keep them warm.

4. Pour out the fat from the skillet. Off the heat, add the shallots and garlic to the pan and stir with a wooden spoon, scraping up any browned bits from the bottom of the pan. Place the skillet over medium-high heat. Add the apples plus any liquid, the remaining hard cider, the beef stock, and minced thyme. Bring to a boil and cook, stirring frequently, until the liquid is reduced by about half and is slightly syrupy. Add the butter, plus any meat juices, swirl the pan by its handle, and continue cooking for 1 to 2 minutes, until the sauce is thick enough to cloak the steaks. Taste and adjust the seasoning with more salt if necessary.

5. Lower the heat to medium-low and add the steaks to the pan. Heat, basting continuously with the sauce for about 1 minute. Serve on warm dinner plates, sprinkled with the parsley and garnished with thyme sprigs.

Beef Short Ribs

The often-neglected meaty tail ends of the ribs, chuck, or beef brisket make succulent and delicious eating. If you can find bone-in short ribs, by all means use them. The bones add great flavor to the meat as it cooks. Four pounds of short ribs may seem like a lot for four people, but most of the weight is bone. (If only boneless short ribs, or, as they are sometimes called, country ribs, are available, they'll do just fine.) The ribs are given an overnight marinade in apple cider, aromatic vegetables, and herbs, then braised slowly in hard cider until the meat practically falls off the bone. After cooking, the pan juices are turned into a barbecue-like sauce. Serve the short ribs with boiled new potatoes or noodles. And don't be bashful about using your hands and licking the delicious sauce off your fingers.

MAKES 4 SERVINGS

MARINADE

4 cups apple cider, plus more if needed
1 large onion, coarsely chopped
1 large carrot, sliced
1 celery stalk, sliced
4 garlic cloves, crushed
4 bay leaves
6 whole cloves
4 parsley sprigs

4 pounds beef short ribs with bone or 3 pounds
   boneless short ribs, trimmed of excess fat
Salt and freshly milled black pepper
1/4 cup olive oil
One 12-ounce bottle hard cider
1 cup beef stock
One 8-ounce can tomato sauce
1 cup smooth unsweetened applesauce
1 tablespoon Dijon mustard
1 tablespoon Worcestershire sauce

1. Combine all the marinade ingredients with 1 cup water in a large nonreactive pot. Add the beef, submerging it in the marinade. If the marinade doesn't cover the beef completely, add enough cider to do the job. Cover the pan and refrigerate overnight.

2. Adjust an oven rack to the lower third position and preheat the oven to 350°F.

3. Remove the beef from the marinade and pat it dry with paper towels. Strain the marinade, reserving the solids. Pick out the cloves and discard them. Season the beef with salt and pepper.

4. Heat the oil in a large ovenproof sauté pan or a Dutch oven over medium-high heat. Add the beef, in batches, and cook until browned on all sides. Set the beef aside and pour out all but 2 tablespoons of fat from the pan. Add the reserved solids from the

marinade and cook over medium heat, stirring, for 2 to 3 minutes. Cover the pan and cook until the vegetables begin to caramelize, about 5 more minutes. Stir in the hard cider and beef stock. Add the short ribs to the pan, with their fleshier sides down. The pieces should fit in a single layer. Bring the mixture to a boil, cover the pan, and set the pan in the oven.

5. Bake bone-in ribs until the meat is completely tender and readily pulls away from the bone, about 2 hours; boneless short ribs will cook in about $1^{1/2}$ hours. Remove the meat from the pan and set it aside.

6. Strain the braising liquid and discard the solids. Wait a few minutes for the fat to rise to the surface, or pour the juices into a fat separator and let stand a few minutes. Skim off the fat and discard it, or pour off the degreased liquid from the fat separator. Return the liquid to the pan (there will be 2 to $2^{1/2}$ cups) and whisk in the tomato sauce, applesauce, mustard, and Worcestershire sauce. Boil over medium-high heat, stirring occasionally, until the sauce is slightly thickened, 5 to 10 minutes. Taste and add salt and pepper if necessary. Add the beef to the pan and baste it well with the sauce.

7. Return the sauce to a simmer, cover the pan, and cook over medium-low heat until the meat is heated through. (You can make this dish a day or two ahead. When cool, cover and refrigerate; reheat it on top of the stove.) Serve hot.

jonagold

many wonderful apple varieties have been around for hundreds of years; others have come about during the last century as random mutations noticed by alert orchardists. Scientists have also gotten into the game, taking over nature's work. Jonagold is a wonderful example of how scientific breeding can result in a winner.

This big, juicy cross between Golden Delicious and Jonathan, bred at New York State's Geneva Station, has a wonderful sweet-tart flavor. In a blind taste test at a 1986 fruit show, Jonagold tied with Gala for second place, after Criterion. Unfortunately for the American consumer who is more concerned with taste than color in an apple, the conventional wisdom that we buy apples with our eyes instead of our taste buds means that this versatile variety can be hard to find. In Western Europe, where people are known to appreciate flavorful fruit, Jonagold is one of the most popular apple varieties, despite its yellow-green color and modest reddish blush.

Jonagold thrives in the moist climate west of the Cascade Mountains in Washington and British Columbia. It doesn't do well in harsher climates. Even though it makes a good sweet eating apple, its tartness and creamy texture hold up when cooked, making it good for pie.

Applesauce Meat Loaf

Applesauce adds moistness and a taste of freshness to an American classic. For the best texture, mix everything together quickly and gently with your hands. Overmixing produces a dense meat loaf. If diehards insist, go ahead and pass the ketchup or a barbecue sauce. Scalloped potatoes and steamed green beans are ideal to serve with this loaf.

MAKES 8 SERVINGS

2 pounds ground chuck
1 pound ground pork
½ cup finely diced red bell pepper
1 cup finely diced celery
1 medium onion, finely chopped
3 garlic cloves, finely chopped
½ cup chopped flat-leaf parsley
2 large eggs
1½ teaspoons salt
1 teaspoon freshly milled black pepper
1 cup unsweetened applesauce
½ cup ketchup
½ cup milk
½ cup fine dry bread crumbs
8 slices bacon

1. Adjust an oven rack to the center position and preheat the oven to 325°F. Coat a shallow roasting pan with cooking spray or lightly oil it.

2. Place the ground chuck, ground pork, bell pepper, celery, onion, garlic, and parsley in a large bowl; don't mix them yet. In another bowl, beat together the eggs, salt, pepper, applesauce, ketchup, and milk with a fork to combine well. Stir in the bread crumbs. Pour the mixture over the meat and fold everything together gently and quickly with your hands. Turn the mixture onto the prepared pan and pat it into a loaf shape about 11 to 12 inches long and 5 to 6 inches wide. Lay the strips of bacon crosswise over the loaf, edges touching, and tuck the ends under the loaf.

3. Bake for about 1½ hours, or until the juices run clear when the loaf is pricked with a fork. Let stand for 10 minutes before serving. Spoon any pan juices over the slices of meat loaf.

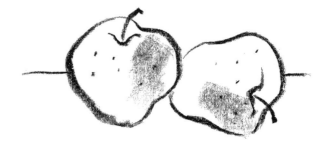

Hard Cider Burgers

These moist burgers can be served plain or on hamburger buns with all the trimmings. You can grill them over hot coals or cook them in a skillet on top of the stove.

MAKES 4 SERVINGS

1 tablespoon olive oil
1/2 cup finely chopped onions
1 garlic clove, minced
1/2 cup loosely packed fresh whole wheat sourdough or rye bread crumbs (see Note)
1 teaspoon salt
1/4 teaspoon freshly milled white or black pepper
1/2 teaspoon dried oregano, crumbled
1/2 cup hard cider
1 pound lean (15 percent fat) ground beef
1 tablespoon olive oil (if panfrying)
4 hamburger buns, split
Mayonnaise (regular or low-fat)
Lettuce leaves
Sliced tomato

1. If grilling, prepare a hot fire in a charcoal grill.

2. Heat the olive oil in a medium skillet over medium heat. Add the onions and garlic and stir occasionally until golden and tender, 5 to 8 minutes. Remove the pan from the heat and add the bread crumbs, salt, pepper, oregano, and hard cider. Stir well and set aside for 2 minutes to cool slightly.

3. Combine the cider mixture with the ground beef in a large bowl, tossing and mixing gently with a fork or your hands. Do not handle the mixture any more than necessary, or you may toughen the burgers. Shape the mixture into four 4-inch patties about 3/4 inch thick.

4. If grilling, place the burgers on the grill rack and cook about 3 minutes per side for medium-rare or to the desired degree of doneness. If cooking on top of the stove, heat the olive oil in a large skillet over medium-high heat. Add the burgers and cook for about 3 minutes on each side for medium-rare or according to your taste.

5. Meanwhile, toast the buns on the grill or under the broiler. Spread both halves with mayonnaise, and assemble the burgers with the lettuce, meat, and tomatoes.

Note: To make the crumbs, remove the crusts from one or two slices of fresh or day-old whole wheat sourdough or rye bread. Tear the bread into pieces and process them in a food processor to make coarse crumbs.

Cider-Marinated Flank Steak

Flank steak, which is very lean, easily picks up the flavors of this marinade. There are two secrets to a tender flank steak: Broil or grill it only until it is rare to medium-rare, and carve it into very thin slices with a sharp knife at an angle, almost parallel to your cutting board. Scoring the steak lightly before cooking prevents the meat from curling. For maximum flavor, marinate the steak for several hours or even overnight. Serve with mashed potatoes and buttered fresh peas or green beans.

MAKES 6 SERVINGS

1 beef flank steak (about 2 pounds)

MARINADE

2 cups apple cider
$1/4$ cup light soy sauce
2 tablespoons olive oil
2 tablespoons fresh lemon juice
2 tablespoons fresh lime juice
2 large shallots, finely chopped
1 tablespoon chopped fresh thyme
1 tablespoon chopped fresh rosemary
$1/2$ teaspoon freshly milled black pepper

1 cup beef stock
1 teaspoon sugar
Salt and freshly milled black pepper

1. Trim the membrane and visible fat and tendons from the flank steak. Lightly score the steak (don't cut into it more than $1/8$ inch) with a very sharp knife in a 2-inch crisscross pattern on both sides. Place the steak in a dish just large enough to hold it.

2. To prepare the marinade, combine the apple cider, soy sauce, oil, citrus juices, shallots, thyme, rosemary, and pepper. Lift the steak and pour some of the marinade under it, then pour the rest over the steak; the liquid should just reach the top of the meat. Cover the pan with plastic wrap and refrigerate for several hours, or overnight. Bring to room temperature before cooking.

3. Either adjust rack as close as possible to the broiler element and preheat the broiler, or prepare a hot charcoal fire. Remove the steak from the marinade, reserving the marinade, and allow the excess to drain off. Place the steak in a broiler pan or on a side dish and set it aside. Strain the marinade into a medium saucepan, add the beef stock, and boil the mixture until it is reduced to 1 cup. Taste carefully. The sauce tends to be a bit on the tart side. Adjust the seasoning with the sugar and, if necessary, salt and pepper. Keep the sauce warm while you cook the meat.

4. Broil or grill the steak for 3 to 4 minutes per side for rare to medium-rare. When done, the meat will feel only slightly springy to the touch; watch it carefully and test often.

5. Lay the steak on a carving board and let it rest for 1 to 2 minutes. Starting about 3 inches from one end, holding a very sharp long knife almost parallel to the board, cut a slice about $\frac{1}{8}$ inch thick, moving to the end of the steak. Continue to slice the meat and arrange the slices, overlapping them slightly, on a heated platter. Moisten the meat with some of the sauce and pass the rest at the table.

snow white and the poisoned apple

we are all familiar with the fairy tale of Snow White. Today, the version in the Disney movie is probably the best known. But how does it compare to the original? The story of Snow White is ancient, having been passed down orally through countless generations. No one knows how many versions exist, but folklorists have compared as many as a hundred at a time. Thus, no one can lay claim to knowing the "original" version. During the 1800s, the Grimm brothers in Germany collected oral tales and put them into books, setting in print limited versions of these old tales.

The story of Snow White evolved over the many Grimm editions too. In the first edition of the Grimms's *Nursery and Household Tales,* it is the girl's mother who becomes consumed with jealousy at her beauty and orders her murder. In the second edition, the mother dies and the wicked stepmother emerges. The version of the Grimm tale in a book from my (Dorothy's) childhood is quite different from Disney's film. The dwarfs play a minor role, and Snow White doesn't meet the prince until after she is in her sleeping trance. The piece of poisoned apple falls from her lips when the prince lifts the glass case in which she lies, not when he kisses her.

The death of the queen comes in at least three different ways. In the old Grimm versions, she dances herself to death in heated iron shoes. In my childhood book, she breaks her magic mirror in fury at finding out Snow White is alive and marrying the prince, and she falls dead as the mirror smashes. In the movie, she falls off a cliff to her death.

Interestingly, one constant through at least many of the versions is the poisoned apple, bright red and too tempting to be resisted. Can we say the same about a modern Red Delicious?

Smoky Pork Chops with Cabbage and Apple

This dish of pork chops, bacon, green cabbage, apples, onions, and garlic is practically a meal in itself. It goes together very quickly and cooks in little more than half an hour. Use a crisp apple that is more sweet than tart. Criterion, Gala, Arlet, and Sunrise are all good choices. Lacking these, opt for Braeburn.

MAKES 4 SERVINGS

4 ounces bacon (about 5 slices)
2 tablespoons olive oil
4 bone-in pork loin chops (about 1³⁄4 pounds)
Salt and freshly milled black pepper
Flour for dredging
1 large onion, thinly sliced
3 garlic cloves, finely chopped
2 large carrots, thinly sliced on the bias
1 medium head green cabbage
    (about 1¹⁄2 pounds), cut lengthwise in half,
    cored, and sliced crosswise into shreds
    (about 10 cups)
3 to 4 bay leaves
¹⁄2 cup dry white French vermouth or hard
    cider
2 large apples (1 pound), quartered, cored,
    peeled, and thinly sliced crosswise

1. Sauté the bacon in a large skillet over medium heat until browned and crisp. Drain on paper towels. Pour out all but 2 tablespoons of the bacon fat and add the olive oil to the skillet. Set the pan aside.

2. Season the chops with salt and pepper and dredge them lightly in flour. Set the skillet over medium-high heat. When the fat is hot, add the chops and cook on both sides until golden brown, 5 to 8 minutes. Remove the chops from the pan and set them aside.

3. Add the onion and garlic to the skillet. Cook and stir for 2 to 3 minutes. Add the carrots and cabbage and stir well, then add the bay leaves, vermouth, apples, 1 teaspoon salt, and ¹⁄2 teaspoon pepper. Stir well, cover the pan, and bring the mixture to a boil. Set the browned chops on top of the cabbage and apple mixture, cover the pan, and return to a boil. Reduce the heat to medium and cook until the chops are tender, 20 to 25 minutes. About 5 minutes before the chops are done, chop the bacon coarsely and sprinkle it over the chops and cabbage.

4. Remove the bay leaves and stir the bacon into the cabbage mixture. Taste and adjust the seasoning with salt and pepper. Serve immediately.

Roasted Pork Tenderloin with Sour Cream Cider Sauce

Apples are featured three times in this classic combination of pork and apples—apple, cider, and Calvados. The fruit is roasted and served with the pork, along with potatoes and onions. Use any crisp tart apple.

MAKES 6 SERVINGS

One 1¾-pound pork tenderloin
3 teaspoons olive oil
12 small red-skinned potatoes (1¼ pounds)
1 large yellow onion, cut into 6 wedges
1 large crisp cooking apple, quartered, cored,
    and cut into ¾-inch pieces
¾ cup apple cider
½ cup chicken stock
¼ cup Calvados or Applejack
Salt and freshly milled black pepper
½ cup sour cream
1 tablespoon minced flat-leaf parsley

1. Remove the tough white silverskin from the tenderloin with a sharp knife.

2. Adjust an oven rack to the center position and preheat the oven to 400°F.

3. Pat the pork dry with paper towels. Heat 2 teaspoons of the olive oil in a large heavy ovenproof nonstick skillet over medium-high heat. Add the pork and cook until well browned on all sides, about 5 minutes. Remove the pork and set it aside, covered loosely.

4. Add the potatoes to the skillet. Stir well and cook for 1 minute. Remove the potatoes and set them aside. Add the onion wedges cut side down to the skillet and cook until browned on their cut sides. Return the potatoes to the skillet and place the pan in the oven. Roast, uncovered, for 30 minutes.

5. Put the apple in a medium bowl and coat with the remaining 1 teaspoon olive oil. Add to the skillet with the potatoes and onion and bake for another 10 minutes. Remove the vegetables and apple to a platter; cover and keep warm.

6. Return the pork to the skillet and roast for 25 to 30 minutes, or until the temperature registers 150°F to 160°F on an instant-read thermometer. Add the pork to the vegetables and apples; cover and keep warm.

7. Add the apple cider, chicken stock, Calvados, and salt and pepper to taste to the skillet and set the pan over high heat. Bring to a boil, scraping up the browned bits from the bottom of the pan. Cook until the liquid is reduced to ½ cup. Add any juices from the vegetables, apples, and pork. Off the heat, whisk in the sour cream, then reheat the sauce briefly until hot but not boiling.

8. To serve, carve the pork into 12 slices and arrange 2 slices each in the center of six heated dinner plates. Place the onion wedges and apples on one side and the potatoes on the other side. Spoon the sauce over the pork and sprinkle with the parsley. Serve immediately.

the apple in the pig's mouth

the tradition of roasting a whole pig with an apple in its mouth goes way back to Germanic pagan rituals. Like other ancient gods, the boar god was thought to be reborn in the process of death, so a boar was sacrificed at Yule. To the old Scandinavians, apples were associated with resurrection, and the apple in the boar's mouth symbolized the rebirth of its heart-soul.

Pork Adobo with Apples

Usually regarded as the national dish of the Philippines, adobo (not to be confused with the Mexican adobo sauce) is a method of cooking in which virtually any kind of meat, fish, or vegetable is marinated in a garlicky cider vinegar brew and then cooked slowly in the marinade. After simmering, the meat is browned and cooked with more garlic, onions, peppers, corn, tomatoes, and apples. The tangy marinade is boiled down and thickened with applesauce. Be sure to use a nonreactive pot for marinating and cooking the pork, since an aluminum one imparts an off taste. The adobo can be cooked a day ahead and reheated. If so, however, don't add the apples until the dish is piping hot, or they will soften and cook too much. Use a crisp, tart apple, such as Granny Smith, Cortland, Criterion, Jonamac, or similar variety. Serve the adobo with hot basmati rice.

MAKES 6 SERVINGS

$^2/_3$ cup cider vinegar
$^1/_4$ cup light soy sauce
2 tablespoons sugar
Salt and freshly milled black pepper
10 garlic cloves, finely chopped
6 bay leaves

3 pounds boneless pork sirloin, cut into
2-inch pieces
1 cup smooth unsweetened applesauce
¼ cup vegetable oil
1 large yellow onion, thinly sliced
1 large jalapeño chile, seeded and finely
chopped
3 large bell peppers (preferably 1 each
green, red, and yellow), cored, seeded, and
cut into 1-inch pieces
2 ears corn, kernels cut from the cobs
4 Roma (plum) tomatoes, peeled, seeded, and
diced
2 large apples (1 pound), quartered, cored,
peeled, and cut into ¼-inch-thick julienne

1. Combine the cider vinegar, soy sauce, 1 cup water, the sugar, 1 teaspoon salt, 1 teaspoon pepper, slightly more than half the garlic, and the bay leaves in a large stainless steel or enameled saucepan. Add the pork and stir well. The liquid should just cover the meat. Cover and marinate at room temperature for 30 minutes to several hours, or in the refrigerator overnight.

2. Bring the adobo to the simmer, covered, over medium heat. Adjust the heat so that the liquid simmers very slowly and cook for about 1 hour, or until the meat is tender.

3. Strain the contents of the pan, reserving the liquid. Discard the bay leaves and cooked garlic and set the pork aside. Return the liquid to the pan and boil it

until it has reduced to 2 cups. Stir in the applesauce and set the mixture aside.

4. Heat the oil in a large skillet or sauté pan over medium-high heat. Add the pork and cook, stirring frequently, until browned on all sides. Remove the pork with a slotted spoon and set it aside. Add the remaining garlic, the onion, and jalapeño to the oil remaining in the pan. Cook, stirring for 3 to 4 minutes, until the onions are almost tender. Add the peppers and corn and cook, stirring, for 3 to 4 minutes. Add the tomatoes, pork, and adobo-applesauce mixture; stir well, cover the pan, and simmer for 3 to 4 minutes. (The adobo can be made several hours or a day ahead to this point; refrigerate when cool and reheat to a simmer before continuing.)

5. Add the apples, cover, and cook for 2 minutes, only until they are piping hot; the apples should remain somewhat firm. Serve immediately.

BEEF, PORK, AND LAMB

Pork Scaloppine with Apples and Calvados

Pork tenderloin makes a fine substitute for veal in this classic dish of apples, Calvados, and a little cream. Fresh tarragon is a surprisingly good pairing with apples. Use a crisp apple on the sweet side. Our first choice is Fuji, but Gala or Golden Delicious will also work. Some steamed green beans and crispy potatoes are wonderful with this.

MAKES 4 SERVINGS

2 large crisp, sweet apples (1 pound), quartered, cored, peeled, and cut into thin slices
1 tablespoon fresh lemon juice
One 1½-pound pork tenderloin
Salt and freshly milled black pepper
Flour for dredging
2 tablespoons unsalted butter
2 tablespoons olive oil
¼ cup Calvados
½ cup chicken stock
½ cup heavy cream
1 to 2 tablespoons finely chopped fresh tarragon, plus whole sprigs for garnish

1. Toss the apples in a bowl with the lemon juice. Set aside.

2. Preheat the oven to the lowest setting.

3. Remove the tough white silverskin fibers from the tenderloin with a sharp knife. Cut the tenderloin crosswise into ¾-inch-thick pieces. Place the slices between two sheets of wax paper or plastic wrap and flatten them gently with a meat pounder until they are about ¼ inch thick. Lightly salt and pepper the pork on both sides. Spread flour on a piece of wax paper.

4. Melt the butter with the oil in a large skillet over medium-high heat. When the butter foam subsides, quickly dredge about half the pork scallops in the flour, shaking off the excess. Add the pork to the skillet, without crowding the pieces, and sauté until browned and cooked through, about 2 minutes per side. Remove the pork from the skillet as it is done and place on a large ovenproof serving platter. Cook the remaining pork scallops the same way and add them to the platter. Keep the pork warm in the oven.

5. Pour the fat out of the skillet, replace the pan over medium-high heat, and add the Calvados and chicken stock. Bring to a boil, scraping up the browned bits in the bottom of the pan with a wooden spoon. Add the apples and any liquid to the pan and cook for 1 to 2 minutes. Add the cream and cook, stirring, until the sauce is slightly thickened. Taste and add the tarragon and salt (about ½ teaspoon) and pepper to taste. Pour the sauce over the pork, garnish with tarragon sprigs, and serve immediately.

Cider House Lamb Stew

An apple cider marinade both tenderizes lamb and imparts a subtle sweetness to the meat. Accompany the stew with crusty bread to sop up the juices.

MAKES 6 SERVINGS

3 pounds fully trimmed boneless lamb, preferably from the leg, cut into 2-inch chunks

4 cups apple cider

¼ cup olive oil, plus more if needed

I large yellow onion, coarsely chopped

3 garlic cloves, finely chopped

½ cup unbleached all-purpose flour

2 cups chicken stock

½ cup dry white French vermouth

Salt and freshly milled black pepper

3 bay leaves

One 3-inch cinnamon stick

Four 3 × 1-inch strips lemon zest (removed with a vegetable peeler)

3 medium carrots, cut into 1-inch pieces

1½ pounds red-skinned potatoes, cut into 1-inch pieces

I large green bell pepper, cored, seeded, and cut into 1-inch pieces

I large red bell pepper, cored, seeded, and cut into 1-inch pieces

1. Combine the lamb and 3 cups of the cider in a large nonreactive saucepan. The cider should just cover the meat. Cover the pan and refrigerate the lamb for several hours, or overnight.

2. Heat 2 tablespoons of the olive oil in a large pot over medium heat. Add the onion and garlic. Cook, stirring occasionally, until the vegetables are tender but not browned, 6 to 8 minutes. Remove from the heat and set aside.

3. Drain the lamb and discard the marinade. Pat the lamb dry with paper towels. Place the flour in a plastic bag. Heat the remaining 2 tablespoons olive oil in a large skillet over medium-high heat. Add about one-third of the lamb to the bag of flour and toss to coat evenly. Shake off the excess flour and add the lamb to the skillet, without crowding the pieces. Brown the lamb on all sides and transfer to the pot with the onions and garlic. Flour and brown the lamb in two more batches, adding more olive oil to the pan if needed.

4. Add the remaining 1 cup cider, the chicken stock, vermouth, 1 teaspoon salt, ½ teaspoon pepper, the bay leaves, cinnamon stick, and lemon zest to the pot. The liquid should just cover the lamb. Bring the mixture to a boil over medium-high heat. Cover the pot, reduce the heat to low, and simmer until the lamb is almost tender, about 1½ hours.

5. Add the carrots and potatoes and return the stew to a boil. Cover the pot, reduce the heat, and simmer until the vegetables are tender, about 15 minutes.

Add the peppers, cover the pot, and cook 5 to 8 minutes more, or until the peppers are crisp-tender. Taste and add more salt and pepper if necessary.

6. To serve, discard the lemon zest, bay leaves, and cinnamon stick and divide the lamb, vegetables, and broth among soup bowls.

Note: If you wish, substitute one 12-ounce bottle of hard cider for the 1 cup sweet cider and the vermouth in Step 4.

Lamb Tagine with Apples

A tagine is either a Moroccan stew or the cooking vessel the stew is cooked in. When made with lamb, tagines are sometimes flavored with preserved lemons for a sweet-sour contrast of flavors. Here we use tart cooking apples instead. Choose a variety that will hold its shape when cooked, such as Jonamac or Granny Smith. This is a robust stew for a fine fall meal. You can make it ahead and reheat it slowly. Serve with steamed couscous, the traditional accompaniment, or with basmati rice.

MAKES 6 SERVINGS

3 pounds fully trimmed boneless lamb, preferably from the leg, cut into 2-inch chunks
3 tablespoons olive oil
2 medium yellow onions, finely chopped
4 garlic cloves, finely chopped
2 tablespoons peeled and finely chopped fresh ginger
1 teaspoon ground cumin
6 cardamom pods
Two 3-inch cinnamon sticks
¹/₄ teaspoon saffron threads, crumbled
Salt and freshly milled black pepper
4 medium carrots, cut into 2-inch pieces
3 large tart cooking apples, quartered and cored
¹/₃ cup fresh cilantro leaves

1. Pat the lamb dry with paper towels. Heat 2 tablespoons of the oil in a wide deep pot over medium-high heat. Add the lamb in batches, and cook until browned on all sides, adding the remaining 1 tablespoon olive oil as needed. Remove the pieces of lamb as they are done and set them aside in a bowl.

2. Add the onions and garlic to the pot and stir well for about 2 minutes to dislodge the browned bits from the bottom of the pan. Add the ginger, cumin, cardamom, and cinnamon sticks and cook, stirring, for 1 minute. Add 3 cups water, the saffron, 1 teaspoon salt, $1/4$ teaspoon pepper, and the browned lamb, with any juices. Bring the tagine to a boil over medium-high heat. Cover the pot, reduce the heat to low, and simmer slowly until the lamb is very tender, about 2 hours.

3. Remove the lamb with a slotted spoon and set aside, covered. Remove the cinnamon sticks and cardamom pods and discard them. Add the carrots to the pot and cook, covered, over medium heat until just tender, about 10 minutes. Remove them with a slotted spoon and set them aside. Add the apples to the pot and cook over medium-low heat until just tender, 8 to 10 minutes. Taste the sauce and adjust seasoning with salt and pepper if necessary. Return the lamb and carrots to the pot and stir in the cilantro. Cover and heat over very low heat until the sauce is bubbling and the lamb and carrots are heated through. (The tagine can be made in advance, cooled, covered, and refrigerated. Reheat, covered, over very low heat, stirring occasionally until the tagine is piping hot.) Serve immediately.

creeping orchards

the love of apples runs deep. In the far, far north of Russia, in the inhospitable region called Siberia, only crab apples are hardy enough to grow naturally. Yet apple orchards cover tens of thousands of acres. How is this possible? The young trees are planted at an angle. As the trees grow and form branches, the branches are held down with wooden pegs. No branch rises more than three feet above the ground. In winter, the orchards are covered with snow, a natural insulator. In spring, the hunched-over trees bloom just like normal apples, and they bear a crop every year.

Lamb Shanks with Garlic

Lamb shanks browned in a little olive oil and braised in their own juices become so tender the meat practically falls off the bone. The key here is to use a heavy pan with a tight-fitting lid to minimize evaporation. Serve with buttered noodles, boiled potatoes, or lentils.

MAKES 4 SERVINGS

4 lamb shanks (about 12 ounces each)
Kosher salt
3 tablespoons olive oil
2 heads garlic, separated into cloves but not
    peeled
1/2 teaspoon herbes de Provence
Freshly milled black pepper
1 cup dry white French vermouth or hard cider
3 medium McIntosh apples, quartered, cored,
    peeled, and cut into 1/2-inch cubes
1/2 cup chopped flat-leaf parsley

1. Trim the excess fat from the lamb shanks and sprinkle them lightly with kosher salt. Heat the oil in a large heavy skillet over medium heat until hot but not smoking. Add the lamb and brown lightly on all sides, turning the shanks frequently. Add the garlic, cover the pan, and reduce the heat to very low. Cook for 1 hour, turning the shanks every 15 minutes or so.

2. Sprinkle the lamb with the herbs and pepper to taste. Continue to cook until the lamb is very tender, 1 1/2 to 2 hours total. If the lamb begins to sizzle and fry in the fat before it is tender, add about 2 tablespoons water, cover the pan, and continue cooking over very low heat, adding water as necessary to allow the lamb to braise, not fry. When the lamb is almost tender, allow any water in the pan to evaporate.

3. Remove the lamb and garlic from the skillet and pour out any fat in the pan. Return the pan to low heat and pour in the vermouth. Scrape the bottom of the pan to release the browned bits and stir in the apples. Return the lamb and garlic to the pan and sprinkle with the parsley. Cover and cook until the apples are completely soft and falling apart, about 15 minutes.

4. Remove the lamb; cover and keep warm. Pour the contents of the pan into a large sieve set over a bowl and press on the garlic and apples to force them through the sieve, leaving the garlic skins in the strainer. Return the mixture to the skillet, add the lamb, and stir to coat evenly with the sauce; there will be enough for a thin coating. Cover the pan and reheat briefly until very hot. Serve immediately.

Side Dishes

But I, when I undress me
Each night, upon my knees,
Will ask the Lord to bless me,
With apple pie and cheese.

—EUGENE FIELD,
APPLE PIE AND CHEESE

Some recipes in this chapter pair apples with cheese because they go so well together. Why is this so? Maybe it's cheese's tanginess in combination with apple's sweetness that makes the match so natural. So, is the sweet/salty principle at work when apples meet cheese? Or is it perhaps the sweet/sour qualities found in both working synergistically, so the resulting flavor is greater than the sum of its parts? I don't want to sound hifalutin' about all of this, but it is somewhat of a puzzlement.

Just about every other recipe in this chapter relies on some aspect of the sweet/sour interaction for its taste. In some cases, the sweet and sour ingredients are obvious (as when vinegar and apples are cooked together in Savoy Cabbage and Hard Cider), but not always (see Tricolor Peppers, Apples, and Onions). What matters is that the combination of apples and all sorts of vegetables, herbs, and seasonings tastes great.

Sautéed Apples

Apple slices cooked in butter are excellent with pork and duck dishes or on top of French toast or waffles. Use crisp, firm apples that will keep their shape when cooked and are more tart than sweet, such as Cortland, Winesap, Rhode Island Greening, Baldwin, or Esopus Spitzenberg.

MAKES 6 SERVINGS

4 large firm, tart apples, quartered, cored,
    and peeled
4 tablespoons (½ stick) unsalted butter
½ teaspoon sugar
Salt and freshly milled black pepper, optional

Cut each apple quarter into two wedges. Melt the butter in a large heavy skillet over medium-high heat. Sprinkle in the sugar. When the butter foam subsides, add the apple slices. Cook, turning the apples occasionally, until they are tender and golden brown with a few darker spots, about 5 minutes. Season lightly with salt and pepper if desired, and serve hot.

Note: You can quarter, core, peel, and cut up the apples ahead and put them into a bowl with 2 cups water and the juice of 1 lemon to prevent discoloration. Drain the slices and pat thoroughly dry on paper towels before cooking.

Apple and Asparagus Risotto

This recipe was inspired by Michele Scicolone's apple risotto in her marvelous book, *A Fresh Taste of Italy* (Broadway Books, 1997). When properly made, risotto is creamy, the rice tender but firm to the bite. Use a sweet, firm apple, such as Fuji for this recipe. For best results, use homemade stock. Beef is my first choice, but a rich chicken stock will also work. Because a risotto retains its perfection for only a few minutes, it should be served as its own course.

MAKES 4 SERVINGS

4 ounces fresh asparagus tips, cut on the bias
    into 1½-inch lengths (about 1 cup) (see Note)
3 to 3½ cups beef or chicken stock
2 tablespoons unsalted butter
1 tablespoon olive oil
1 medium sweet, firm apple, quartered, cored,
    peeled, and diced
¼ cup finely chopped shallots
1 cup arborio rice
½ cup dry white French vermouth
Salt and freshly milled black pepper
⅓ cup freshly grated Parmesan

1. Blanch the asparagus in 1 quart lightly salted boiling water for 1 minute. Drain well and place in a large bowl of cold water until cool. Drain and pat dry with paper towels. Set aside.

2. Bring the stock to a simmer in a medium saucepan; keep at a gentle simmer over medium-low heat.

3. Melt 1 tablespoon of the butter with the olive oil in a heavy medium saucepan over medium-high heat. Add the apple and stir and cook 2 to 3 minutes until the apple is golden brown. Remove with a slotted spoon and set aside. Add the shallots to the pan and stir for 30 seconds. Add the rice and stir constantly for 2 minutes, or until you hear a decided "clicking" sound as the rice is moved around the pan. Add the vermouth and continue stirring until it has evaporated.

4. Add 1½ cups of the beef stock, ½ cup at a time, cooking and stirring after each addition until it is absorbed. Add the apple, asparagus, and another ½ cup stock. Stir and cook until most of the liquid is absorbed. Add salt and pepper to taste and another ½ cup of stock and cook until it is absorbed. Stir in another ½ cup stock and continue stirring and cooking until the rice is tender but firm to the bite and the risotto has a creamy consistency. If necessary, add up to ½ cup more stock. Remove the pan from heat and stir in the remaining 1 tablespoon butter and the cheese. Serve immediately in heated bowls.

Note: Buy slightly more than 8 ounces of asparagus and cut 3 to 4-inch-long tips. Cut these tips into 1½-inch lengths on the bias. Save the stems for another use.

winesap

winesap is an apple that has stood the proverbial test of time. It is one of our oldest varieties and was once one of our favorites. No one knows for sure where it came from, but it's been around for more than two hundred years. However, its commercial popularity is waning. It used to be one of the most widely grown varieties in eastern Washington, but Red Delicious and Winesap's own offspring, Stayman, have pushed it out of many orchards. This is unfortunate, for this is an especially versatile apple. If cooked with the skin on and passed through a colander, it makes a delightfully pink sauce, and its slices hold their shape well in a pie, but it is such a good juice apple that much of the commercial crop is shunted into juice production. Unfortunately, that lowers the price growers receive, which discourages them from growing it.

Winesap is a good apple for the home orchard. It has lovely pink blossoms and produces abundant dark red fruit. It can be grown throughout the normal range of apple country, but the fruit tends to be small in more northerly areas. Another advantage for the home grower is that Winesap keeps well in the fluctuating temperatures of an unheated winter garage.

Red Cabbage with Apples

The classic combination of apples and red cabbage is associated with the cuisine of Alsace. The usual long, slow cooking is dispensed with in this recipe in order to preserve some of the cabbage's crunch. Use a tart, crisp, apple, such as Cortland or Granny Smith.

MAKES 6 SERVINGS

4 slices bacon, cut crosswise into ¼-inch strips
1 large onion, finely chopped
2 garlic cloves, finely chopped
1 small head red cabbage (about 1¼ pounds),
    cored and thinly sliced
3 tablespoons red wine vinegar
2 tablespoons sugar
2 large crisp, tart apples (about 1 pound),
    quartered, cored, and shredded
Pinch of ground cloves
¼ cup dry white French vermouth
Salt and freshly milled black pepper

1. Cook the bacon in a large skillet over medium heat, stirring occasionally, until crisp. Remove the bacon with a slotted spoon and set aside.

2. Add the onion and garlic to the fat in the pan and cook, stirring, for 2 to 3 minutes. Add the cabbage, vinegar, and sugar and stir well. Add the apples, cloves, vermouth, and salt and pepper to taste. Toss and stir constantly over medium-high heat for 3 to 4 minutes, or until the cabbage is tender but still has a bit of crunch.

3. Add the reserved bacon and stir well. Serve hot or warm.

Note: If you want the cabbage tender, cover the pan after all the ingredients have been added and cook over low heat for about 1 hour, stirring occasionally.

Savoy Cabbage in Hard Cider

Savoy cabbage is milder and sweeter than regular green cabbage, and it pairs exceedingly well with onions and apples. Apples get used three ways here—sliced fresh, as hard cider, and as cider vinegar. It's important to use a tart apple, such as Granny Smith. Serve this with pork roast or with just about any stew or ragout. Double the recipe if you have a large enough pan. Leftovers taste even better the next day.

MAKES 4 SERVINGS

2 tablespoons olive oil
2 large yellow onions, cut lengthwise in half
    and sliced $1/4$ inch thick
2 tablespoons cider vinegar
I teaspoon sugar
I pound savoy cabbage, cored and cut into
    $1/2$-inch-thick pieces (about 8 cups)
I large tart apple (8 ounces), quartered, cored,
    peeled, and thinly sliced crosswise
$1/2$ cup hard cider
$1/2$ cup chicken stock
$1/2$ teaspoon fennel seed, crushed
Salt and freshly milled black pepper

1. Heat the olive oil in a large skillet or sauté pan over medium heat. Add the onions, vinegar, and sugar. Stir well and cook, covered, until the onions have softened, about 10 minutes. Add the cabbage, apple, hard cider, chicken stock, fennel seed, $1/2$ teaspoon salt, and $1/4$ teaspoon pepper. Stir well and cover the pan. Cook, stirring occasionally, until the cabbage is completely tender, about 30 minutes.

2. At the end of cooking, there should be very little liquid left in the pan. If there is too much, cook uncovered over high heat, stirring and tossing the cabbage mixture, to evaporate excess moisture and to concentrate the juices. Add salt and pepper to taste and serve hot.

Cider-Glazed Carrots

Baby carrots cooked in sweet cider develop an almost creamy texture when simmered in a cider glaze and tossed with fresh mint and parsley.

MAKES 4 SERVINGS

One 1-pound bag peeled baby carrots
2½ cups apple cider
1 tablespoon finely grated orange zest
Salt and freshly milled black pepper
2 tablespoons unsalted butter
1 tablespoon sugar
1 tablespoon red wine vinegar
1 tablespoon finely chopped fresh mint
2 teaspoons finely chopped flat-leaf parsley

1. Place the carrots, 2 cups of the cider, 2 cups water, the orange zest, 1 teaspoon salt, and a few grindings of pepper in a medium saucepan. Cover the pan and bring to a boil over high heat. Reduce the heat to medium and cook until the carrots are almost tender, 8 to 10 minutes. Drain well and discard the liquid.

2. Melt the butter in a medium skillet over high heat. Add the remaining ½ cup cider, the sugar, red wine vinegar, and the carrots. Boil, stirring almost constantly, until the liquid is reduced to a syrupy glaze. Add the mint and parsley and salt and pepper to taste. Stir well and serve.

Sweet-and-Sour Mushrooms and Apples

Tender shiitake mushrooms and crisp, tart apple are a great combination to serve with other sweet-sour dishes or with grilled salmon or chicken. Because the apple should remain somewhat firm, make this just before serving. Use a crisp, tart apple, such as Granny Smith.

MAKES 4 TO 6 SERVINGS

2 tablespoons cider vinegar
2 tablespoons sugar
1 medium Granny Smith apple, quartered and cored, but not peeled
¼ cup olive oil
1 medium yellow onion, thinly sliced
1 pound fresh shiitake mushrooms, stems removed and caps sliced ¼ inch thick
Salt and freshly milled black pepper
3 tablespoons finely chopped flat-leaf parsley

1. Combine the cider vinegar and sugar in a medium bowl. Thinly slice the apple quarters on the bias and add them to the cider mixture; stir to combine well and set aside.

2. Heat the olive oil in a large skillet over medium heat. Add the onion and cook, stirring, for 2 to 3 minutes. Add the mushrooms and salt and pepper

to taste and stir well. Cover the pan and cook for 3 to 4 minutes, until the mushrooms are tender. Add the apple mixture and stir briefly just to heat the apples through. Don't cook them too much, or they'll lose their crunch. Stir in the parsley and serve immediately.

magic apples in greek legend

ancient greek myths sometimes feature the "golden apples of the Hesperides." You may have heard the phrase, but what were these magical fruits and what, or who, were the Hesperides? The Hesperides were, at most, seven maidens—sometimes only three or four—who guarded the golden apples, which were a wedding gift from Gaea, the earth goddess, to Hera when she married Zeus. The apples themselves are pretty mysterious and probably weren't apples at all, since the Greeks didn't grow them. The fruit came from the mysterious land where the Hyperboreans lived. Acquiring the fruit was a feat in itself, for the tree was guarded by a dragon who never slept.

The apples, which were said to bring eternal life, figure into Greek legend in a number of ways. The eleventh of the Greek hero Hercule's twelve labors was to get his hands on them. In one version of the story, Hercules took over the burden of carrying the world on his shoulders from Atlas. Atlas acquired the apples and refused to take back the world. But clever Hercules got him to hold the world "for just a moment," while he got shoulder pads. Needless to say, Atlas was stuck again, and Hercules took off with the apples. In other versions of the story, Hercules somehow manages to either kill the dragon or make it fall asleep and thereby gain the apples.

The apples really got around, despite the difficulty in obtaining them. In another story, the famous huntress Atalanta, who had killed Centaurs and could run like the wind, was encouraged by her father to marry. She challenged suitors to a race, stipulating that if they lost, they would die. But if anyone could beat her, he would gain her hand in marriage. A clever fellow named Meilanion took up the challenge, but he had a secret weapon. As he ran, he tossed out three golden apples given to him by Aphrodite (don't ask how she got her hands on them!). Atalanta stopped to pick them up and thereby lost the race—and gained a husband.

Apples in general seemed to mean trouble in ancient Greece—one, nicknamed the apple of discord, even led to the downfall of the legendary city of Troy. It seems that Paris, son of King Priam, was given the perilous task of choosing the fairest of the three highest Greek goddesses. The winner would get that pesky apple as her reward. Aphrodite won by bribing Paris, telling him she would get him the beautiful Helen as his bride—never mind that Helen was already married to Menelaus, King of Sparta. Paris snatched Helen away from Menelaus and took her to Troy. The Spartans and their allies eventually won, bringing about the fall of Troy.

Tricolor Peppers, Apples, and Onions

This pretty mixture of colored bell peppers, apples, and onions goes with just about any grilled meat or fish. Use a tart, crisp variety, such as Cortland, Winesap, Jonamac, or Granny Smith.

MAKES 4 TO 6 SERVINGS

2 tablespoons olive oil
1 large green bell pepper, cored, seeded, and
    cut into thin strips
1 large red bell pepper, cored, seeded, and cut
    into thin strips
1 large yellow or orange bell pepper, cored,
    seeded, and cut into thin strips
1 large yellow onion, thinly sliced
1 garlic clove, minced
$\frac{1}{4}$ cup beef or chicken stock
$\frac{1}{4}$ cup apple juice
Salt and freshly milled black pepper
1 large apple (8 ounces), quartered, cored, and
    thinly sliced crosswise
1 tablespoon finely chopped fresh thyme

1. Heat the olive oil in a large skillet over medium heat. Add the peppers, onion, and garlic. Cook, stirring occasionally, until the vegetables are almost tender, 5 to 8 minutes. Add the stock, apple juice, and a sprinkling of salt and pepper and raise the heat to high. Cook, stirring constantly, until the liquid has almost evaporated.

2. Add the apple slices and cook, stirring well, just to heat them through and soften them slightly. Taste for salt and pepper, adding more if necessary. Stir in the thyme and serve hot.

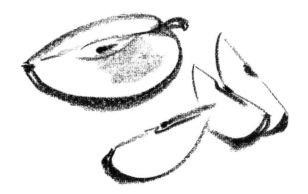

Apple and Potato Gratin

Serve this spicy, tangy side dish with grilled meats, fish, or poultry. Be sure to use a crisp apple that is sweet to the taste, not one that is tart. And use a boiling potato, such as Yellow Finn or Yukon Gold. I don't peel the apple or the potatoes, but I do slice them thin with the 2-mm slicing disk of a food processor. A mandoline or a sure hand with a large chef's knife will also do the trick.

MAKES 8 SERVINGS

I tablespoon olive oil
I cup thinly sliced leeks (including some
   of the tender green)
2 fresh poblano chiles, seeded and chopped
   (see Note)
I large crisp, sweet apple (8 to 9 ounces),
   quartered, cored, and thinly sliced crosswise
I large egg
2 cups milk
³/₄ teaspoon salt
¹/₄ teaspoon freshly milled black pepper
I¹/₂ pounds Yukon Gold potatoes, thinly sliced
I cup (4 ounces) shredded sharp or
   extra-sharp Cheddar cheese
2 tablespoons freshly grated Parmesan

1. Adjust an oven rack to the center position and preheat the oven to 425°F. Coat a 12 × 8 × 1³/₄-inch baking dish lightly with olive oil.

2. Heat the olive oil in a heavy medium saucepan over medium heat. Add the leeks and poblano chiles, stir well, and cook, covered, for 2 to 3 minutes. Add the apple slices and cook for 2 minutes, covered. Set aside.

3. In a medium bowl, whisk together the egg, milk, salt, and pepper until smooth. Arrange one-third of the sliced potatoes, slightly overlapping, in the prepared dish. Spread half the leek-apple mixture over the potatoes and sprinkle with half the shredded Cheddar. Repeat the layering with half the remaining potatoes, the rest of the leek-apple mixture, and the Cheddar cheese. Complete the layering with the last of the potatoes.

4. Bake for 20 minutes. Remove the baking dish from the oven and press on the potatoes firmly with a wide metal spatula to immerse them in the milk mixture. Return the gratin to the oven and bake for another 20 minutes.

5. Remove the dish from the oven and press down on the potatoes again. Sprinkle the Parmesan evenly over the top and bake until the top layer of potatoes is nicely browned with a thin crust, about 10 minutes more. Let the gratin stand for 5 to 10 minutes, then cut into squares and serve hot.

Note: If fresh poblanos aren't available, substitute 2 or 3 seeded and chopped fresh jalapeño or serrano chiles or a 4-ounce can of diced green chiles.

Potato, Onion, and Apple Pancakes

You can call these latkes if you want to. We think of them as creamy-centered, crusty potato pancakes. Be sure to use starchy potatoes such as Russet, red-skinned, or Yukon Gold. Or use a mixture. The apple adds a subtle mysterious presence. We like Jonagold or Braeburn. Serve the pancakes with applesauce.

MAKES 8 PANCAKES

1½ pounds potatoes
1 large yellow onion
1 large crisp apple, quartered, cored, and
   peeled
1 large egg
1 teaspoon salt
½ teaspoon freshly milled black pepper
3 tablespoons snipped fresh chives
Vegetable oil for pan frying

1. Peel the potatoes and coarsely shred them. Place in a bowl and shred the onion and then the apple into the potatoes. Mix well.

2. Turn the mixture into a large wire strainer set over a bowl. Press and squeeze the mixture forcefully so that the liquid drains into the bowl. Allow the liquid to stand for a few minutes. A layer of potato starch will settle to the bottom of the bowl.

3. Carefully pour off the liquid, leaving the starch in the bowl. Add the potato mixture, egg, salt, pepper, and chives and mix thoroughly.

4. Add vegetable oil to a large heavy skillet to a depth of about ¼ inch. Set the pan over medium heat. When the oil is shimmering and hot—but not smoking—divide the potato mixture into 8 portions. One by one, shape each between your palms into a round, about 3 inches in diameter and a scant ¾ inch thick. Squeeze firmly so that the mixture holds together (some liquid will be released in the process) and add to the pan. Cook for about 5 minutes per side, until nicely browned and cooked through. Transfer the pancakes to paper towels to drain briefly and serve immediately.

Note: You can make these several hours ahead and reheat them before serving. Place the pancakes on a baking sheet and reheat them in a 375°F oven for about 10 minutes, turning them once.

Cider Scalloped Potatoes with Smoked Gouda

Here is another dish that takes advantage of apple's natural affinity for cheese. Although cider will cause milk to curdle, a little flour prevents that from happening. Serve these potatoes with any grilled meat, sausage, or fish.

MAKES 8 SERVINGS

2 tablespoons unbleached all-purpose flour
1 cup milk
1 cup apple cider
$^1\!/_2$ cup chicken stock
$^1\!/_2$ teaspoon salt
$^1\!/_4$ teaspoon freshly milled black pepper
$^1\!/_8$ teaspoon freshly grated nutmeg
$^1\!/_2$ cup (2 ounces) shredded smoked Gouda cheese
$^1\!/_2$ cup (2 ounces) shredded Jarlsberg cheese
2 pounds Yukon Gold or Yellow Finn potatoes, peeled and thinly sliced

1. Adjust an oven rack to the center position and preheat the oven to 425°F. Lightly butter a round 10 × 2-inch baking dish or a rectangular 12 × 8-inch baking pan.

2. Place the flour in a heavy medium saucepan. Gradually add the milk, whisking until smooth. Whisk in the cider, chicken stock, salt, pepper, and nutmeg. Bring the mixture to the boil over high heat, whisking constantly. Cook for a few seconds more, then remove the pan from the heat and set aside.

3. Combine the cheeses and set them aside. Arrange half of the sliced potatoes, slightly overlapping, in the baking dish. Sprinkle with half of the cheese mixture and arrange the remaining potatoes on top. Pour the hot cider mixture over the potatoes.

4. Bake for 25 minutes. Remove the pan from the oven and press down on the potatoes with a metal spatula. Sprinkle with the remaining cheese and return the pan to the oven. Bake for another 20 minutes, or until the potatoes are tender and the top is browned. Let stand for 10 minutes before serving.

SIDE DISHES

Roasted Winter Vegetables with Herbs

The bounty of fall and winter is celebrated in this dish, a mixture of tastes, textures, and colors. Choose a firm, tart apple that will hold its shape during cooking. Granny Smith or Cortland are good choices.

MAKES 6 SERVINGS

**2 bunches small turnips (1 to 2 inches
    in diameter)**
2 large fennel bulbs
2 medium rutabagas
3 medium parsnips
**2 medium apples, quartered, cored, peeled,
    and cut crosswise in half**
3 tablespoons olive oil
⅛ teaspoon freshly grated nutmeg
Salt and freshly milled black pepper
¼ cup chopped flat-leaf parsley
2 teaspoons chopped fresh thyme

1. Adjust an oven rack to the center position and preheat the oven to 400°F. Coat a 15 × 10 × 1-inch nonstick jelly-roll pan with cooking spray.

2. Trim the root and stem ends from the turnips and cut the turnips into halves or quarters, depending on their size, so that the pieces are about 1 inch.

It's not necessary to peel the turnips if they're small. Trim the stalks and tough outer layers from the fennel bulbs. Halve and remove cores, and cut each half into ½-inch wedges. Peel the rutabagas and cut into 1-inch pieces. Do the same with the parsnips.

3. Combine the vegetables, apples, olive oil, nutmeg, and salt and pepper to taste in a large bowl, tossing to coat evenly. Spread the mixture in a single layer in the prepared pan and bake, stirring occasionally, for about 45 minutes, or until the vegetables and apples are tender and nicely caramelized; don't let them burn, or they might turn bitter. (The vegetables can be prepared hours ahead to this point, kept at room temperature, and reheated in the oven.)

4. Add the parsley and thyme to the pan and stir gently to combine well. Serve hot.

Italian Apple Stuffing

Pancetta, fennel, and fresh oregano give this stuffing a decided taste of Italy. Apples and hard cider contribute tartness and freshness. For best results, use a firm, tart apple such as Winesap or Granny Smith. Whether you stuff this into a turkey or simply bake it in a dish, start it a day ahead to allow the bread to dry out slightly. And don't feel you have to serve this just with turkey. A spoonful on the plate with meat loaf, roast chicken, roast pork, or grilled fish would be most welcome.

MAKES ABOUT 3 QUARTS

12 cups ½-inch bread cubes (made from day-old sourdough, Italian, or French bread; about 1¼ pounds crustless bread from a 2-pound loaf)
1 large fennel bulb, trimmed, cored, and diced; feathery tops reserved and chopped
½ pound pancetta
1 tablespoon olive oil
2 large yellow onions, chopped
3 large celery stalks, diced
1 large red bell pepper, cored, seeded, and diced
3 garlic cloves, finely chopped

4 medium crisp, tart apples (1½ pounds), quartered, cored, peeled, and diced
¼ cup chopped fresh oregano
2 tablespoons chopped fresh thyme
2 teaspoons salt
1 teaspoon freshly milled black pepper
2 large eggs
1 cup hard cider

1. Spread the bread cubes out on two shallow baking sheets. Leave at room temperature to dry overnight.

2. Chop enough of the reserved fennel tops to equal ½ cup and set aside (discard the remainder).

3. Cut the pancetta into strips about ¾ inch long and ¼ inch wide. Cook the pancetta in the olive oil in a large skillet or sauté pan over medium heat until browned and crisp. Remove with a slotted spoon and drain on paper towels. Reserve 3 table-spoons of fat and discard the remainder; set the pan aside.

4. Finely chop the pancetta and set it aside. Return the reserved fat to the pan and set the pan over medium heat. Add the onions, celery, bell pepper, fennel, garlic, and apples. Cook, stirring occasion-ally, until the vegetables and apples are crisp-tender about 10 minutes. Remove the pan from the heat and add the chopped fennel tops, oregano, thyme, salt, and pepper. Mix well and set aside to cool to room temperature.

5. Beat the eggs and hard cider together just to combine well. Place the bread cubes in a large bowl and add the cooled apple mixture, pancetta, and egg mixture. Fold everything together well.

6. The stuffing is now ready to be put into a 16-pound turkey. Stuff just before roasting. Or, if baking the stuffing alone, preheat the oven to 350°F. Turn the stuffing mixture into a 13 × 9 × 2-inch baking pan and cover tightly with foil. Bake for 1 hour and serve hot.

henderson lewelling, orchard pioneer

for some people, the challenges of daily life are not enough. They need big, perhaps insurmountable, obstacles to overcome, or they become bored. We can be thankful to such people, for they often bring about revolutions of one kind or another that otherwise might not have happened.

Such a man was Henderson Lewelling. After establishing a successful fruit nursery in Iowa in the 1830s, Lewelling heard the call of the west. So, in the spring of 1847, he prepared to depart for Oregon to bring fruit trees to the new land. He designed a covered wagon especially to carry his young trees, with two boxes filled with charcoal and earth. He selected about seven hundred plants—grapes, berries, quinces, pears, plums, cherries, and, of course, apples. With seven wagons in their party, Lewelling, his family, his business partner, and his precious cargo headed out on April 17.

In Missouri, the group joined up with a wagon train heading for Oregon. But before long, the other members of the train were complaining about Lewelling and his portable orchard. The heavily loaded nursery wagon moved slowly. The trees leafed out and required regular watering to stay alive. The others tried to get him to give up, to throw away his nursery stock, but he refused. Eventually, the rest of the train went on without him, and his little group had to go it alone.

Lewelling never gave up. His partner died along the way, as did some of his oxen and half of his trees, but Lewelling and his family finally arrived in the Willamette Valley on November 17, seven months after leaving Iowa.

Corn Bread, Pork, and Apple Stuffing

A southern-style stuffing made with an abundant amount of fresh herbs is ideal for a bird or as a side dish with just about any kind of meat. The jalapeño corn bread must be made a day ahead so that it dries out and will not fall apart. The best type of apple is a firm, tart one such as Winesap or Granny Smith, which will make a nice contrast to the sweetness of the pork and the spiciness of the corn bread.

MAKES ABOUT 3 QUARTS

CORN BREAD

2 cups yellow cornmeal

1 cup (4½ ounces) unbleached all-purpose flour (spooned into the cup and leveled)

2 tablespoons sugar

1 teaspoon salt

2½ teaspoons baking powder

½ teaspoon baking soda

3 large eggs

1½ cups buttermilk

2 large jalapeño chiles, seeded and finely chopped

⅓ cup corn oil

12 ounces pork sausage

3 tablespoons unsalted butter

½ pound crimini or oyster mushrooms, cleaned and diced

2 large onions, chopped

1 large red or yellow bell pepper, cored, seeded, and diced

4 medium firm, tart apples (1½ pounds), quartered, cored, peeled, and diced

¼ cup finely chopped flat-leaf parsley

2 tablespoons finely chopped fresh rosemary

2 tablespoons finely chopped fresh thyme

2 teaspoons salt

1 teaspoon freshly milled black pepper

1 cup chopped pecans

2 large eggs

½ to 1 cup hard cider

1. Adjust an oven rack to the center position and preheat the oven to 350°F. Coat a 13 × 9 × 2-inch baking pan with cooking spray.

2. To make the corn bread, in a large bowl combine the cornmeal, flour, sugar, salt, baking powder, and baking soda. In a medium bowl, beat the eggs lightly with a fork. Add the buttermilk, jalapeño peppers, and corn oil. Add this mixture to the dry ingredients and fold together with a rubber spatula just until the dry ingredients are thoroughly moistened. Spread evenly in the prepared pan.

3. Bake until the corn bread springs back when lightly pressed and a toothpick comes out clean, 25 to 30 minutes. Cool the corn bread in its pan for 10

minutes, then invert it onto a cooling rack and let stand for several hours to firm up a bit.

4. With a sharp serrated knife, cut the corn bread into ¾-inch cubes. Spread the cubes out on two shallow baking sheets and let stand at room temperature overnight.

5. Crumble the sausage into a large skillet or sauté pan and cook over medium heat, stirring occasionally, until browned. Transfer the sausage to paper towels to drain and discard the fat.

6. Put the butter in the pan and melt over medium heat. When the butter is hot, add the mushrooms. Stir and cook for 3 to 4 minutes, until the mushrooms are lightly browned and begin to release their juices. Add the onions, bell pepper, and apples and cook, stirring occasionally, until the vegetables and apples are crisp-tender, about 10 minutes. Remove the pan from the heat and add the parsley, rosemary, thyme, salt, pepper, and pecans. Mix well and set aside to cool to room temperature.

7. Beat the eggs and ½ cup of the hard cider together just to combine well. Place the corn bread cubes in a large bowl and add the cooled apple mixture, pork sausage, and egg mixture. Fold everything together well. If the stuffing seems dry, gradually add up to ½ cup more hard cider.

8. The stuffing is now ready to be put into a turkey; if so, stuff it just before roasting. Or, if baking the stuffing alone, preheat the oven to 350°F. Turn the mixture into a 13 × 9 × 2-inch baking pan and cover it tightly with foil. Bake for 1 hour and serve hot.

Apple Thises 'n' Thats

There's small choice in rotten apples.

—AMERICAN PROVERB

Apples may keep, but they don't keep forever. Fortunately, we can preserve them in all sorts of ways to have on hand all year round. Whether you're cooking apples for jelly, leather, chutney, butter, or relish, the key is to use the freshest in-season varieties. There's just no point in using apples that have been held in storage, because the apples won't be at their peak of flavor. Similarly, apple beverages will be most flavorful if made with pasteurized fresh cider or juice. So, for the best results and maximum enjoyment, think of the recipes in this chapter as pleasurable kitchen activities for the fall and early winter.

Caramel Apples

Apples and chewy caramel are made for each other. Sure, you could opt for store-bought caramels, melt them, and dip apples into the caramel. But where's the fun in that? Here you make your own caramel candy, which is far better than any supermarket variety you could buy. The caramel takes time and requires almost constant attention, but it is not difficult. You will need a candy thermometer.

MAKES 6 SERVINGS

6 medium crisp, tart apples
3 cups sugar
³/₄ cup light corn syrup
2 cups evaporated milk
  (not sweetened condensed milk)
1 tablespoon pure vanilla extract

1. Wash the apples and dry them thoroughly with paper towels. There must be no trace of water when the apples are dipped. Remove the apple stems and insert wooden skewers, chopsticks, or ice cream sticks through their stem ends, extending to their base. Set aside. Line a cookie sheet with aluminum foil.

2. Combine the sugar, corn syrup, and 1 cup of the evaporated milk in a heavy medium saucepan. Cook over medium to medium-high heat, stirring frequently with a wooden spoon, until the mixture comes to a boil. Stir constantly as the mixture boils and bubbles and rises almost to the top of the pan; if you keep stirring, the mixture will not overflow. Then cook, stirring constantly, for another 10 minutes.

3. Very gradually, add the remaining 1 cup evaporated milk. Continue stirring constantly as the mixture sputters and bubbles. The syrup will rise again almost to the top of the pan. Insert a candy thermometer and keep stirring and cooking until the syrup is very thick, bubbly, and caramel-colored and reaches 242°F (firm ball stage).

4. Immediately remove the pan from the heat and stir in the vanilla. Then, tipping the pan slightly so that the hot caramel collects in one spot, immerse an apple in the caramel. Twirl it a few times to coat completely, then remove the apple from the caramel and twirl it a few more times as the excess coating falls back into the pan. Lightly drag the base of the apple over the lip of the pan to remove additional caramel. Set the apple on the foil. Working quickly, coat the remaining apples with the remaining caramel. (If you have caramel left over, scrape it into a small foil-lined dish. Let it cool, then cut it into individual caramel candies.)

5. Let the apples stand until the caramel is completely cool and set, about 1 hour. They will keep at room temperature for 24 hours. Don't refrigerate them, as this makes them tacky.

Toffee Candy Apples

These apples are coated with a toffee-like syrup that hardens into a brittle candy. Anyone with a sturdy set of teeth will love them. You can use any crisp, tart apple. Granny Smith is a good choice. You will need a candy thermometer.

MAKES 6 TO 8 SERVINGS

6 to 8 medium Granny Smith apples
One 1-pound box dark brown sugar
$^3/_4$ cup unsulphured molasses
$^1/_4$ cup unsalted butter
1 tablespoon distilled white vinegar
Pinch of salt

1. Wash the apples and dry them thoroughly with paper towels. There must be no trace of water when the apples are dipped. Remove the apple stems and insert wooden skewers, chopsticks, or ice cream sticks through their stem ends, extending to their base. Set aside. Line a cookie sheet with aluminum foil.

2. Combine the remaining ingredients and $^1/_3$ cup water in a heavy medium saucepan and set the pan over medium heat. Cook, stirring occasionally, until the mixture comes to the boil. Cover the pan and boil for 3 minutes. (This dissolves any sugar crystals on the side of the pan.) Uncover the pan, increase the heat to medium-high, and attach a candy thermometer to the side of the pan. *Do not stir the sugar mixture.* Cook, swirling the pan occasionally by the handle, until the syrup reaches 290°F, (the hard crack stage) about 10 minutes. Swirl often toward the end of cooking to prevent scorching.

3. Immediately remove the pan from heat. Wait 20 seconds, then, tipping the pan slightly so that the hot syrup collects in one spot, immerse an apple in the syrup. Twirl it a few times to coat completely, then remove the apple from the syrup and twirl it a few more times as the excess syrup falls back into the pan. Lightly drag the base of the apple over the lip of the pan to remove additional syrup. Set the apple on the foil. Working quickly, coat the remaining apples with the remaining syrup.

4. Let the apples stand until the coating is completely cool and set, about 1 hour. The apples will keep at room temperature for 24 hours. Don't refrigerate them, as this makes them tacky.

Candy Apples

If there's one treat that brings back old memories of county fairs, this is it. I (Greg) remember running straight for the candied apple concession as soon as I entered the fairgrounds. Those bright red apples were absolutely irresistible. Considering the bad rap artificial dyes have gotten, I decided to omit them from the recipe. The results are far more interesting without dye, since the natural color of the apple skins shines through the glass-like candy coating. You will need a candy thermometer.

MAKES 6 TO 8 SERVINGS

6 to 8 medium crisp, tart apples
3 cups sugar
I cup light corn syrup

I. Wash the apples and dry them thoroughly with paper towels. There must be no trace of water when the apples are dipped. Remove the apple stems and insert wooden skewers, chopsticks, or ice cream sticks through their stem ends, extending to their base. Set aside. Line a cookie sheet with aluminum foil.

2. Combine the sugar, corn syrup, and I½ cups water in a heavy medium saucepan and set the pan over medium heat. Cook, stirring occasionally, until the mixture comes to a boil. Cover the pan and boil for 3 minutes. (This dissolves any sugar crystals on the side of the pan.) Uncover the pan, increase the heat to medium-high, and attach a candy thermometer to the side of the pan. *Do not stir the sugar mixture.* Cook, swirling the pan occasionally by the handle, until the syrup reaches 290°F, (the hard crack stage) about 10 minutes. Swirl often toward the end of cooking.

3. Immediately remove the pan from the heat. Wait 20 seconds, then, tipping the pan slightly so that the hot syrup collects in one spot, immerse an apple in the syrup. Twirl it a few times to coat completely, then remove the apple from the syrup and twirl it a few more times as the excess syrup falls back into the pan. Lightly drag the base of the apple over the lip of the pan to remove additional syrup. Set the apple on the foil. Working quickly, coat the remaining apples with the remaining syrup.

4. Let the apples stand until the coating is completely cool and set. The apples will keep at room temperature for 24 hours. Don't refrigerate them, as this makes them tacky.

Apple Trail Mix

When heading out for a hike or strenuous walk, carry some of this fruity mix in your backpack for a jolt of quick energy. Use dried apples that are pliable and on the moist side.

MAKES 3 CUPS

1 cup diced dried apples
⅓ cup dried blueberries
⅓ cup golden raisins
⅓ cup dark raisins
⅓ cup dried cranberries
½ cup dry-roasted mixed nuts or peanuts
½ cup sunflower seeds

Combine all ingredients in a zip-top plastic bag and refrigerate. The mix will keep for 1 week.

Apple Salsa

With its sweet/tart/spicy flavors, this colorful salsa goes with almost anything—chicken, fish, beef, pork, or grilled vegetables. I make it in the fall, when our garden has more green tomatoes than red, and local sweet apples are available at our farmers' market. Use a crisp, sweet apple, such as Fuji, Gala, or Honeycrisp. The food processor makes quick work of the chopping, but it's important to follow the method closely so that the salsa will be finely chopped and not mushy. If you prefer, chop the ingredients with a large chef's knife. Like all salsas, this one is best when freshly made, but it will keep for one to two days.

MAKES 2½ CUPS

**1 medium sweet apple (6 ounces), quartered
    and cored, but not peeled**
One 3-inch cube peeled jicama
½ medium red onion
½ seeded red bell pepper
¼ cup fresh cilantro leaves
**2 small tomatillos, husked, rinsed, and
    quartered**
1 medium green tomato, cut into 8 wedges
**1 fresh hot red chile, such as cayenne, seeded
    and finely chopped**
½ teaspoon salt
1 tablespoon fresh lime juice

APPLE THISES 'N' THATS

Cut each apple quarter into fourths. Cut the jicama into 8 pieces. Cut the onion and bell pepper into fourths. Place the apple, jicama, onion, bell pepper, and cilantro to the work bowl of a food processor fitted with the metal blade. Pulse 3 times (about 1 second each). Scrape the side of the work bowl. Add the tomatillos, green tomato, hot pepper, salt, and lime juice. To achieve an even fine chop, pulse very rapidly about 6 times. (Very rapidly means each pulse should last a fraction of a second.) Scrape the work bowl and check the consistency. If you like your salsa finer, pulse very rapidly 2 or 3 times more. Serve, or transfer to a container, cover, and refrigerate until needed. (The salsa will keep for 1 to 2 days. Bring to room temperature before serving.)

Note: If you can't find jicama, use another medium apple instead of the jicama. If a green tomato isn't available, substitute a red one. Be careful handling the hot pepper; use rubber gloves and wash your hands thoroughly after preparing it. Irritating oils, particularly in the membrane and the seeds, can cause serious irritation.

roxbury russet

roxbury russet is the antique of antique American apples—no other American variety worth growing has been around so long. Experts figure it came from a seedling that sprouted early in the 1600s near Roxbury, Massachusetts. That early, its parents would almost certainly have been English varieties, since that was just about all that lived along the East Coast in those days.

You'll never find Roxbury Russet in your grocery store—its russeted green skin and somewhat irregular shape won't sell it. But if you're lucky enough to taste one, you'll wish you could buy them. The flavor is difficult to describe—it has a tart richness at first bite, but actually contains plenty of sugar. If you like it, you'll need either to cultivate the right friends or grow a tree for yourself. Juice made from only Roxbury Russet is quite sweet, and this variety is popular for use in cider mixes. Fortunately, Roxbury Russet does well in the home garden, even here in Montana, where winters can be pretty harsh. It is resistant to the most common apple diseases—fire blight, scab, and mildew—and it stores well.

Apple, Beer, and Green Chile Relish

This quickly made cooked relish is especially good with roast turkey, pork, or beef or turkey burgers. Use a crisp, tart apple, such as Granny Smith, Cortland, Winesap, or Newtown Pippin. Braeburn will also work well.

MAKES ABOUT 4 CUPS

2 tablespoons olive oil
2 garlic cloves, finely chopped
1 large onion, finely chopped
4 large apples (about 2 pounds), quartered,
    cored, peeled, and diced
³/₄ cup light Mexican beer, such as Corona
One 7-ounce can diced green chiles
2 jalapeño chiles, seeded and finely chopped
¹/₄ cup distilled white vinegar
2 tablespoons firmly packed light brown sugar,
    or more to taste
Salt and freshly milled black pepper

Heat the olive oil in a large nonreactive skillet over medium heat. Add the garlic, onion, and apples. Cook, stirring, for 5 to 8 minutes, until the onion and apples are translucent but not completely tender. Add the beer, ³/₄ cup water, the canned and fresh chiles, the vinegar, brown sugar, ¹/₂ teaspoon

salt, and ¹/₄ teaspoon pepper. Bring the mixture to a simmer and adjust the heat so that the mixture simmers slowly, uncovered, until the relish is the consistency of applesauce, 20 to 30 minutes. Add more water, if necessary. Taste and adjust the seasoning with salt, pepper, or brown sugar if necessary. Cool completely before serving. The relish will keep, covered in the refrigerator, for about 3 weeks.

APPLE THISES 'N' THATS

Apple-Rhubarb Chutney with Lemongrass and Ginger

Take advantage of worldwide shipping and make this chutney in the spring when rhubarb is plentiful and the first apples from south of the equator are in the markets. Any firm, sweet/tart cooking apple, such as Braeburn or Gala, will work well. Chutneys develop flavor during storage, and this one is no exception, but it is also delicious freshly made. Serve it as is, or combine it with yogurt to make a raita. It is excellent with grains, grilled fish, pork, or poultry. Double the recipe if you wish.

MAKES 5 TO 6 CUPS

2 pounds crisp cooking apples, quartered, cored, peeled, and cut into $1/2$-inch dice (about 6 cups)
$1/2$ pound rhubarb, trimmed and cut into $1/4$-inch dice (about 2 cups)
1 cup golden raisins
1 tablespoon mustard seed
1 cup cider vinegar
$1^1/3$ cups granulated sugar
$1/4$ cup firmly packed light or dark brown sugar
2 tablespoons fresh lime juice
$1/4$ to $1/2$ teaspoon hot pepper flakes
2 tablespoons peeled and finely shredded ginger
1 stalk lemongrass, bulb end flattened with a knife, cut into 2-inch lengths, and tied in a bundle with kitchen twine

1. Stir all the ingredients together in a heavy nonreactive saucepan. Cover the pan and bring the mixture to a simmer over medium-low heat. Uncover the pan and simmer, stirring occasionally with a wooden spatula, until the chutney is thick enough to hold a soft shape, about 2 hours. When you draw the spatula through the chutney, the bottom of the pan will be visible for a second or two. Discard the lemongrass.

2. Transfer the chutney to sterilized half-pint canning jars, leaving $1/2$ inch of headroom. Seal and process in a boiling-water bath for 10 minutes. Cool completely. Properly processed and sealed, the chutney will keep for at least 1 year. Otherwise, store it in the refrigerator, where it will mellow for up to 1 month.

Apple-Cranberry Relish

A nice change-of-pace relish to serve with hamburgers or hot dogs—actually, it's delicious with roast or grilled pork and chicken too. Use a firm, tart apple that will not fall apart during cooking, such as Granny Smith, Newtown Pippin, Jonamac, or a similar variety.

MAKES ABOUT 4 CUPS

**3 medium firm, tart apples (about 1 pound),
   quartered, cored, peeled, and diced**
3 cups fresh or frozen cranberries
²/₃ cup maple syrup
2 tablespoons peeled and minced fresh ginger
Grated zest of 1 lemon
2 tablespoons fresh lemon juice
Pinch of ground allspice

Combine all the ingredients with ¹/₂ cup water in a heavy nonreactive saucepan. Bring the mixture to a boil over medium-high heat, stirring occasionally. Reduce the heat to low and cook, stirring constantly, until the apples are tender and the relish is thickened, about 10 minutes. Cool. (Stored airtight in the refrigerator, the relish will keep for 2 to 3 weeks. Bring to room temperature before serving.)

Variation: For more heat, add 1 jalapeño chile, seeded and finely chopped, before cooking.

Spicy Apple-Kumquat Chutney

Serve this chutney with curries, grilled meats, lentils, or just about anything. Be sure to use firm, tart, apples—Granny Smith or Newtown Pippin—that will hold their shape when cooked so that the chutney maintains a chunky texture.

MAKES ABOUT 5 CUPS

¹/₂ pound kumquats
**6 medium firm, tart apples (2 to 2¹/₄ pounds
   total), quartered, cored, and peeled**
2 jalapeño chiles, seeded and finely diced
**1 ounce fresh ginger, peeled and finely
   shredded**
1 teaspoon salt
1 cup (5 ounces) dried cherries
1 cup cider vinegar
1¹/₄ cups firmly packed light brown sugar
¹/₂ cup fresh cilantro leaves

1. Drop the kumquats into 2 quarts boiling water and cook for 30 seconds. Drain and put the fruit into a large bowl of cold water. When cool, drain well and pat dry on paper towels. Cut the kumquats into quarters.

2. Cut each apple wedge lengthwise into thirds and then crosswise into thirds. Combine all the ingredients in a heavy nonreactive saucepan and set the pan over medium-high heat. Stir occasionallly as the mixture comes to the boil. Reduce the heat to medium-low and cook at a slow simmer, stirring occasionally, until the chutney is thick and the fruit tender, about 1 hour. The liquid should be syrupy, don't cook until all the liquid is absorbed.

3. Transfer the chutney to sterilized half-pint canning jars, leaving $^1/_2$ inch of headroom. Seal and process in a boiling-water bath for 10 minutes. Cool completely. Properly processed and sealed, the chutney will keep in a cupboard for at least 1 year. Alternatively, if you're going to use the chutney within 1 month, you can cool the cooked chutney and store it airtight in the refrigerator.

pioneer fruit

one reason apples are so identified in our minds as an American fruit is their importance to early pioneers. Apples harvested in the fall were stored in the root cellar, which was dug away from the house. Because it was underground, the fruits and vegetables stored there stayed cold but were protected from freezing. Apples were laid between layers of straw and then removed as needed. Varieties that stored well were especially prized. Apples that would not last in storage were cut into rings and dried for other uses.

Not only did apples provide a vital source of vitamins and other nutrients during the long winter, they were also a source of material for artistic endeavors. Twigs from apple trees were boiled to yield a lovely pale green dye for wool from the farmer's sheep. Circles of dried apples were used to decorate the Christmas tree simply by hanging them over branches or by stringing them and looping the strings onto the tree. Whole small fruit also made shiny red decorations.

Making apple dolls, which you can still find today at crafts fairs during the holidays, was a favorite pastime during the long winter months. The apple was peeled and the rough features of a human face were carved into the fruit; then it was salted, brushed with lemon juice, and hung up to dry. As the apple shriveled, the face began to take on a personality, and the artist would help it along by shaping, gently pinching here and there. She used pins or cloves for eyes and might fashion a pair of glasses from a bit of wire. Eventually the face would inspire the rest of the doll, and the dollmaker would add a bit of carded wool for hair, make a cap, and add a stick for a body and the clothes. The charming result was a unique and special creation.

Apple Barbecue Sauce

This thick, caramel-colored sauce is easy to make, cooks quickly, and can be used as a baste on hamburgers, buffalo burgers, grilled chicken, turkey, or roast pork. Add some to meat loaf mixtures to flavor and moisten the meat. Use a cooking apple that is on the tart side, such as McIntosh or Jonamac, or any local variety that will cook to a thick purée without becoming watery.

MAKES ABOUT 4 CUPS

1 tablespoon vegetable oil
1 large red onion (8 ounces),
    coarsely chopped
4 garlic cloves, coarsely chopped
2 tablespoons peeled and coarsely chopped
    fresh ginger
1 jalapeño chile, seeded and
    coarsely chopped
2 pounds apples, quartered, cored, peeled, and
    cut into chunks
3/4 cup cider vinegar
1/4 cup firmly packed dark brown sugar
1/4 cup unsulphured molasses
1 tablespoon Dijon mustard
2 tablespoons tomato paste
1 tablespoon sweet paprika
1 teaspoon salt

1. Heat the oil in a heavy nonreactive medium saucepan over medium heat. Add the onion, garlic, ginger, and jalapeño. Stir well, cover the pan, and cook over medium-low heat, stirring occasionally, until the vegetables are tender, about 10 minutes. Add the apples and vinegar. Cook, covered, stirring occasionally, until the apples are very tender and beginning to fall apart, about 30 minutes.

2. Beat the sauce with a wooden spoon to make a smooth mixture and add all the remaining ingredients. Cook, stirring constantly, over medium-high heat for 5 minutes. Cool, and serve at room temperature. (The sauce keeps in the refrigerator, in an airtight container, for up to 1 month.)

Apple Butter

Thick, homemade apple butter makes a wonderful spread on toasted bread or English muffins. Apple butter should be made with late-season fall apples: Winesap, Cortland, Northern Spy, York Imperial, and the like. Use a mixture of tart and sweet varieties for best results.

MAKES ABOUT 3 CUPS

3 cups apple cider
3 pounds apples (a mixture of sweet and tart),
    quartered, cored, peeled, and thinly sliced
Finely grated zest of 1 lemon
3 tablespoons fresh lemon juice
¹/₂ teaspoon salt
1 cup sugar, or more to taste
¹/₂ teaspoon ground cinnamon
¹/₂ teaspoon ground mace

1. Boil the cider in a heavy nonreactive saucepan until reduced by half, about 10 minutes. Add the apples, lemon zest, lemon juice, and salt. Return the mixture to a boil, cover the pan, and reduce the heat to medium to medium-low. Cook, stirring occasionally, until the apples are completely tender, 30 to 40 minutes.

2. Purée the apple mixture with an immersion blender or in batches in a blender or food processor.

Return the purée to the pan and add the sugar and spices. Stir well and taste the mixture. If you feel it needs more sugar, add a little but not too much, since the mixture will cook down considerably and concentrate the sweetness.

3. There are several options for cooking the apple butter: If you have a slow cooker, you can cook the purée, covered, on a medium-high to high setting for about 8 hours, or until it is very thick. Or transfer the purée to a 13 × 9 × 2-inch baking pan and place it in the center of a preheated 350°F oven. Stir occasionally until the mixture reaches a boil, then reduce the heat to 250°F and bake, stirring occasionally, until the butter is very thick. This may take 4 to 6 hours. You can also cook the apple butter on top of the stove in a large saucepan over medium heat. Stir almost constantly as the mixture bubbles, and cook until it is thick, about 2 hours. In all of these methods, taste the butter as the mixture cooks down and add more sugar if necessary. The butter is ready when it measures about 3 cups.

4. Divide the apple butter among hot sterilized ¹/₂-pint jars, seal tightly, cool to room temperature, and refrigerate. Or transfer the butter to airtight freezer containers, and cool uncovered, then cover and refrigerate or freeze. The apple butter will keep, refrigerated, for at least 1 month, and for 6 months or more in the freezer.

crab apples are a familiar feature of the American landscape, especially the tiny-fruited decorative varieties that burst into giant pillows of pink blossoms in the spring. The term *crab apple* is confusing, for it doesn't refer to a particular species of fruit. Most people use the word for any small-fruited member of the genus *Malus,* to which the apple belongs. Some experts define a crab apple as any species of *Malus* with fruits under two inches in diameter. The problem with that definition is that a very old apple variety, the Lady apple, is in that size range.

The crab apple is a different group of species and hybrids from the regular apple, but its pollen will fertilize apple flowers, which makes even crab apples with miniscule fruit useful as well as decorative. Crab apples are partly derived from two species from frigid Manchuria, so the trees are especially hardy and can be grown farther north than regular apples. This gives northern gardeners, even in Quebec, northern Vermont, and Minnesota, an opportunity to grow something at least resembling an apple and to have beautiful flowering trees in their spring gardens. And even though they are cold-weather champs, crab apples also do well in the southern part of the apple's range.

The small fruits of crab apples are generally tarter in flavor than regular apples and contain generous quantities of pectin, making them ideal for jelly. Good varieties for the home garden are Centennial, Young America, Wickson, Whitney, and Martha. All of these are good for eating raw, pickling, and mixing with apples for cider. Dolgo is especially fine for making jelly; it is also one of the hardiest of fruit varieties. Other good varieties include Chestnut, Hyslop, and Rescue. All of these are beautiful additions to any garden.

Apple Jelly

Homemade jellies are easy to make and are great gifts. Use any tart, crisp fall apples or crab apples. You will need a candy thermometer, jelly bag, and canning jars, lids, and rims, all of which you can usually find during the summer and fall months in well-stocked supermarkets or hardware stores.

MAKES ABOUT 4 CUPS

4 pounds crisp, tart apples, cut into eighths, or crab apples, quartered
1 lemon, quartered
Sugar

1. Place the apples and lemon in a large nonreactive saucepan and add water to barely reach the top of the fruit. Bring to a boil over medium-high heat, then cover the pan and adjust the heat so that the mixture simmers slowly. Cook, stirring occasionally, until the apples are very soft, about 1 hour.

2. Pour the contents of the pan into a jelly bag suspended over a bowl and leave it for several hours to drain. Do not agitate the bag or press on the fruit, or the jelly will be cloudy instead of sparkling.

3. Measure the juice and transfer it to a medium saucepan. Add ¾ cup sugar for each cup of juice. Stir over medium heat, without boiling, until the sugar has dissolved. Raise the heat to medium-high and boil the mixture, stirring occasionally, until the jelling point, 221°F is reached (see Note). As the mixture cooks, skim off any scum that forms. When the jelly is ready, take the pan off the heat and let it stand for 10 minutes.

4. Ladle the jelly into hot sterilized jars, cover with the lids, and secure them tightly with the metal bands. Invert the jars for 5 minutes, then stand the jars upright. They should seal on their own as they cool. Or process the filled jars in a boiling-water bath for 10 minutes. Cool them completely. Jars that have sealed, whether in a processed water bath or not, can be stored in a cool cupboard for 6 months or more. Any unsealed jars should be stored in the refrigerator, where the jelly will keep for 3 to 4 weeks.

Note: Jellies usually set at a temperature of 8°F above boiling at sea level (220°F). To be sure of a proper set, place two or three saucers in the freezer to chill before you begin cooking the juice with the sugar. When a candy thermometer registers close to the gelling point, remove the pan from heat and place a small dab of jelly onto a chilled plate. Push into the jelly from the edge with the tip of a metal teaspoon. If wrinkles form on the surface of the jelly, it's ready. If not, return the pan to the heat and continue cooking. Repeat the gel test. Once in jars, it may take a day or more for the jelly to set completely.

Minted Apple Jelly: Add 6 to 8 sprigs of fresh mint to the apples and lemon. Cook and strain in the jelly bag as directed.

Apple Leather

Homemade apple leathers are moist and chewy and taste only of apple, with no added sugar. Apples with a good sweet/tart balance such as Newtown Pippin or any russet variety are our first choices. The best time to make apple leather is in the late fall, when these varieties become available. Make several batches while the apples are really good, since the leathers keep for weeks in the cupboard and months in the freezer.

MAKES TWO 15 × 10-INCH SHEETS

4 pounds apples, quartered, cored, and peeled
1½ cups apple cider, plus more if needed
Pinch of ground cinnamon
Cornstarch for dusting

1. Lightly oil two nonstick 15½ × 10½ × 1-inch jelly-roll pans or coat with cooking spray. Adjust two oven racks to divide the oven into thirds, but don't turn the oven on.

2. Process the apples in batches in a food processor until finely chopped. Transfer the apples plus any juices to a large saucepan. Add the cider and cinnamon and set the pan over medium-low heat. Cover the pan and cook, stirring occasionally, until the apples are very soft, about 20 minutes.

3. Uncover the pan and continue cooking, stirring frequently, until the apples hold a soft shape in a spoon, 20 to 30 minutes. The consistency will be somewhat like apple butter or soft jam. To prevent scorching, stir the apples often toward the end of cooking. If the mixture seems too dry, add a bit more cider. You should have about 3 cups of cooked apple.

4. Place half of the mixture on each prepared baking sheet and spread it into a thin even layer with a spatula. Place the pans in the oven, prop the door ajar, and turn the oven on to the lowest setting. Apple leather takes anywhere from 12 to 24 hours (sometimes less, sometimes more) to dry out, depending on the type of apple you used, how thick a layer you spread in the pan, and the ambient humidity. If you begin this at night, you can simply leave the pans in the oven all night long. If you start it in the morning or afternoon, rotate the pans top to bottom and front to back every 3 hours or so. The leather is done when it is pliable and no longer feels sticky. If the leather still feels sticky after being in the oven for most of the day, let it sit at room temperature during the night and resume the drying the next day.

5. Remove the pans from the oven and let the leather stand until cool. Carefully peel the leather off the pans and place on your countertop. Sprinkle both sides lightly with cornstarch and rub with your fingers to make a thin even coating. To store, enclose each sheet of leather between two layers of plastic wrap, roll it up, tuck it into a plastic bag, and seal the bag.

the story of aplets

in the 1920s, two young Armenian immigrants, Mark Balaban and Armen Tertsagian, purchased an orchard in Washington State's fertile Vale of Cashmere. Blessed with a climate that was perfect for apple trees, the two partners soon were harvesting more fruit than they could sell. They hit upon the idea of making *lokoum,* the candy they had enjoyed as children, using fresh apple juice and walnuts. The results were better than they had expected, and the candy became a hit. At first, they sold their candy at county fairs, but after receiving numerous requests by mail, the confection became a highly successful mail-order business. Today, Liberty Orchards, which markets Aplets and other candies, is in its third generation of family management.

Apple Gels

Apple candies known as Aplets are sold commercially. They have a marvelous chewy texture and great apple flavor. The real thing is made with apple pectin, citrus pectin, natural flavors, and other ingredients and is based on the Turkish classic *rahad lokoum.* This recipe comes mighty close to what you can buy. You'll need to make your own silky-smooth applesauce for the candies. If you have a power strainer attachment for your food processor, it will make a gossamer-like applesauce. Lacking that, use the finest holes of a food mill. Use a sauce apple, such as McIntosh or Macoun, if possible. For best results, let the candy age for several days at room temperature for its special texture to develop.

MAKES ABOUT 4 DOZEN PIECES

2½ pounds apples, cut into eighths
2 envelopes unflavored gelatin
½ cup apple juice or apple cider
2 cups granulated sugar
¼ teaspoon salt
¼ cup fresh lemon juice
1 cup chopped walnuts
Confectioners' sugar for dusting

1. Combine the apples with ½ cup water in a large heavy saucepan. Cook, covered, over medium heat,

stirring occasionally, until the apples are very soft, about 45 minutes. Add up to ½ additional cup of water if needed during cooking. Strain the apples through the power strainer attachment of a food processor or through the finest holes of a food mill. You will have about 2½ cups of purée. You only need 2 cups for this recipe.

2. In a cup, sprinkle the gelatin over the apple juice; set it aside. Combine 2 cups of the applesauce with the sugar and salt in a heavy medium saucepan. Bring to a boil over high heat, stirring constantly. Reduce the heat to medium and cook, stirring frequently, until the mixture is as thick as apple butter, 30 to 40 minutes.

3. Add the gelatin mixture to the saucepan and stir and cook for 1 minute, only until the gelatin is dissolved. Do not cook too long, or the gelatin may lose its setting capacity. Remove the pan from the heat and stir in the lemon juice. Cool to room temperature, stirring occasionally, then stir in the walnuts.

4. Lightly coat an 8-inch square baking pan, preferably nonstick, with cooking spray. Scrape the apple mixture into the pan and spread it level. Let the candy set at room temperature, or refrigerate it for an hour or two to speed the process.

5. Unmold the candy (it will come loose with the aid of a table knife) onto a work surface lightly dusted with confectioners' sugar. With a sharp heavy knife, cut the candy into 48 squares. Coat each piece lightly with confectioners' sugar and space them about 1 inch apart on a wax paper–lined jelly-roll pan. Leave them at room temperature, loosely covered with another inverted jelly-roll pan, for 4 to 5 days. Keep the top pan slightly askew so air can circulate around the candies. Turn the gels over once a day. During this time, the sugar will deliquesce and the candies will develop a marvelous chewy texture, reminiscent of the commercial Aplets.

6. Just before serving, coat the candies again with confectioners' sugar, and arrange them on a plate. (Once the candies have cured, they keep well, refrigerated, for about 2 weeks.)

APPLE THISES 'N' THATS

Winter Apple Punch

This heady combination of citrus, cider, rum, and spices is a great cold-weather pick-me-up.

MAKES 1½ QUARTS; 12 SERVINGS

3 oranges (use blood oranges, if available)
2 lemons (Meyer lemons, if available)
One 3-inch cinnamon stick
6 cardamom pods
6 allspice berries
6 whole cloves
6 cups apple cider
I cup light rum
Sugar, if necessary

1. Remove the zest from the oranges and lemons in strips with a swivel-bladed vegetable peeler. Tie the zests, cinnamon stick, cardamom, allspice, and cloves in a square of rinsed cheesecloth and place the bag in a large nonreactive saucepan. Squeeze the juices from the oranges and lemons and set aside.

2. Add the apple cider to the saucepan and bring to a boil over medium-high heat. Reduce the heat to a simmer, cover the pan, and cook for 20 minutes.

3. Add the citrus juices and rum and heat, without boiling, until the mixture is piping hot. Taste and add a little sugar if necessary. Remove the spice bag and serve the punch in glass cups or mugs. (Leftovers can be reheated.)

Hot Mulled Cider and Cranberry

This is a soothing, mildly spiced fruity hot drink for a frosty day. Make it instead of tea and sip it by a crackling fire. In the evening, you could add a splash of Calvados.

MAKES 1½ QUARTS; ABOUT 12 SERVINGS

3½ cups apple cider
2½ cups cranberry juice cocktail
Zest of I lemon—removed in strips with
  vegetable peeler
Zest of I orange—removed in strips with
  vegetable peeler
Two 3-inch cinnamon sticks
I teaspoon allspice berries
6 whole cloves
One ¼-inch-thick slice unpeeled fresh ginger

1. Combine all the ingredients in a heavy nonreactive saucepan. Heat over very low heat, at a bare simmer, for 30 minutes. Let stand for several hours to allow the flavors to blend.

2. When ready to serve, reheat slowly. Strain and serve in small cups

Growing Your Own Apples

Fine fruit is the flower of commodities. It is the most perfect union of the useful and the beautiful that the earth knows. Trees full of soft foliage; blossoms fresh with spring bounty; and, finally, fruit, rich, bloom–dusted, melting, and luscious."

—ANDREW JACKSON DOWNING,
THE FRUITS AND FRUIT TREES OF AMERICA

Even if you live in an apartment with only a balcony, you can grow your own apples, thanks to modern science. Some nurseries offer tiny trees that grow and produce fruit even when grown in pots. Miniature trees that may grow no taller than six feet can decorate your patio or deck with springtime blossoms and autumn fruit that nourishes your taste buds through the winter. For those really cramped for space, or those who want to grow an entire orchard in a small space, Stark Brothers nursery offers their Colonnade® apples, columnar trees that get no wider than two feet and no taller than eight. As long as you have room for a few twenty-inch pots, you have enough space for these unique trees.

If you are lucky enough to have a yard, you have many more options. As we've pointed out, some of the most flavorful and interesting apples are not available in stores. The only way to find them is to order by mail, to live near a small, commercial orchard that sells them, or to grow them yourself.

Planning Your Orchard

Before you order any trees, you need to plan carefully where you will plant them—they will be with you for many years, and you don't want to make mistakes at the outset that will cause you trouble later on. All fruits like to grow in the sun—it takes a lot of energy to produce big, juicy apples, and the sun is the source of that energy. Apples will grow best on the south side of any buildings or tall trees. After you've picked a likely spot, watch the path of the shadows of trees and houses during the day to make sure they don't dominate the area you've chosen. Think ahead too—if you or your neighbor have some young trees in the yard that will grow to be big and bushy, don't plant your apple trees in what will become their shadows.

It's also important to consider the ultimate size of the apple trees themselves. It takes some imagination to see that the modest sticks you plant can mature into trees with branches that extend several feet in all directions. You want to make sure that both the roots and the branches of your trees have plenty of space to grow over the years. Science comes to the rescue here, too—apple trees are available in a number of sizes—miniature (up to 6 feet tall), dwarf (8 to 10 feet), semidwarf (12 to 15 feet), and standard (18 to 25 feet). Whatever the size of the tree, it will grow full-sized fruit.

Few home growers plant standard trees these days—they take up lots of room and don't bear fruit for many years after planting. And once they begin to bear, they can produce a huge crop that's difficult to harvest and impossible to use in its entirety. In addition, orchard tasks such as spraying and pruning are very difficult to accomplish with large trees. However, if you have plenty of room and fond memories of climbing the backyard apple tree when you were a child, you might want to consider a standard tree. It can become a legacy for future generations.

Once you've found a good spot for your orchard, you need to decide what varieties to plant. Our feeling is that if you want to grow your own fruit, there's no point in choosing the varieties you can find easily in the store—go out on a limb and plant the rarities that offer unique qualities otherwise not available. The most flavorful varieties, such as Calville Blanc d'Hiver, the classic dessert apple of France; Cox's Orange Pippin, one of the most richly flavored apples and a popular favorite in England; and Esopus Spitzenberg, described by one expert as "the finest eating apple in the world when perfectly ripe," are almost impossible to find in stores. Yet you can grow them for yourself, along with newer disease-resistant varieties such as Liberty and Enterprise.

The potential for disease is one of the most important considerations in planning your orchard. A quick call to your local county agricultural extension office can get you the information you need—what apple diseases are prevalent in your area, what varieties do well where you live. The latter list is likely to focus on the more familiar, readily available varieties. But once you know about which diseases you need to be concerned, you can query nurseries as to whether the varieties that interest you are likely to thrive or succumb where you live.

You also need to take into consideration your climate and the length of your seasons. How cold does it become in the winter where you live?

The United States is divided into planting zones, numbered from zone 3 to zone 10, based on the climate (fortunately, you don't need to concern yourself with frigid zones 1 and 2 or hothouse-warm zones 11 and 12.) Residents of the colder zones 3 and 4 must choose varieties carefully and be sure to inquire about the hardiness of the rootstock used by the nursery they order from. Many wonderful varieties can be grown in the north, including Cortland, Honeycrisp, State Fair, Sweet Sixteen, Wealthy, and Wolf River. But they do need to be grown on hardy rootstocks.

Fortunately, most of the populated areas of the United States are in zones 5 through 8, prime growing regions for apples. Zones 9 and 10,

saving rare fruit

it is fortunate that people with the power to do something care about preserving rare and unusual apple varieties and educating the public about them. The best way to explore the range of apple flavors is to order an assortment from Applesource or another mail-order provider of antique varieties (see Mail-Order Sources). Applesource offers about a hundred kinds of apple, from Arkansas Black to York Imperial.

If you want to grow your own unusual apples, your best bet is Southmeadow Fruit Gardens. They sell more than a hundred and fifty varieties, from Adams Pearmain to Zabergau Reinette. All their apples are available on dwarfing rootstocks.

Fruit-growing enthusiasts should know about NAFEX—North American Fruit Explorers (see Mail-Order Sources). Some of the members of this organization are professionals, but most are amateurs with a passion for growing fruit. Members help one another by sharing information and varietal material, such as wood for grafting. While many members grow apples, others raise unusual fruits such as mayhaws, pawpaws, and persimmons. Perhaps the best thing about NAFEX is the annual meeting, held in different parts of the country, when members get a chance to savor some of the best fruit ever.

it's hard to believe that each of those delicate flowers on an apple tree has the potential to develop into a big, robust, crunchy apple, but it does. However, fruit trees have many more flowers than will result in a harvest. The impressive display of blossoms makes the tree obvious to pollinating bees. When the bee snuggles its head into the flower to gather pollen or sip the sweet nectar, the tiny hairs on its body pick up grains of pollen, which contain the male germ cells of the flower. At the next blossom, some of the grains come off and adhere to the tops of the female part of the flower, called the style. Each style of an apple flower has five of these sticky projections, called stigmas.

When a pollen grain settles on a stigma, it begins to grow a tube that penetrates into the stalk of the stigma. The pollen tube grows down through the style to the ovary, at the base of the flower. There a nucleus from the pollen unites with an egg cell nucleus in one of the ovary's ten ovules, forming the beginnings of a seed. For most apples, a grain of pollen from the same variety can't produce a viable pollen tube, so it can't fertilize the egg cell. It needs pollen carried by the bee from another appropriate variety. That's why more than one variety should be planted in your garden.

Once the eggs in a flower are fertilized, big changes happen. The young seeds produce a hormone called auxin. Auxin keeps the fruit on the plant and promotes the fruit's growth, so the more seeds are fertilized, the larger it will usually be. The part of the apple you eat grows from the ovary of the flower. That means it is part of the parent tree, which is why all the fruit on a tree is the same, no matter what kind of pollen fertilized its flowers.

If you examine an apple tree after the blossoms fall, you can see tiny green apples that have started to form. A stem connects each to the tree, and at the opposite, or blossom, end, you can see the remnants of the flower. If not enough seeds have been formed, the fruit will fall from the tree. This is not usually a problem, as apple trees are more likely to produce too much rather than too little fruit.

During the summer, the fruit undergoes many changes. A young apple grows to a certain size as its cells divide, then stops for a period of weeks. At that point, the apple contains as many cells as it ever will, and you may wonder if you're going to be stuck with a harvest of miniature fruit. But not to worry—during the last few weeks before harvest the cells in the fruit swell with water, air spaces develop between them, and the apple enlarges to its final, satisfying size. At the same time, the starch inside is converted into sugar, and the chemical that causes the astringent taste characteristic of unripe apples disappears.

As harvest draws near, the skin develops its final color. The fruits on the same tree may vary considerably in color, since color is very dependent on the amount of light each fruit receives. The more sun, the redder the fruit.

however, present problems. Apples have adapted to a temperate climate and typically require a minimum of nine hundred to a thousand hours of temperatures between 32° and 45°F during the winter. Without this winter chill, the tree might not come out of dormancy at all, or growth will be late and generally weak. Fortunately for those in the South who love apples, a few varieties of low-chill apples (requiring fewer cold hours) have been developed, including Dorsett Golden and Anna, which will bear fruit as far south as the Gulf Coast. If you live in either the northern or southern climate extremes, order your apple trees from a regional nursery that specializes in fruit for your area.

The majority of Americans, however, can plan an orchard that bears fruit over a long season. In zone 5, the earliest varieties, such as Lodi, are ready to pick in early July, while the latest, like Granny Smith, shouldn't be harvested before early November. If you have room for several trees and plan carefully, you can pick fruit from midsummer through early winter and savor your harvest by storing fruit through the following spring.

The final consideration in choosing varieties is pollination. Most apple varieties are not self-fruitful. This means their flowers won't produce full-sized fruit unless they are fertilized by pollen from a different variety. Some, like Baldwin and Stayman, can't even pollinate other varieties. That means that in order to guarantee a harvest, you need to plant more than one tree. A few kinds, such as Golden Delicious and Grimes Golden, are self-fruitful, but even these produce more abundantly when cross-pollinated. If you live in an area with lots of apple trees nearby, bees might bring pollen from other trees to yours. But in order to guarantee a harvest, you must plant trees of more than one variety.

Of the more commonly offered varieties, Golden Delicious is one of the best pollinizers. It blooms over a longer period than most kinds, so its flowers are available for cross-pollination of varieties with staggered blossom times.

If you choose antique or unusual varieties, be sure to ask the nursery if your choices will do a good job of pollinating one another.

Planting and Early Care

Apple trees can be planted in the fall or in the spring. If you choose fall planting, be sure to plant them early enough so that they can establish some new roots before really cold weather

sets in. If you plant in the spring, you want to be sure to get the trees in the ground while the weather is still cool. Spring or fall, it's important that the trees be dormant—bare wood with no leaves or unfurling buds. Before the trees arrive, you need to prepare the orchard area for them. Grass and other plants compete with trees for water and nutrients, so you should clear a circle about six feet in diameter around the spot you've picked for each tree.

Check mail-order trees as soon as they arrive to be sure the roots are still moist. You may have trouble telling if the young trees are alive or not. They will look like unpromising little sticks with a few twigs coming out, and their roots will be wrapped in burlap or other protective material, with a little peat moss around them. But if you rub away a bit of bark and find green underneath, the tree is fine. If the tree is black or brown under the bark, test a spot farther down on the trunk, looking for green. If you find none, chances are the tree is dead, and you should request a refund. Fortunately, most mail-order nurseries are careful to ship only healthy, dormant trees.

One to twenty-four hours before planting, unwrap the trees and place them in buckets of water. While your trees soak up a good dose of fluid, you need to provide them with abundant living space. Digging a hole to plant a fruit tree is hard work, but it's worth every drop of sweat. Just remember, how you plant the tree will affect it for the rest of its life. You need to dig a hole deep enough and wide enough so you can spread the roots out naturally as you cover them with soil. If burrowing rodents are a problem in your area, you may want to help protect your trees by lining the planting holes with wire fencing with one-inch mesh.

Plant the tree with the graft union about an inch-and-a-half above the soil line. You can recognize the graft as a small ridge around the trunk, often with different-colored or -textured bark above and below it. Be careful not to cover the graft with soil, or you'll negate the desired effects of the rootstock when the interstem or scion sends out roots.

It's a good idea to plant a metal stake along with each tree, since even a tree that will develop a strong root system can use a little help staying upright during its first year or two. Place the stake six to eight inches away from the trunk. After planting, use a bit of soft cloth to tie the tree to the stake. Once the tree and stake are in place, firm the soil down around them. Then build a moat around the tree, with the inner wall an inch or two away from the trunk. The moat will catch water for the roots, and the inner wall will keep the water from pooling around the trunk, where it could encourage rot. Fill the moat with water to give your new tree a nice, long drink and further settle the soil around the roots.

Rodents don't only burrow under the soil, they also look for food, such as the bark of young trees, at the surface. The easiest way to protect your trees from them is to wrap each one with a spiral plastic tree guard you can purchase at any nursery. The spiral expands as the tree grows, so you don't need to worry about strangling a growing trunk. Finally, mulch your new trees from the border of the inner moat wall outward to the edge of the cleared area. Three to six inches of mulch such as compost or straw will help hold in water and keep down weeds.

For the first few weeks after planting, make sure your new orchard is well watered. The trees are establishing their root systems and need help. Whenever you water your trees, give them a good soaking. Trees are much healthier if given a good soaking once a week or so rather than a short daily sprinkling. Light, superficial watering encourages shallow roots; less frequent watering helps deeper roots develop. Don't fertilize new fruit trees—that can encourage too much top growth for the developing root system, weakening the tree. Normally, keeping the trees mulched with compost or straw fortified with some manure will provide plenty of fertilizer for the trees.

Tending the Orchard

For the first year or two, tending your trees consists mainly of keeping them watered and weeded. However, pruning is a third chore that may seem intimidating at first but is very important to making your trees produce the best harvest possible. It takes little time, but you need to invest in a good pair of sharp pruning shears, and later on you'll also need a pruning saw. When you plant your new trees, be brave and cut the trunk, called the leader, back to about three feet tall. Trim off any twigs growing from the leader, as they are not likely to grow into worthwhile branches. When cutting off the twigs, be careful not to cut too close to the trunk. Leave a short stump so you don't damage the protective area called the "branch collar," which helps form scar tissue after a cut. It's important to cut back the above-ground portions of the tree because some of the roots will have been damaged in transit and thus the root system will not support as many branches and leaves as before. You may think you've destroyed the possibility that you'll ever have trees, but don't despair—fruit trees put on an amazing amount of growth their first year.

From then on, the ideal time for pruning fruit trees is in late winter, after the coldest days have passed but before the buds begin to swell. The second winter after planting, you'll see that the leader of each tree has shot up about thirty inches during the growing season. You need to cut it back by about a third. Leave three or four strong lower branches that stick out in different directions at wide angles from the trunk. These will serve as the first scaffolds for the adult tree.

Cutting back the lateral branches on the scaffolds will encourage the scaffolds to branch, making a stronger tree. Prune away the other shoots that grow higher off the trunk and are likely to be more upright in their growth.

By the third year, each of your trees should have grown two good sets of scaffold branches. Again, cut away the more vertical branches that are closest to the top and trim back the leader. The fourth and fifth years, repeat this procedure so that your trees each have five good sets of scaffold branches.

When pruning, remove any shoots on the scaffold branches that grow straight up or straight down. If two branches rub against each other, prune one off. In order to bear fruit, the leaves of the fruit-bearing branches need to be exposed to at least 30 percent of the available sunlight. Keep this in mind as you snip off crowded twigs. Think of yourself as a sculptor as you prune. Your goal is to produce an open, wide tree that can harvest maximum sunlight. When you cut back crowded branches, always cut close to, but not right at, a bud. Ideally, you should prune your trees every winter to keep the branches uncrowded. Be sure to cut away any suckers that have grown around the base of the tree, too.

manmade trees

when you get to the bottom line in the catalog description of an apple tree, where the price is given, you may gasp. How can they charge twenty dollars for a skimpy little stick that won't reward you with fruit for at least two years? It might help for you to know what went into making that unimpressive little twig. In order to create it, at least two different varieties had to be grown, one for the roots and one for the bearing part of the tree.

Many different rootstocks are used for apple trees. The cheapest is seedling rootstock. The grower simply plants lots of apple seeds and waits until the trees have reached the appropriate size for grafting. But apple seedlings are variable, and no one can be sure just how they will grow. So most commercial nurseries use what are called "clonal rootstocks," ones that are genetically identical, so they will know what characteristics the rootstock will impart to the eventual tree. Clonal rootstocks can be grown in the field by mounding sawdust around a dormant year-old tree, letting it grow for a season, and then removing the sawdust to expose and harvest the rooted branches that have grown. This provides several pieces of rootstock. Clonal rootstocks can also be produced in the laboratory through tissue culture.

Rootstocks confer characteristics to the entire tree, such as disease-resistance, size of harvest, and size of the tree. No one understands just how a rootstock affects the entire tree, but it does. A number of different rootstocks are used for making dwarf trees. Most were developed at the East Malling Research Station in England, and they are designated by the letter "M" preceding a number. Unfortunately, nurseries don't use a consistent notation for these rootstocks—EM9, M.9, and M–IX all refer to the same rootstock, one of the most dwarfing. Dwarf trees advertised for growing in a tub are usually grafted onto M9 rootstock. The roots are weak and shallow, so M9 trees often require staking to help hold them up.

M7 rootstock is also popular with nurseries. A tree on M7 will reach eight to twelve feet. It adapts well to heavy soils. M26 trees, which are somewhat smaller than those on M7, need well-drained soil. Some specialty nurseries ask you when you order about your soil type so they can provide you with the best tree for your growing conditions.

When the rootstock reaches the right size, the top of the tree, called the scion, is grafted onto it. The ultimate size of the tree depends on the scion variety as well as on the rootstock. Nurseries obtain their scion wood from "mother trees" that are known to bear reliably. The mother tree is cut back heavily each year so it will produce plenty of vigorous new growth. These young branches are harvested and each is grafted onto a rootstock to make a new tree. Then the tree must grow for at least another year before you buy it.

Producing just the right tree can be even more complicated. Sometimes the desired scion doesn't graft well onto the desired rootstock. Or the orchardist may want a small tree with generous roots. In these cases, another piece is grafted between the rootstock and the scion, an "interstem." Interstems can dwarf a tree to varying degrees, depending on the length of the piece used. Just a half-inch to one-inch difference in length can result in a larger or smaller tree. The longer the interstem, the smaller the tree.

The ultimate tree has *four* pieces—the rootstock, one interstem for dwarfing, another interstem piece that induces hardiness in the tree, and the scion! No wonder apple trees can be expensive.

Apple Enemies

Be on the lookout for diseases. One of the most common and deadliest apple diseases is fire blight. An infected branch dies and becomes blackened with shriveled leaves, as if it had been burned. Other members of the rose family, such as pears, mountain ash, and hawthorne, can also develop fire blight. If this disease is a problem in your area, the best way to avoid it is to plant resistant varieties, such as Roxbury Russet, Liberty, and Enterprise. There is no cure for fire blight, but you can fight it by cutting back affected branches at least twelve inches away from any evidence of disease. Throw the trimmings into the garbage, not into the compost pile. Between cuts, clean your clippers or saw with a 10 percent bleach solution or rubbing alcohol to keep from spreading the bacteria that cause the disease.

After your trees leaf out in the spring, check the undersides of the leaves every week or so for caterpillars. If you find any, pick up some *Bacillus thuringiensis* spray at the local nursery and follow the directions. This bacterial spray kills caterpillars on the spot but is harmless to humans and pets.

Once your trees begin to bear fruit, you will probably need to watch for the apple coddling moth, whose larva is the infamous worm in the apple. The best defense against this pest is cleanliness—pick up all windfall apples and be sure to remove all wormy apples from the trees.

If your trees seem troubled by pests or diseases, it's always a good idea to contact your county agricultural extension agent or local nurseryman for suggestions for treatment. We favor organic means whenever possible, as they are healthier for plants, people, and the environment. If you agree, be sure to ask about organic treatments when you seek help. Because chemical fixes are often the easiest to suggest and to use, you may not be told about alternatives unless you ask.

Harvesttime!

If you planted dwarf or semidwarf trees, you are likely to see those welcome apple blossoms the second or third spring after planting. Now you can look forward to apples in the fall.

Apples often need thinning to prevent the harvest from exhausting the tree. Some varieties have a tendency to bear a good crop only every other year, and overbearing only makes this habit more likely. Also, the right-sized crop means fruit of good size and flavor.

How do you know how many apples your tree can comfortably nourish and bear until harvest? The trees actually thin themselves early on with what's called the "June drop," which occurs when auxin production slows as the embryos within the seeds are developing. You'll want to do any thinning after the June drop. Keep in mind that each apple needs thirty to forty leaves to provide it with enough energy to grow and mature properly and enough sugar to give it full flavor. If estimating leaf numbers seems too time-consuming, make sure each fruit has six to eight inches of leaf-bearing branch. Thin out clusters of the small fruit to avoid having them rub together when they swell, leaving the largest one. Twist the fruit off carefully so you don't damage the fruit-bearing spurs.

Deciding when to harvest your fruit can be tricky. Some varieties, such as McIntosh, begin to fall from the tree before they are fully ripe. Cortland, on the other hand, doesn't come off easily even when the fruit is overripe. Most apples are getting ripe when the green background color begins to turn yellow. This can be hard to see on deep red fruit, such as some kinds of Red Delicious. When you suspect your fruit may be ready to pick, carefully twist one off so as not to damage the spur and taste it—that's always the best test of ripeness.

liberty

disease resistance is a very important quality for home orchardists, and the Liberty apple is aptly named. This variety, developed at the Geneva, New York, Station of Cornell University, is immune or resistant to the most devastating apple diseases. Liberty is an attractive apple with plenty of red in the skin. The fruit is small to medium in size and has a crisp, aromatic flesh with a tart, refreshing flavor, good both for eating raw and for cooking. It usually matures in early October and stores well at temperatures around freezing until December.

To produce this wonderful variety, breeder Dr. Robert Lamb included flowering crab apple in the mix, which provided the disease-resistance. One of the parents, Macoun, itself a member of the McIntosh family, is an especially delicious, versatile fruit, which contributed to the delightful balanced flavor.

Liberty grows well in the cooler climates, from Wisconsin to the mountains of northern Georgia. It also thrives in the Willamette Valley of Oregon. It's an abundant bearer, and the fruit needs to be thinned, or the apples will be very small.

Storing the Crop

Even dwarf apple trees usually produce more fruit than you can use right away, presenting you with the delightful problem of how best to store your harvest. Any windfalls or bruised fruit should be used right away. The best storage conditions for apples are 90 percent humidity and a temperature between 30° and 32°F, colder than most refrigerators. Cold temperatures slow the respiration of the fruit, which helps keep it from overripening, and the sugar in the fruit keeps it from freezing at these temperatures. If you have an old refrigerator in the basement or garage, you can probably tinker with the temperature control until it provides the right temperature for storing apples.

Varieties vary greatly in how long they will keep in storage. Spigold won't really store for more than two months, while York will keep into April under good conditions. Honeycrisp keeps well, and its flavor improves in storage. Generally, the earlier the variety, the poorer the storage. Some varieties keep well at refrigerator temperatures for several weeks. Fuji is probably the storage champion, staying crisp and delicious even at room temperature for up to two weeks.

Mail-Order Sources

Equipment

The Baker's Catalog
King Arthur Flour
RR2, Box 876
Norwich, VT 05055–0876
800–827–6836

Rotary apple peeler, baking equipment including silicon baking-pan liners, baking stones, scales, instant-read thermometers, baking pans, and books

Sur La Table
Pike Place Farmers' Market
84 Pine Street
Seattle, WA 98101
800–243–0852

Wide variety of baking and cooking equipment including crème brûlée dishes, soufflé molds, and books

Williams-Sonoma
P.O. Box 7456
San Francisco, CA 94120–7456
800–541–2233

Baking stones, baking pans, blowtorches, and cookware

Ingredients

The Baker's Catalog
(see above)

Fiori di Sicilia, extracts, tapioca flour, SAF-Instant yeast, apple nuggets, and other dried fruits

D'Artagnan
399–419 St. Paul Avenue
Jersey City, NJ 07306
800–DARTAGN

Ducks, pheasants, buffalo, and game meats

Penzeys, Ltd.
P.O. Box 933
Muskego, WI 53150
414–679–7207

Spices (including true Ceylon cinnamon), vanilla beans, vanilla
extract, and more

Apples to Eat

To have a wide range of apples at your fingertips for tasting during
the fall harvest, we encourage you to order from the following. Call
early in the season for the best selections.

Applesource
Tom and Jill Vorbeck
1716 Apples Road
Chapin, IL 62628
800–588–3854

The Vorbecks ship dozens of apple varieties, from late October to
early January. They also carry the rotary apple peeler.

Browning Orchard
RR 1
Wallingford, KY 41093
606–849–2881

They offer a large selection of early and late season apples. Because
of their southern location, this orchard harvests Lodi apples in early
July. Arkansas Black, a late-season variety, is picked at the end
of October. The shipping season ends in late December or early
January.

North American Fruit Explorers (NAFEX)
1716 Apples Raod
Chapin, IL 62628
217–245–7589

An organization for sharing information and varietal material, such
as wood for grafting.

Apple Trees

Because climate plays a crucial role in apple growing, it's important
to order trees that will do well where you live. Consult local county
extension agents for advice. The following are additional helpful
sources for advice or for ordering trees.

Adams County Nursery
P.O. Box 108
Aspers, PA 17304
717–677–8105

Carry many apple cultivars, especially for the eastern U.S.

Applesource
(see above)

Bailey Nursery, Inc.
1325 Bailey Road
St. Paul, MN 55119
612–459–9744

Good source for cold-hardy apples on cold-hardy rootstock

Bear Creek Nursery
Box 411
Northport, WA 99157
509–732–4417
Apple trees for the Northwest

Carlos Manning
Mannings Nursery
681 Maplewood Road
Lester, WV 25865
304–934–6558
Grows at least 200 different cultivars of hard-to-find apples such as Rainbow, Red Winter Pearmain, and Black Twig. Approximately 25 varieties are available during any one season.

Dave Wilson Nursery
19701 Lake Road
Hickman, CA 95323
800–654–5854
A reliable nursery in operation for over 60 years, featuring the varieties Pink Lady and Sundowner, among many others.

Lawsons Nursery
Route 1, Box 473
Ball Ground, GA 30107
This orchard carries apple trees for the south and southeast U.S. Many cultivars are old and hard to find.

Sonoma Antique Apple Nursery
4395 Westside Rd.
Healdsburg, CA 95448
707–433–6420
Offers 94 varieties of apple trees

Stark Bro's
P.O. Box 10
Louisiana, MO 63353
800–325–4180
The nation's largest supplier of apple trees; in business since 1816

Southmeadow Fruit Gardens
c/o Grootendorst Nursery
Lakeside, MI 49116
616–469–2865
Carries more than 200 grafted apple cultivars from all over the world

BIBLIOGRAPHY

Beach, S.A., N.O. Booth, and D.M. Taylor. *Apples of New York* (Volumes I and 2). J.B. Lyon Company, 1905. This is a report of the New York Agricultural Experiment Station for the year 1903. A historic and exhaustive study.

Bilderback, Diane E. and Dorothy Hinshaw Patent. *Backyard Fruits & Berries.* Emmaus, PA: Rodale Press, 1984. Basic information on growing popular fruits in the home orchard and berry patch, with information on how plants function that can aid understanding the "whys" behind the "hows."

Browning, Frank. *Apples.* New York: North Point Press, 1998. Lots of interesting apple information; no illustrations or recipes.

Davidson, Alan. *Fruit: A Connoisseur's Guide and Cookbook.* New York: Simon & Schuster, 1991. A wonderful coffee-table book with beautiful paintings of fruits and lots of historical information and a few recipes.

Grigson, Jane. *Jane Grigson's Fruit Book.* New York: Atheneum, 1982. A standard reference, with many fine savory recipes for apples.

Lape, Fred. *Apples & Man.* New York: Van Nostrand Reinhold Co., 1979. The history of our interactions with apples, including information on topics like pesticide use and the disappearance of rare varieties.

Manhart, Warren. *Apples for the 21st Century*. Portland, OR: North American Tree Company, 1995. Written primarily for commercial growers, but also very useful for anyone who wants to establish a home apple orchard; discusses the characteristics of both old and new varieties.

Martin, Alice A. *All About Apples*. Boston: Houghton Mifflin, 1976. Difficult to find book with lots of historical information about apples.

Proulx, Annie and Lew Nichols. *Cider: Making, Using & Enjoying Sweet & Hard Cider*. Pownal, VT: Storey Communications, 1997. A how-to manual and historic reference for anyone seriously interested in cider.

Ruttle, Jack. "Training New Apple Trees." *Organic Gardening*, December 1987, 48–49. A compact but detailed article with clear drawings showing how to prune apple trees.

Sass, Lorna J. *To the King's Taste: Richard II's book of feasts and recipes adapted for modern cooking*. New York: Metropolitan Museum of Art, 1975. An interesting small book showing historical uses of apples and other foods.

Yepsen, Roger. *Apples*. New York: W. W. Norton & Co, 1994. A beautiful small book with portraits and descriptions of many apple varieties, both popular and little known.

Index